SOLD OUT

SOLD OUT

How Marketing in School Threatens Children's Well-Being and Undermines Their Education

Alex Molnar and Faith Boninger

ROWMAN & LITTLEFIELD
Lanham • Boulder • New York • London

Published by Rowman & Littlefield
A wholly owned subsidiary of The Rowman & Littlefield Publishing Group, Inc.
4501 Forbes Boulevard, Suite 200, Lanham, Maryland 20706
www.rowman.com

Unit A, Whitacre Mews, 26-34 Stannary Street, London SE11 4AB

British Library Cataloguing in Publication Information Available

Library of Congress Cataloging-in-Publication Data

Molnar, Alex.
Sold out : how marketing in school threatens children's well-being and undermines their education / Alex Molnar and Faith Boninger.
pages cm.
Includes bibliographical references and index.
ISBN 978-1-4758-1360-9 (cloth : alk. paper) -- ISBN 978-1-4758-1361-6 (pbk. : alk. paper) -- ISBN 978-1-4758-1362-3 (electronic)
1. Business and education--United States. 2. Commercialism in schools--United States. 3. Public schools--United States--Finance. 4. Consumption (Economics)--United States. I. Boninger, Faith. II. Title.
LC1085.2.M66 2015
371.19'5--dc23
                              2015009895

Printed in the United States of America

CONTENTS

ACKNOWLEDGMENTS

Alex has been studying commercialism in schools since the mid-1980s. He and Faith have been collaborating for over a decade. Taken together, their work on school commercialism includes two books as well as twenty reports, briefs, and studies (available on the National Education Policy Center website: nepc.colorado.edu). With all of that, we have a lot of collaborators, colleagues, and supporters to thank.

Our collaborators and research assistants over the years contributed their ideas and did a lot of the difficult and tedious work associated with complex research projects: Elizabeth Buchanan and Jennifer Morales (University of Wisconsin-Milwaukee); Max B. Sawicky (Economic Policy Institute); Joseph A. Reaves, Sharon Lake, Rafael Serrano, David R. Garcia, and Bruce Merrill (Arizona State University); Elaine Duggan (independent researcher); Gary Wilkerson (University of Hull, Great Britain); Bill Koski (Stanford University); Sean Geary (Arizona State University); Tiana Tagami (independent researcher); Michael D. Harris and Ken M. Libby (University of Colorado-Boulder); and Joseph Fogarty (Corballa National School, Ireland).

Our colleagues at the National Education Policy Center—Erik Gunn, Pat Hinchey, Bill Mathis, Kevin Welner, and many anonymous reviewers—have been invaluable to us as we struggled with ideas, tracked down leads, and wrote and then rewrote manuscripts. The annual school commercialism trends reports have been made possible by the support of Consumers Union, particularly that of Rhoda Karpatkin (president emeritus), whose initial support was crucial, and Chuck Bell (program director), who has kept the faith all these years. The national survey of marketing of foods of minimal nutritional value was made possible by a grant from the Robert Wood Johnson Foundation.

Margo Wootan and Kate Klimczak (Center for Science in the Public Interest), Susan Linn and Josh Golin (Campaign for a Commercial-Free Childhood), Jeff Chester and Joy Spencer (Center for Digital Democracy), Sabrina Adler (ChangeLab Solutions), and Khaliah Barnes (Electronic Privacy Information Center) always answered their phones and replied to our e-mails, offering us information, leads to follow, and encouragement. They are committed, principled advocates for children. Peggy Charren, whose tireless work led to the passage of the Children's Television Act, was an inspiration. We are indebted to Sheila Harty for her groundbreaking exploration of schoolhouse commercialism.

Farida Shaheed, the United Nations Special Rapporteur in the Field of Cultural Rights, took up the issue of the threat that commercialism poses to cultural freedom and provided her report to the U.N. General Assembly in October 2014. We're very grateful.

Barbara, David, Alisa, and Talia deserve special mention. They put up with our commitment to and endless talk about school commercialism, and kept the home fires burning. Finally, our children and grandchildren all should know that they were and will always be our first source of inspiration and encouragement. They provide constant reminders about why this work is important.

1

THE PROBLEM OF SCHOOLHOUSE COMMERCIALISM

As we were starting to write this book, a colleague's third-grade daughter was honored by her elementary school for her mileage in the school's "running group." Our colleague was invited to the school for the award presentation, where the principal and representatives of a local Nike store awarded Nike-branded "fuel bands," which assess users' workouts, to ten children for their accomplishments. After the ceremony, the Nike employees showed the children and their parents how to use their new fuel bands by syncing them with their iPhones.

According to the school's principal, the collaboration between the school and Nike was a stroke of good luck: the Nike store's manager had decided to build a relationship with a school when the school's nurse happened to mention the newly created running group while shopping at the Nike store. As a result the store was soon sending employees to the school a couple of times a week to encourage students to run more.[1] This type of activity is consistent with Nike, Inc.'s more general interest in schools. In 2013, for example, the corporation committed $50 million to support Michelle Obama's Let's Move! Active Schools initiative.[2]

Nike is hardly alone. It is now common for schools to seek corporate sponsorship for programs, activities, or building renovations; to work with corporations on fundraising projects; or to use corporate-produced educational materials. Marketing activities are a routine part of many, perhaps most, students' experience in schools.

"Advertising" consists of the creation and delivery of specific messages presented to potential customers via print or other media, and "marketing" refers to any type of promotional activity intended to bring together a brand and its customers.[3] Thus, advertising and marketing are the mechanisms that propagate commercialism, a value system defined by the Oxford English Dictionary as "excessive adherence to financial return as a measure of worth."[4]

In his book, *Lead Us into Temptation*, James Twitchell argues that commercialism consists of two processes: "commodification," or stripping an object of all other value except its value for sale, and marketing, "the insertion of the object into a network of exchanges, only some of which involve money."[5] The Center for the Study of Commercialism characterizes commercialism as "ubiquitous product marketing that leads to a preoccupation with individual consumption to the detriment of oneself and society."[6]

In our work, commercialism is defined as a value system that promotes profit above all other concerns and that seeks to transform all relationships into commodities that can be exchanged for money. An important question, though rarely asked, is, what are the implications for students and for public education when commercialism influences what children learn and how they learn it?

Commercializing activities in schools take many forms. Some are easy to spot, such as when a company places ads in a school. Other commercializing activities, such as when a company sponsors a school activity or provides sponsored educational materials that promote a worldview consistent with its business aims, are more subtle. Very often these days, commercializing activities in schools are commonly and misleadingly framed as "partnerships."

SCHOOL-CORPORATE "PARTNERSHIPS" AND OTHER MISLEADING TERMS

Corporations are eager to engage in commercializing activities in schools as part of broader efforts to reach a desirable market of children, whose worth has been variously estimated at up to $700 billion.[7] The terms used to describe these activities are typically "corporate partnership," "school-business partnership," or "public-private partnership"—terms that suggest corporations and schools share a common purpose. As we shall see, they do not.

Since corporations exist for the sole purpose of profiting their owners, corporate activities in schools must also, by definition, serve that purpose. Public schools, however, unlike corporations, are intended to promote the general welfare. Thus, although some corporate marketing programs in schools may at times address matters of educational value, it is not necessarily in the interest of corporate sponsors to promote, for instance, the development of critical thinking and the habits of mind associated with it;[8] and, when corporate interests and the public interest clash, corporations will inevitably choose to promote their own interests.

Consider the case of critical thinking. It is hard to find anyone willing to oppose the idea of students thinking critically in the abstract. However, real critical thinking is an inherent threat to corporate self-promotion, because such thinking might lead students to question the story that sponsors tell about their brands.[9]

For this reason, corporate-sponsored programs in schools avoid touching on anything that might lead to conclusions inconsistent with the corporation's self-serving message. They contribute to the creation of a school environment that discourages students from developing the critical thinking skills that might lead them to question the stories that corporate sponsors tell about their brands—in contrast to an environment that would encourage students to ask questions, to think critically, and to develop habits of mind that would enable them to transfer any critical thinking skills they learn in school to other, unrelated, situations.[10]

The fundamental incompatibility between the self-interested commercial goals of corporations and the public interest goals of schools makes it misleading to refer to corporate involvements in the schools as "partnerships." For this reason, throughout this book we refer to corporate involvements with schools simply as "relationships."

"Partnership" is not the only misleading term associated with school commercialism. Corporate activities in schools are sometimes explained, for example, as stemming from corporations' desire to "give back," and in so doing to demonstrate that they are good "corporate citizens." This is positive language that paints a picture of corporations engaged in civic activity to promote the common good. However, what corporations have received that they are now "giving back" is rarely, if ever, explained.

When, or to whom, they choose to "give back" does offer some insight into what "giving back" actually means in practice.

Twentieth Century Fox Home Entertainment chose to "give back" right about the time it released the DVD of *Glee: The Complete Second Season*, in 2011, by "partnering" with the National Association for Music Education to sponsor the *"Glee*—Give a Note" contest. The contest offered grants to support school musical theater programs.[11]

To win a grant, students had to submit a video in which they creatively demonstrated why they needed and deserved the grant, and also conduct massive grass-roots efforts to win a popular vote conducted on Facebook. In reaching out to their families and friends to get the vote out, they simultaneously promoted *Glee* in their communities. This is an example of how the term "giving back" obscures the self-interested and exploitive nature of the relationship.

In the language of corporate "partnerships" and "giving back," however, the *"Glee*—Give a Note" contest would most likely be described as "win-win": the lucky school gets a grant to provide a musical theater program and the corporation gets increased sales of its product. Overall, however, the corporation is the big winner in this situation.

SCHOOLS ARE VALUABLE MARKETING VENUES

Whereas other marketing venues tend to be cluttered with a lot of advertising and might reach only specific segments of the child market (the "athletic kids," the "nerdy kids," and so on), schools, by comparison, still provide relatively uncluttered access to a captive audience of all children for most of the year. The Nike-clad running-club facilitators, for example, well-meaning and enthusiastic as they may be, also regularly promote their brand in school and encourage children to develop a relationship with them as means of developing loyalty to Nike—or, in marketing terms, to "brand" them.

The Motives of Marketers

Advertisers are limited only by their imaginations. And the financial stakes are high, as corporations strive to "brand" children early. Asked by the *Pittsburgh Business Times* why sports firms are interested in sponsorship agreements with schools, Ted Black, an attorney with the Pittsburgh firm Katarincic & Salmon, replied: "The number-one reason is to build brand loyalty and to build it as early as possible." Kevin Popovic, a marketing specialist with the St. George Group, noted in 1997: "Once you have a loyal customer, you really have to do something to lose him. Companies are making the investment and buying that market early."[12]

Apparently the strategy is a success. According to James McNeal, about 90 percent of the product requests made by children to their parents are by brand name. "Customers cultivated as children may be critical of changes in products, both those they love and hate," he argues. "But they will probably be less resistant to price increases and size reductions."[13]

George Carey, the president of Just Kid, Inc., a Stamford, Connecticut, marketing company, noted that his firm's research found that when his company "asked kids to draw something cool, they overwhelmingly drew a brand."[14] *Technos* magazine reported that market research shows that

> brand names are important to kids, because they help young consumers forge and express their identities. If marketers can capitalize on that need for self-expression, if they can woo and win the child, they're likely to enjoy his or her loyalty for the next 70 years.[15]

Thus, the message to marketers is clear: Establish product loyalty as soon as possible. In other words, to paraphrase the apocryphal comment attributed to Willy Sutton, the bank robber, who allegedly said he robbed banks "because that's where the money is," schools attract advertisers because that's where the children are, and because they represent one of the least ad-saturated environments available.

The Motives of School Leaders

Schools push for partnerships with corporations because school leaders often believe that they will benefit financially.[16] Further, they may also perceive that being seen as good "partners" with business will enhance their broader political support and thereby further enhance their financial security.[17]

Research findings support these notions. A 2012 report released by Public Citizen cited district officials who described a "desperate need for funding that they believe warrants the intrusion of advertising into the educational system," and who believed that advertising brought financial benefits worth what they perceived to be relatively insignificant risk. [18]

Although several states had started to cut education funding even before the Great Recession that began in 2007, the economic downturn led to an ongoing reduction in spending across the United States. [19] Not only has federal aid to states fallen, but most states have continued to fund education at lower than prerecession levels. [20]

A review of state funding by the Center on Budget and Policy Priorities found that thirty-five states provided less funding per student, in constant dollars, to local school districts in the fiscal year 2014 than they provided in 2008. Even among states that increased spending in 2014, as the economy was recovering, most did not bring spending back to 2008 levels. [21]

Arizona, for instance, cut spending by $633 per student between 2008 and 2013 and increased it by $4 in 2014, for a total reduction of $629 between 2008 and 2014. [22] School districts across the nation are fiscally stressed, leaving them ever more open to the enticements of corporate "partnerships" that promise to bring in any money at all. [23]

Limited Financial Payout

Despite the promise of millions of dollars in marketing revenue for schools, it is by no means clear that the fiscal benefits are as great as supporters of sponsorship programs and other commercializing activities suggest. In 1993, Colorado Springs School District 11 was the first in the nation to launch a comprehensive campaign to offer advertisers a chance to rent space in its hallways, on its buses, and at other locations on its property. *Marketing News* reported that between 1993 and 1997, the district received $338,680 from advertisers. With approximately 36,000 students, that works out to about $2.50 per student per year over the four-year period. [24]

This finding is consistent with our own research. Our nationwide study of school leaders found that in the 2003–2004 school year, 67.4 percent of schools that engaged in commercial activities that were meant to generate income received none at all, and that only 0.4 percent of schools generated more than $50,000. [25] Public Citizen reported in 2012 that seemingly big-money contracts such as that in Colorado Springs tend to bring at most 0.03 percent of districts' budgets.[26]

It is likely that the real financial winners in the trend toward sponsorship and exclusive sales agreements are not schools but the firms that broker the deals, because marketing firms that help negotiate agreements between school districts and corporations can take up to 40 percent of corporate payout.[27]

CONCERNS RAISED ABOUT COMMERCIALISM IN SCHOOL

Some stakeholders believe that corporations are good partners who will eventually employ students, or that since corporations market to children anyway, they should do it in a way that will benefit schools.[28] They tend to argue either that children need to learn how to navigate the marketing to which they are exposed in every other aspect of their lives, or that children are already too savvy about it to be negatively influenced by more exposure in school.[29]

Often when stakeholders worry about the potential implications for students, their concern centers on the character of the marketing to which children will be exposed (e.g., sexual or alcohol-related content).[30] For this reason, regulations and district advertising guidelines typically restrict the nature of products that can be advertised at school (eliminating alcohol, tobacco, and illegal drugs, for example) and also restrict features of the advertising itself (eliminating sexual, political, religious, criminal, violent, or profane content, undertones, or depictions).[31] Such regulations address stakeholders' concerns about ad content while establishing the legitimacy of advertising within the district.

Broadly, stakeholders are concerned with balancing a variety of demands: they want to increase income to struggling districts without adding to residents' tax burden.[32] Ideally, this would come with no or little up-front cost. Marketing companies that set up an advertising program in exchange for a percentage of the returns satisfy this need, even when their compensation percentage is high (20 to 50 percent, according to a Public Citizen report).[33]

THREATS POSED BY COMMERCIALIZING ACTIVITIES IN SCHOOL

Since 2010, our research has explored the dangers of exposing children to corporate commercializing activities at school. If activities such as fundraising programs, sponsored educational materials, and incentive programs were not at all harmful, it could reasonably be argued that they are a benign way for schools to pick up a few extra dollars and to demonstrate engagement with the business community.

Our analysis, however, suggests specific, serious threats to children's physical and psychological well-being, and to the integrity of their education, associated with corporate commercializing activities at school.[34] This is partly a result of the nature of products typically advertised at school: food and beverages (of the not-good-for-you kind) are, for example, the class of product most marketed in schools.[35] This marketing, by encouraging children to eat more and more of foods that are harmful to them when eaten to excess, may contribute to the development of metabolic syndrome, obesity, and illnesses associated with them.[36]

In addition to promoting a particular product, every advertisement reinforces the assumption that the path to happiness and satisfaction lies through consumption. This powerful belief is all the more effectively taught because it is promoted invisibly as an *a priori* assumption and is therefore seldom questioned.[37]

At the same time, research suggests that the materialistic values promoted by advertising and marketing are associated with higher rates of anxiety, depression, psychological distress, chronic physical symptoms, and lower self-esteem.[38] In teenagers, higher materialistic values also correlate with increased smoking, drinking, drug use, weapon carrying, vandalism, and truancy.[39]

Especially for teenagers, advertising exploits psychological vulnerabilities—in particular, their reduced ability to control impulsive behaviors and to resist immediate gratification—and increases their susceptibility to peer influence and image advertising.[40] In other words, advertising creates or amplifies adolescents' insecurities, then sells them a "solution" for those insecurities in the form of a product that cannot solve the problem the advertising itself created or attached itself to.

Finally, marketing in schools poses a threat to the quality of the education students receive, in several possible ways.[41] Specifically, it can undermine curricular messages, as Coca-Cola– or Pepsi-branded vending machines in school do, delivering by their presence a standing challenge to the school's nutrition lessons.[42] Marketing can also displace educational activities, as when students go on a field trip to their local supermarket, assisted by Field Trip Factory.[43]

Advertising and marketing are also ways to encourage children to hold a positive attitude toward a corporation's sponsored brand or worldview, as when Shell's *Energize Your Future* sponsored curriculum addresses the importance of developing many energy sources and casts Shell as a leader in alternative technologies.[44]

Shell's materials may not explicitly contradict what the children learn about energy in their regular curriculum. But when a corporate worldview is taught as objective and relevant fact, rather than as a self-interested perspective or corporate public relations, and when that worldview is transmitted by a trusted source of information—the teacher—the corporate-provided materials influence students to accept the legitimacy of Shell's self-interested message.

Marketing programs pose threats of varying intensity, however, because the characteristics of the sponsoring entity, the nature of the product, and the advertising itself vary and appear in different combinations. Many school board members tacitly acknowledge this reality when they struggle to develop their advertising guidelines to distinguish between permissible and non-permissible advertising in their district schools.

A marketing program that poses the multiple types of threats we have defined (i.e., to children's psychological well-being, to their physical well-being, or to the integrity of their education) may or may not be more potent than a marketing program that poses only a single type of threat.

Additionally, certain features of the school setting are likely to increase the effectiveness, and concurrently the threat, of individual promotions and programs. For instance, we and others have pointed out that students are likely to assume that their school and teachers approve of the promoted products, which enhances the credibility of commercial messages.[45] To the extent that children perceive the school as an authoritative or credible source of information, they would be more likely to "take its word" for products it seems to endorse. The same is true with respect to teachers: the more credible teachers are as a source of information, the more credibility students are likely to assign to marketing linked to their teachers.

It is not quite as simple as one New Jersey administrator put it when he asked rhetorically, "If you can sell a little space and bring in discretionary money for student programs, why not?"[46] We believe all advertising poses some threat to children—but also that not all threats are equal. At the same time, it is also not as simple as saying that if a school allows a given advertisement, it necessarily presents a serious threat to children's education.

HOW WE GOT HERE

Commercial activity in public spaces generally, not just in schools, has expanded at an exponential rate over the past century.[47] It is so ubiquitous in modern Western nations that we tend to assume that it is natural, even necessary.[48]

Advertising, marketing, and commercialism are omnipresent in most of the environments in which children find themselves. Marketing messages are constantly transmitted through children's televisions, computers, and phones. Schools, however, have historically been seen as qualitatively different from these other environments. Children are, after all, required to be in school for the commonly understood civic purpose of being guided toward learning and growth by adults who have special training and qualifications to provide them with educative experiences.

Regardless of how gullible or how savvy children may be about advertising, situational factors of the school environment make children susceptible to advertisements and marketing that are essentially "embedded" product placements, in a relatively uncluttered space.[49]

Although unlikely to think about it explicitly, students are likely to expect that the gatekeepers of the information transmitted to them at school are, in fact, serving their best interests by presenting accurate information and weeding out attempts at manipulation. The students are, therefore, likely to assume that their administrators and teachers endorse products promoted in school, and they are unlikely to discount advertising and marketing in school in the same ways that they might in clearly commercial settings such as shopping malls. These situational factors contribute to a persuasive environment that would be difficult for even the most sophisticated marketing targets to negotiate, much less children.[50]

The presence of marketing in school is not a new phenomenon. It results from the volume and intensity of marketing in our society in general and increased focus on children and youth in particular.

Marketing to children has existed in American society for the past century, but its development has picked up in pace. The National Education Association was worried enough about the introduction of corporate "propaganda" in the classroom to investigate and publish a report about it in 1929. Over the last three decades two policy trends—fewer regulatory restrictions on business activities, including advertising, and a chronic lack of adequate public funding for public education—helped to erode barriers to commercialism in schools. With regulatory restrictions weakened, corporations intensified their efforts to market in schools.

Estimates of the amount of money spent marketing to children vary. The Center for Science in the Public Interest (CSPI) estimated in 2005 that marketing aimed at young people totaled $15 billion a year, twice what it had been the decade before.[51] More recently, the Federal Trade Commission's 2012 research on food marketing found that this sector alone accounted for $1.79 billion in 2009 spending.[52] Forty-eight major national food and beverage corporations spent $149 million to market in schools in that year.[53] For businesses that want to target the youth market, any opportunities to reach it are highly sought after. And as schools continue to face funding challenges, they continue to be tempted by schoolhouse commercializing activities. Our 2006 study found 82.6 percent of district public schools had advertising by corporations.[54]

In the early 1990s, some particularly overt types of commercialism, especially the commercial television company Channel One's advertising to students,[55] moved school leaders, parents, and other stakeholders to protest and led some states to pass legislation limiting commercialism in schools.[56]

Times have changed, however. Two organizations that had expressed strong concern about school commercialism in the early 1990s, the National PTA and the American Association of School Superintendents, have since shelved their anticommercialism resolutions and no longer consider commercialism a priority concern. In 2001, administrators and organizations such as the National Association of Secondary School Principals joined forces with local bottlers, vending machine lobbyists, and Channel One to defeat a bill aimed at limiting commercialism in Maryland public schools.[57] In 2014, the School Nutrition Association, concerned about the "long-term financial solvency of child nutrition pro-grams," joined the food industry in trying to weaken the school food standards authorized by the Healthy Hunger-Free Kids Act of 2010.[58]

Supported by the concern about job loss in the recent recession, policy makers have promoted introducing corporations into schools as a way of ensuring jobs for children when they graduate. In his State of the Union address in 2013, President Obama emphasized the importance of educa-tion for putting students "on a path to a good job" and lauded IBM for providing funds, sponsoring school programs and educational materials, and helping design curricula at P-TECH, a Brooklyn, New York, school oriented toward science, technology, engineering, and math (STEM).[59]

Corporate domination of public space, including schools, seems obvi-ous and natural to those who grew up in recent years. The corporate capture of public space is, however, neither natural nor necessary.[60] And while postschool employment is certainly important, giving corporate marketers access to schoolchildren is not the obvious best way of assur-ing students' job prospects.

Policy tends to support commercial activities in schools, mostly by omission: in other words, by not addressing it. As was the case in the early 1990s, however, when a particular type of commercial activity, such as electronic marketing, catches the attention of parents and advocates, it can lead to policy reform. Currently, stakeholders' concern about student privacy has led to a rash of bills to address particular aspects of student privacy, some of them touching on commercial use of student data. Over-all, however, to this point policy reform has been halting and piecemeal.

In the absence of a countervailing ethic backed up by strong policies putting schools off-limits to corporate marketing plans, the combination of temptations for both schools and corporations leads almost inevitably to pervasive schoolhouse commercialism. It has become clear to us that although school commercialism is often wrapped in the benign trappings of a "partnership" with a public-spirited corporation, as we shall see, advertising and marketing in schools is anything but benign.

Schools are one of the only places still available where children can exist outside of our pervasive consumer culture. They can be places where children explore possibilities for their lives, their values, and their selves other than those that corporations define for them.

NOTES

1. Root, K. (2014, June 2). Personal communication (telephone) with Faith Boninger.

2. Nike, Inc. (2013, February 23). Nike Announces $50 Million Commitment to Get Kids Moving. Retrieved May 22, 2014, from http://nikeinc.com/news/nike-announces-50-million-commitment-to-get-kids-moving.

3. Dictionary.com (n.d.). Marketing. Author. Retrieved February 25, 2014, from http://dictionary.reference.com/browse/Marketing; Dictionary.com (n.d.). Advertising. Author. Retrieved February 25, 2014, from http://dictionary.reference.com/browse/advertising?s=t.

4. Brown, L., ed. (1993). *The New Shorter Oxford English Dictionary*. Oxford: Clarendon Press, p. 451.

5. Twitchell, J. B. (1999). *Lead Us into Temptation*. New York: Columbia University Press, p. 30.

6. Jacobson, M. F., & Mazur, L. A. (1995). *Marketing Madness*. Boulder, CO: Westview Press, p. 12.

7. The exact amount of child spending is difficult to pin down, both because most estimates are proprietary and because of variables (such as the age range of children) included in any estimate, whether the estimate includes children's direct purchases only or also their influence on parent purchases, and what product categories are included in the estimate. The Institute of Medicine's report cited below has a good discussion of child spending on pp. 153–55. It cites a 2003 proprietary study that found $500 in direct and indirect spending by two- to fourteen-year-olds. In 2006, the *Economist* cited James McNeal, a noted and oft-cited expert in this area, as estimating that children under fourteen influenced as much as 47 percent of American household spending in 2005, amounting to more than $700 billion. This overall number is based on estimates of $40 billion in children's own spending power, $340 billion in direct influence, and $340 billion in indirect influence. *The Economist*. (2006). Trillion-Dollar Kids. Retrieved February 4, 2015, from http://www.economist.com/node/8355035; Institute of Medicine. (2006). *Food Marketing to Children and Youth: Threat or Opportunity?* Washington, DC: The National Academies Press. Retrieved January 31, 2013, from http://www.nap.edu/books/0309097134/html/; Packaged Facts (2003). The U.S. Market for Kids Foods and Beverages—5th Edition. [cited in Institute of Medicine, 2006]. Abstract retrieved June 20, 2014, from http://www.marketresearch.com/Packaged-Facts-v768/Kids-Foods-Beverages-Edition-849192/#pagetop.

8. Molnar, A., Boninger, F., & Fogarty, J. (2011). *The Educational Cost of Schoolhouse Commercialism—The Fourteenth Annual Report on Schoolhouse Commercializing Trends: 2010–2011*. Boulder, CO: National Education Policy

Center. Retrieved December 5, 2012, from http://nepc.colorado.edu/publication/schoolhouse-commercialism-2011/; Jhally, S. (1997). *Advertising and the end of the world.* Media Education Foundation. Retrieved January 3, 2013, from http://www.mediaed.org/assets/products/101/transcript_101.pdf/; Kanner, A. D. (2008, November). *Now, Class, A Word from Our Sponsors . . .* Boston, MA: Campaign for a Commercial-Free Childhood. Retrieved January 29, 2013, from http://commercialfreechildhood.org/sites/default/files/kanner_nowclassaword.pdf.

9. Molnar, A., Boninger, F., & Fogarty, J. (2011). *The Educational Cost of Schoolhouse Commercialism—The Fourteenth Annual Report on Schoolhouse Commercializing Trends: 2010–2011.* Boulder, CO: National Education Policy Center. Retrieved December 5, 2012, from http://nepc.colorado.edu/publication/schoolhouse-commercialism-2011/.

10. For a review, see Molnar, A., Boninger, F., & Fogarty, J. (2011). *The Educational Cost of Schoolhouse Commercialism—The Fourteenth Annual Report on Schoolhouse Commercializing Trends: 2010–2011.* Boulder, CO: National Education Policy Center. Retrieved December 5, 2012, from http://nepc.colorado.edu/publication/schoolhouse-commercialism-2011/.

Halpern (1998) points out (p. 453) that the transfer and use of critical thinking skills in a variety of real-world situations is facilitated by the creation of elaborated cognitive structures associated with those skills. Although she does not focus on the classroom and school environments as a source of developing those elaborated cognitive structures, she emphasizes that any program to teach thinking should draw questions and scenarios from the real-world contexts of the workplace and "in the exercise of citizenship" (p. 453). To the extent that students get practice extending the thinking skills they learn in class to the "real-life" contexts they face out of class, they may be more likely to recognize when other real-life situations emerge that warrant the application of their skills. Halpern, D. F. (1998, April). Teaching critical thinking for transfer across domains: Dispositions, skills, structure training, and metacognitive monitoring. *American Psychologist, 53*(4), 449–55. See also Rogoff, B., & Lave, J. (eds.) (1984). *Everyday Cognition: Its Development in Social Context.* Cambridge, MA: Harvard University Press; Perkins, D. N., & Grotzer, T. (1997). Teaching intelligence. *American Psychologist, 52*(10), 1125–33. For an example of a school environment that actively encourages critical thinking, see Weinstock , M., Assor, A., & Broide, G. (2009). Schools as promoters of moral judgment: The essential role of teachers' encouragement of critical thinking. *Social Psychology in Education, 12,* 137–51.

11. Give a Note Foundation (2011, September 9). Press Release: *Glee* Season 2 DVD strikes a chord with "Give a Note" Campaign to help save arts programs in schools. Mustech.net. Retrieved June 16, 2014, from http://mustech.net/2011/09/glee-music-education/.

12. Carlisle, A. T. (1997, July 7). Be true to your school (sponsor). *Pittsburgh Business Times.*

13. McNeal, J. U. (1998, April). Tapping the three kids' markets. *American Demographics.* 37–41.

14. *Selling to Kids* (1997, April 2). Global Study: A Roadmap for Marketers. Author.

15. Reese, S. (1996, Winter). Kidmoney: Children as Big Business. *Technos.* 19–22.

16. Molnar, A., Garcia, D. R., Boninger, F., & Merrill, B. (2006, 1 January). *A National Survey of the Types and Extent of the Marketing of Foods of Minimal Nutritional Value in Schools.* Commercialism in Education Research Unit, Arizona State University. Retrieved June 16, 2014, from http://nepc.colorado.edu/publication/national-survey-types-and-extent-marketing-foods-minimal-nutritional-value-schools.

17. Brent, B. O., & Lunden, S. (2009). Much ado about very little: The benefits and costs of school-based commercial activities. *Leadership and Policy in Schools, 8*(3), 307–36.

18. This report found not only that district officials were often unaware of exactly how much they were making from commercial arrangements, but also that the financial gain usually accounted for less than 1 percent of their district budgets. Ben Ishai, E. (2012, February). School commercialism: High cost, low revenues. *Public Citizen.* Retrieved June 16, 2014, from http://www.commercialalert.org/PDFs/SchoolCommercialismReport_PC.pdf. In 2013, the New Jersey School Boards Association conducted an informal survey of members that corroborated findings that districts make little money from advertising programs in school: New Jersey School Boards Association (2013, March 26). Advertising in schools. For most schools, only a modest money-maker. *School Board Notes, XXXVI* (33). Retrieved April 2, from http://www.njsba.org/news/sbn/20130326/advertising-in-schools-for-most-schools-only-modest-money-maker.php. See also Molnar, A., Garcia, D. R., Boninger, F., & Merrill, B. (2006, 1 January). *A National Survey of the Types and Extent of the Marketing of Foods of Minimal Nutritional Value in Schools.* Commercialism in Education Research Unit, Arizona State University. Retrieved June 16, 2014, from http://nepc.colorado.edu/publication/national-survey-types-and-extent-marketing-foods-minimal-nutritional-value-schools.

19. Baker, B. (2010, December 23). The new normal? An extension of the old normal in many states. National Education Policy Center. Retrieved May 27, 2014, from http://nepc.colorado.edu/thinktank/new-normal. Leachman, M., & Mai, C. (2014, May 20). Most states funding schools less than before the recession. Center on Budget and Policy Priorities. Retrieved May 23, 2014, from http://www.cbpp.org/files/9-12-13sfp.pdf.

20. This analysis included forty-eight states. Indiana and Hawaii's education funding data are published in ways that make it difficult to make accurate historical comparisons. Leachman, M., & Mai, C. (2014, May 20). Most states funding schools less than before the recession. Center on Budget and Policy Priorities. Retrieved May 23, 2014, from http://www.cbpp.org/files/9-12-13sfp.pdf.

21. Leachman, M., & Mai, C. (2014, May 20). Most states funding schools less than before the recession. Center on Budget and Policy Priorities. Retrieved May 23, 2014, from http://www.cbpp.org/files/9-12-13sfp.pdf.

22. Leachman, M., & Mai, C. (2014, May 20). Most states funding schools less than before the recession. Center on Budget and Policy Priorities. Retrieved May 23, 2014, from http://www.cbpp.org/files/9-12-13sfp.pdf.

23. Blank, C. (2012). Missouri lawmakers mull allowing school bus ads. *Associated Press*. Retrieved on April 26, 2012, from http://hosted.ap.org/dynamic/stories/M/MO_XGR_SCHOOL_BUS_ADS_MOOL-?SITE=MOCAP&SECTION=STATE&TEMPLATE=DEFAULT; Ben Ishai, E. (2012, February). School commercialism: High cost, low revenues. *Public Citizen*. Retrieved June 16, 2014, from http://www.commercialalert.org/PDFs/SchoolCommercialism-Report_PC.pdf; D'Amico, D. (2012). Cash-strapped schools look to fund arts programs through online competitions. Press of Atlantic City. Retrieved May 8, 2012, from http://www.pressofatlanticcity.com/news/press/atlantic/cash-strapped-schools-look-to-fund-arts-programs-through-online/article_9aae8502-05d3-11e1-af29-001cc4c03286.html; Education Funding Partners (2012, September). Cause marketing: The case for corporate marketing investments in public education to grow minds and mindshare. Golden, CO: Author. Retrieved January 23, 2011, from http://edufundingpartners.com/cause-marketing-and-education-white-paper; Hardy, D. (2011, October 16). To balance budgets, schools allow ads. www.philly.com/*Philadelphia Inquirer*. Retrieved October 16, 2011, from http://www.philly.com/philly/news/131929973.html; Reeves, A. (2011, October 9). Desperate times call for ads in schools. *Patriot-News*. Retrieved October 10, 2011, from http://www.pennlive.com/midstate/index.ssf/2011/10/anne_reeves_desperate_times_ca.html; Roberts, R. (2012, January 25). School funding 101: District looking at bus advertising, sales tax. *Lee's Summit Journal*. Retrieved April 30, 2012, from http://www.lsjournal.com/2012/01/25/78718/school-funding-101.html; Wainfor, S. (2012, April 23). Westerville School Board Finalizes Cuts. *Ohio Votes 2012*. Retrieved April 30, 2012, from http://www2.ohio-votes.com/news/2012/apr/23/4/westerville-school-board-finalizes-cuts-ar-1010287/.

24. Associated Press (1997, October 3). Schools grant Coke exclusive rights. *Marketing News*, Marketing Perspective, sec. 9.

25. Molnar, A., Garcia, D. R., Boninger, F., & Merrill, B. (2006, 1 January). *A National Survey of the Types and Extent of the Marketing of Foods of Minimal*

Nutritional Value in Schools. Commercialism in Education Research Unit, Arizona State University. Retrieved June 16, 2014, from http://nepc.colorado.edu/ publication/national-survey-types-and-extent-marketing-foods-minimal-nutritional-value-schools.

26. Ben Ishai, E. (2012, February). School commercialism: High cost, low revenues. *Public Citizen.* Retrieved June 16, 2014, from http://www. commercialalert.org/PDFs/SchoolCommercialismReport_PC.pdf. A smaller study of districts in New York and Pennsylvania found similar results: Brent, B. O., & Lunden, S. (2009). Much ado about very little: The benefits and costs of school-based commercial activities. *Leadership and Policy in Schools, 8*(3), 307–36.

27. *Dallas Business Journal* (1997, July 11–17). Advertisers Must Treat Schools with Kid Gloves (editorial). Author, 26; Ben Ishai, E. (2012, February). School commercialism: High cost, low revenues. *Public Citizen.* Retrieved June 16, 2014, from http://www.commercialalert.org/PDFs/SchoolCommercialism-Report_PC.pdf.

28. For example, see Rundquist, J. (2013, March 17). More New Jersey schools turning to advertising to make ends meet. Nj.com. Retrieved August 15, 2013, from http://www.nj.com/news/index.ssf/2013/03/schools_look_at_advertising_to.html; Castillo, A. (2014, February 13). Hillsboro School District to consider allowing corporate sponsorships, naming rights for extra funding. Oregonlive.com. Retrieved June 9, 2014, from http://www.oregonlive.com/ hillsboro/index.ssf/2014/02/hillsboro_school_district_to_c.html.

29. Rundquist, J. (2013, March 17). More New Jersey schools turning to advertising to make ends meet. Nj.com. Retrieved December 9, 2014, from http:/ /www.nj.com/news/index.ssf/2013/03/schools_look_at_advertising_to.html .

30. For examples, see Los Angeles Unified School District (2011, May 24). *Sponsorship Guidelines.* Retrieved April 27, 2012, from http://notebook.lausd. net/portal/page?_pageid=33,501466&_dad=ptl&_schema=PTL_EP; Roberts, R. (2012, January 25). School funding 101: District looking at bus advertising, sales tax. *Lee's Summit Journal.* Retrieved April 30, 2012, from http://www.lsjournal. com/2012/01/25/78718/school-funding-101.html; Curtis, D. (2012, November 22). In-school advertising stays out of Greater Nashua, for now. *The Telegraph.* Retrieved November 26, 2012, from http://www.nashuatelegraph.com/news/ 984742-469/in-school-advertising-stays-out-of-greater-nashua.html; Castillo, A. (2014, February 13). Hillsboro School District to consider allowing corporate sponsorships, naming rights for extra funding. Oregonlive.com. Retrieved June 9, 2014, from http://www.oregonlive.com/hillsboro/index.ssf/2014/02/hillsboro_school_district_to_c.html.

31. For example, see Cole, B. (2011, September 28). Norwood school committee considers advertisements at school. *Wicked Local Norwood.* Retrieved

October 1, 2011, from http://www.wickedlocal.com/norwood/town_info/history/ x504737131#axzz1ZjcuJrRU [no longer available].

32. *Advertisement Journal* (n.d.). School bus advertisements in Jordan. Retrieved September 12, 2012, from http://www.advertisementjournal.com/2012/ 09/school-bus-advertisements-in-jordan/.

33. *Advertisement Journal* (n.d.). Advertising possibilities for Verona Schools. Retrieved September 12, 2012, from http://www.advertisementjournal. com/2012/09/advertising-possibilities-for-verona-schools/; Ben Ishai, E. (2012, February). School commercialism: High cost, low revenues. *Public Citizen* (p. 17). Retrieved June 16, 2014, from http://www.commercialalert.org/PDFs/ SchoolCommercialismReport_PC.pdf.

34. Molnar, A., Boninger, F., Wilkinson, G., Fogarty, J., & Geary, S. (2010). *Effectively Embedded: Schools and the Machinery of Modern Marketing—The Thirteenth Annual Report on Schoolhouse Commercializing Trends: 2009–2010.* Boulder, CO: National Education Policy Center. Retrieved January 29, 2014, from http://nepc.colorado.edu/publication/Schoolhouse-commercialism-2010; Molnar, A., Boninger, F., & Fogarty, J. (2011). *The Educational Cost of Schoolhouse Commercialism—The Fourteenth Annual Report on Schoolhouse Commercializing Trends: 2010–2011.* Boulder, CO: National Education Policy Center. Retrieved December 5, 2012, from http://nepc.colorado.edu/publication/ schoolhouse-commercialism-2011/; Molnar, A., Boninger, F., Harris, M. D., Libby, K. M., & Fogarty, J. (2013). *Promoting Consumption at School: Health Threats Associated with Schoolhouse Commercialism—The Fifteenth Annual Report on Schoolhouse Commercializing Trends: 2011–2012.* Boulder, CO: National Education Policy Center. Retrieved August 13, 2013, from http://nepc. colorado.edu/publication/schoolhouse-commercialism-2012.

35. Molnar, A., Garcia, D. R., Boninger, F., & Merrill, B. (2006, 1 January). *A National Survey of the Types and Extent of the Marketing of Foods of Minimal Nutritional Value in Schools.* Commercialism in Education Research Unit, Arizona State University. Retrieved June 16, 2014, from http://nepc.colorado.edu/ publication/national-survey-types-and-extent-marketing-foods-minimal- nutritional-value-schools.

36. Institute of Medicine. (2006). *Food Marketing to Children and Youth: Threat or Opportunity?* Washington, DC: The National Academies Press. Retrieved January 31, 2013, from http://www.nap.edu/books/0309097134/html/.

37. Cultural observers long have noted that propaganda is most effective when it goes unnoted: "This is the secret of propaganda: those who are to be persuaded by it should be completely immersed in the ideas of the propaganda, without ever noticing that they are being immersed in it." Attributed to Nazi propagandist Joseph Goebbels, cited in, among many other places, Anthony Pratkanis and Elliot Aronson (2001), *Age of Propaganda: The Everyday Use and*

Abuse of Persuasion. New York: Holt Paperbacks (87); "Individuals are controlled through the power of the norm and this power is effective because it is relatively invisible. In modern society, the behaviour of individuals is regulated not through overt repression, but through a set of standards and values associated with normality which are set into play by a network of ostensibly beneficent and scientific forms of knowledge." McNay, L. (1994). *Foucault: A Critical Introduction.* Cambridge: Polity (94–95); "So the images, the values, the ideas of advertising are lodged inside us because that's the way all culture works. To not be influenced by advertising would be to live outside of culture. No human being lives outside of culture." Jhally, S. (1997). Advertising and the end of the world. Media Education Foundation. Retrieved January 3, 2013, from http://www.mediaed.org/assets/products/101/transcript_101.pdf/.

The "third-person effect" refers to the phenomenon that people tend to think that advertising and other such communications influence others more than themselves. See Davison, W. P. (1996). The third-person effect revisited. *International Journal of Public Opinion Research, 8* (2), 113–119. Retrieved September 28, 2010, from http://ijpor.oxfordjournals.org.ezproxy1.lib.asu.edu/content/8/2/113.full.pdf+html; Shavitt, S., Lowrey, P., & Haefner, J. (1998, July 1). Public attitudes toward advertising: More favorable than you might think. *Journal of Advertising Research, 38*, 7–22; *Advertisement Journal* (n.d.). School bus advertisements in Jordan. Author. Retrieved September 26, 2012, from http://www.advertisementjournal.com/2012/09/school-bus-advertisements-in-jordan/.

Other research shows that people are often unaware of the factors that influence their thoughts and attitudes: Nisbett, R. E., & Wilson, T. D. (1977). The halo effect: Evidence for unconscious alteration of judgments. *Journal of Personality and Social Psychology, 35*, 250–56. Retrieved March 31, 2010, from http://osil.psy.ua.edu/672readings/T6-SocCog2/haloeffect.pdf/; Wilson, T. D., & Bar-Anan, Y. (2008). The unseen mind. *Science, 321*, 1046–47. Retrieved June 23, 2010, from http://www.sciencemag.org.ezproxy1.lib.asu.edu/cgi/reprint/321/5892/1046.pdf/.

38. Schor, J. B. (2004). *Born to Buy.* New York: Scribner.

39. Kasser, T. (2002). *The High Price of Materialism.* Cambridge, MA: MIT Press.

40. For simplicity's sake we include "adolescents" in with "children," but adolescents are even more susceptible than younger children to the psychological harms caused by advertising because of the sensitivities associated with their developmental stage. Self-regulation guidelines for advertisers have only very recently begun to recognize adolescents' susceptibility; and up until now adolescents have been grouped with adults. For research on adolescents, see Food Marketing Workgroup (2011, July). Re: Interagency Working Group on Food Marketed to Children: General Comments and Proposed Marketing Definitions:

FTC Project No. P094513 (Comment on Marketing Definitions) (pp. 10–13). Retrieved September 9, 2011, from http://www.ftc.gov/os/comments/ foodmarketedchildren/07843-80010.pdf/; Montgomery, K. C., & Chester, J. (2009). Interactive food and beverage marketing: Targeting adolescents in the digital age. *Journal of Adolescent Health, 45*, S18–S29; Giedd, J. N. (2008). The teen brain: Insights from neuroimaging. *Journal of Adolescent Health, 42*, 335–43. Retrieved October 15, 2010, from http://download.journals. elsevierhealth.com/pdfs/journals/1054-139X/PIIS1054139X0800075X.pdf? refuid=S1054-139X(09)00149-9&refissn=1054-139X&mis=.pdf/; Pechmann, C., Levine, L., Loughlin S., & Leslie, F. (2005). Impulsive and self-conscious: Adolescents' vulnerability to advertising and promotion. *Journal of Public Policy Marketing, 24*, 202–21; Steinberg, L. (2008). A social neuroscience perspective on adolescent risktaking. *Development Review, 28*, 78–106.

41. Kanner, A. D. (2008, November). Now, Class, A Word from Our Sponsors . . . Boston, MA: Campaign for a Commercial-Free Childhood. Retrieved January 29, 2013, from http://commercialfreechildhood.org/sites/default/files/ kanner_nowclassaword.pdf/; Molnar, A., Boninger, F., & Fogarty, J. (2011). *The Educational Cost of Schoolhouse Commercialism–The Fourteenth Annual Report on Schoolhouse Commercializing Trends: 2010–2011.* Boulder, CO: National Education Policy Center. Retrieved December 5, 2012, from http://nepc. colorado.edu/publication/schoolhouse-commercialism-2011/.

42. Molnar, A., Boninger, F., & Fogarty, J. (2011). *The Educational Cost of Schoolhouse Commercialism--The Fourteenth Annual Report on Schoolhouse Commercializing Trends: 2010–2011.* Boulder, CO: National Education Policy Center. Retrieved December 5, 2012, from http://nepc.colorado.edu/publication/ schoolhouse-commercialism-2011/.

43. Field Trip Factory (n.d.). Retrieved June 19, 2014, from http://fieldtrip-factory.com/.

44. Shell Oil Company (n.d.). Educators. Retrieved February 4, 2013, from http://www.shell.us/environment-society/education/teacher.html/; Shell Oil Company (2006). Teacher's guide: Energizing your future with Shell. Retrieved February 4, 2013, from http://s03.static-shell.com/content/dam/shell/static/usa/ downloads/education/poster-intro.pdf/; Shell Oil Company (2006). Energizing your future with Shell (classroom poster). Retrieved February 4, 2013, from http://s03.static-shell.com/content/dam/shell/static/usa/downloads/education/ poster-final.pdf/. Shell is not the only energy interest attempting to influence children in schools. Climate Science Watch, a sponsored project of the Government Accountability Project, cites BP, Chevron, ConocoPhillips, Halliburton, and Pacific Gas and Electric as funders of energy education programs in schools. The American Coal Foundation also sponsors programs in coal-producing states. CEDAR, Inc. (2011). CEDAR, Inc.: Coal Education Development and Resource.

Retrieved February 4, 2013, from http://www.cedarinc.org/; *Climate Science Watch* (2010, December 23). Corporate funding in public education—is anyone watching? Author. Retrieved February 4, 2013, from http://www. climatesciencewatch.org/2010/12/23/corporate-funding-in-public-education-is-anyone-watching/; National Energy Education Development Project (n.d.). Sponsors. Retrieved October 28, 2011, from http://www.need.org/Sponsors-Partners/.

45. Molnar, A., Boninger, F., Harris, M. D., Libby, K. M., & Fogarty, J. (2013). *Promoting Consumption at School: Health Threats Associated with Schoolhouse Commercialism—The Fifteenth Annual Report on Schoolhouse Commercializing Trends: 2011–2012.* Boulder, CO: National Education Policy Center. Retrieved August 13, 2013, from http://nepc.colorado.edu/publication/schoolhouse-commercialism-2012.

46. Rundquist, J. (2013, March 17). More N.J. schools turning to advertising to make ends meet. Nj.com. Retrieved December 9, 2014, from http://www.nj.com/news/index.ssf/2013/03/schools_look_at_advertising_to.html.

47. Jhally, S. (1997). *Advertising and the end of the world.* Media Education Foundation. Retrieved January 3, 2013, from http://www.mediaed.org/assets/products/101/transcript_101.pdf.

48. Jhally, S. (2005). *Advertising as social communication* (online course; part one: Why study advertising?). Retrieved July 22, 2009, from http://www.comm287.com/partone/; McLaren, C., & Torchinsky, J. (2009). *Ad Nauseum.* New York: Faber and Faber, Inc. Retrieved July 31, 2009, from http://www.adnauseum.info.

49. According to market research firm PQ Media, companies worldwide have continued to increase their spending on product placement, even during the recession when they cut other advertising spending, because they know it works. Psychological research also supports the effectiveness of embedding persuasive messages so that the messages' target audiences do not counterargue against them. PQ Media (2010, June). *PQ Media Global Branded Entertainment Marketing Forecast 2010–2014.* Stamford, CT: Author, 12.

50. Eagly, A. E., & Chaiken, S. (1983). Process theories of attitude formation and change: The elaboration likelihood model and the heuristic systematic models. In Alice E. Eagly and Shelly Chaiken (eds.), *The Psychology of Attitudes.* Fort Worth, TX: Harcourt Brace Jovanovich, 305–25; Mallinckrodt, V., & Mizerski, D. (2007). The effects of playing an advergame on young children's perceptions, preferences and request. *Journal of Advertising, 36,* 87–100; Nairn, A., & Fine, C. (2008). Who's messing with my mind? The implications of dual-process models for the ethics of advertising to children. *International Journal of Advertising, 27*(3), 447–70; Petty, R. E., & Cacioppo, J. T. (1986). *Communication and Persuasion: Central and Peripheral Routes to Attitude Change.* New

York: Springer; Tellis, G. J. (2004). *Effective Advertising: Understanding When, How, and Why Advertising Works*. Thousand Oaks, CA: Sage.

51. Dunnewind, S. (2005, September 24). And now, class, a word from our sponsors. *Seattle Times*, p. C1.

52. Federal Trade Commission (2012, December). A review of food marketing to children and adolescents: Follow-up report (p. 5). Washington, DC: Author. Retrieved December 1, 2014, from http://www.ftc.gov/opa/2012/12/foodmarketing.shtm/.

53. Federal Trade Commission (2012, December). A review of food marketing to children and adolescents: Follow-up report (p. 23). Washington, DC: Author. Retrieved December 1, 2014, from http://www.ftc.gov/opa/2012/12/foodmarketing.shtm/.

54. Molnar, A., Garcia, D. R., Boninger, F., & Merrill, B. (2006, 1 January). A national survey of the types and extent of the marketing of foods of minimal nutritional value in schools. Commercialism in Education Research Unit, Arizona State University. Retrieved June 16, 2014, from http://nepc.colorado.edu/publication/national-survey-types-and-extent-marketing-foods-minimal-nutritional-value-schools.

55. Channel One is a company founded in 1988 that provides television equipment to schools under the condition that teachers show a daily, mandatory twelve-minute news program that includes two minutes of commercials. See, for example, Campaign for a Commercial-Free Childhood (2012, July 30). CCFC asks states to study Channel One news; letter outlines concerns, urges review of controversial in-school advertiser. Author. Retrieved December 9, 2014, from http://www.commercialfreechildhood.org/ccfc-asks-states-study-channel-one-news-letter-outlines-concerns-urges-review-controversial-school.

56. For example, Cal Ed Code §§ 35181-35186 (2013). Retrieved February 1, 2015, from http://leginfo.legislature.ca.gov/faces/codes_displayText.xhtml?lawCode=EDC&division=3.&title=2.&part=21.&chapter=2.&article=4.7.

57. Manning, S. (2001, June 15). The littlest Coke addicts: Soft drinks in schools. *Nation*. Retrieved June 24, 2014, from http://www.thenation.com/article/littlest-coke-addicts.

58. Hamburger, T. (2014, May 27). First lady gets moving against House measure to let school districts duck lunch mandates. *Washington Post*. Retrieved June 25, 2014, from http://www.washingtonpost.com/politics/first-lady-gets-moving-against-house-measure-to-let-school-districts-duck-lunch-mandates/2014/05/26/f3da60ae-e507-11e3-afc6-a1dd9407abcf_story.html; School Nutrition Association (2014, June 12). *SNA Comments on Senate Child Nutrition Hearing*. Author. Retrieved June 25, 2014, from http://www.schoolnutrition.org/Blog2.aspx?id=20575&blogid=564.

59. City University of New York (2014, February 13). President Obama praises CUNY's P-TECH HS in State of the Union speech. CUNY Newswire. Retrieved August 20, 2014, from http://www1.cuny.edu/mu/forum/2013/02/13/obama-praises-cunys-p-tech-hs-in-state-of-union-speech/.

60. Jhally, S. (2005). *Advertising as Social Communication* (online course; part one: Why study advertising?). Retrieved July 22, 2009, from http://www.comm287.com/partone/. McLaren, C., & Torchinsky, J. (2009). *Ad Nauseum*. New York: Faber and Faber, Inc. Retrieved July 31, 2009, from http://www.adnauseum.info.

2

SCHOOLHOUSE COMMERCIALIZING TRENDS, 1990–2006

In 1998 Greenbrier High School in Evans, Georgia, made international news when principal Gloria Hamilton suspended senior Mike Cameron. Mike, along with 1,200 or so of his classmates, was lined up in the school parking lot to spell out the word "Coke." Each class had an assignment. Standing on letters carefully marked off by the band director, seniors formed the letter *C,* juniors *O,* sophomores *K,* and freshmen *E.* Photographers in a crane captured the moment on film as Coke executives, who had flown in to participate in Greenbrier's Coke in Education Day, looked on. During the photo opportunity, Cameron unveiled a Pepsi shirt.[1] According to Mike, while delivering a dressing-down in her office, Ms. Hamilton not only told him he was being suspended for his disrespect but admonished him for potentially costing the school a lot of money.[2]

Ms. Hamilton was apparently worried that Greenbrier's chances of winning the $10,000 prize in a national contest sponsored by Coke, as well as the opportunity to collect $500 from the local Coke bottler, had been damaged by Mike's irreverent act. Greenbrier High was competing to win the $10,000 offered by the Coca-Cola Company to the high school that developed the best plan for marketing Coke-sponsored promotional business discount cards. Local Coke bottlers offered an additional $500 to the winning school in their territory. On the day that Mike Cameron exposed his Pepsi shirt in the Greenbrier High School parking lot, about twenty Coke officials were on hand to lecture on economics, provide technical assistance to home economics students who were baking a Coke cake, and help chemistry students analyze the sugar content of Coke. Coke in Education Day at Greenbrier High was described by Principal Hamilton as a "fun, instructional event." The school received no money from the Coca-Cola Company for organizing the day's activities.[3]

Surprised by intense media attention to the incident at her school, Principal Hamilton nevertheless stuck to her guns, commenting: "I don't apologize for expecting my students to behave in school." District super-intendent Tom Dorhmann defended his principal and pronounced himself "flabbergasted" by the media attention. He accused Mike Cameron of manipulating the press and called Cameron's act "premeditated." Super-intendent Dorhmann told the *Washington Post*, "The kid is preying on the press. He's used you."[4] Indeed, press coverage of the incident was hardly flattering to the school.

The director of the ACLU in Atlanta told the *Atlanta Constitution*, "This concerns me because basically, it's pimping our kids. Is it worth $500 for students to be out there hustling Coke?"[5] Editorial opinion was no kinder, with editorial writers raising a host of questions such as, from the (Baton Rouge, Louisiana) *Advocate*, ". . . has American society fallen so far that teens can be punished for not following the corporate party line?"[6] The *Omaha World-Herald* asked, "What exactly is a school doing sponsoring a 'Coke in Education Day' anyway? Promoting a commercial product to its captive audience of young people?"[7]

The (Raleigh, North Carolina) *News and Observer* was scathing: "Without even knowing it, der furious fuhrer [Greenbrier principal Gloria Hamilton] was imparting to the students a civics lesson in obsequiousness and greed. It is disquieting to think that a kid could be kicked out of school for refusing to regard an impersonal multinational corporation with the same reverence that the principal does."[8]

And, according to *Miami Herald* columnist Carl Hiaasen, the incident at Greenbrier taught students ". . . that money is more important than freedom of choice. It taught them that silence is more desirable than dissent, that conformity is better than being different. And it taught them that there is no shame in selling out, if the price is right."[9]

The $10,000 to be awarded by Coke to the winning school in the national contest and the $500 offered by a local bottler were, relatively speaking, minuscule. This is a tiny fraction of the advertising dollars Coca-Cola committed to its campaign to market its Coke discount card. *Advertising Age* reported that the company had a multimillion-dollar budget for "one of its most elaborate consumer promotions ever." One Coke distributor called the marketing effort ". . . one of our strongest programs ever. We're mainly going after kids, the junior and senior high crowd."[10]

At Greenbrier, at least, it seems the company got the school administration into the bargain.

In addition to concerns about civil rights and about the values being taught, some commentators worried about the health implications of Greenbrier's Coke in Education Day. Writing for the *Fort Worth Star-Telegram*, Bud Kennedy noted that "colas and other caffeinated soft drinks cause anxiety, irritability and loss of concentration" and commented puckishly, "I don't know whether Greenbrier had enough students to spell out Caffeine Free Coca-Cola Classic."[11]

The *South China Morning Post* questioned the motives of corporations pitching products in schools. "The reason why the saga [at Greenbrier High School] strikes such a chord among students and parents alike is because of the light it sheds on the steamroller tactics of soft drinks and other corporations to turn schools into nothing more than supermarkets where children can also take lessons."[12]

And the *Chicago Tribune* argued:

> Schools shouldn't be in the position of selling captive students to advertisers, whatever the excuse. They are entrusted with children's minds and they have no right to sell access to them. Even a quick glance at the sales pitches made by marketing companies peddling promotion ideas to schools makes it clear the whole point is to make money for advertisers, not to help kids.[13]

In a story published in London by the *Independent*, Marlin Schneider, a Wisconsin lawmaker, pointed out the potential conflict of interest arising from corporate marketing activities in schools. He asked, "What's next? Some large company coughing up money and then telling the school's social studies department, 'We don't want you saying anything bad about our labour or investment practices?'"[14]

Officials at Greenbrier High School might be forgiven for being caught off guard by the intense and largely negative press coverage of their response to a student wearing a Pepsi shirt at a Coke in Education Day photo op. Devoting school time, school space, and student energy to corporate-sponsored activities had become so widespread that perhaps the most surprising thing about the Greenbrier incident was that it hadn't happened before.

SCHOOLHOUSE COMMERCIALIZING TRENDS

Commercialism was not new in schools when Mike Cameron helped draw attention to it. It was already entrenched, and growing. In our reports on trends in commercialism in schools published between 1998 and 2006, we identified and traced media references to eight sometimes-overlapping categories of commercial activity in schools between 1990 and 2006 (all of which continue to be common marketing practice in 2015):

1. Sponsorship of Programs and Activities: Corporations paying for or subsidizing school events and/or one-time activities in return for the right to associate their name with the events and activities. This may also include school contests, scholarships, or support for particular school programs.
2. Exclusive Agreements: Agreements between schools and corporations that give corporations the exclusive right to sell and promote their goods and/or services in the school or school district. In return the district or school receives a percentage of the profits derived from the arrangement. Exclusive agreements may also entail granting a corporation the right to be the sole supplier of a product or service and thus associate its products with activities such as high school basketball programs.
3. Incentive Programs: Corporate programs that provide money, goods, or services to a school or school district when its students, parents, or staff engage in a specified activity, such as collecting particular product labels or cash register receipts from particular stores.
4. Appropriation of Space: The allocation of school space such as scoreboards, rooftops, bulletin boards, walls, and textbooks on which corporations may place corporate logos and/or advertising messages.
5. Sponsored Educational Materials: Materials supplied by corporations and/or trade associations that claim to have an instructional content.

6. Electronic Marketing: The provision of electronic programming and/or equipment in return for the right to advertise to students and/or their families and community members in school or when they contact the school or district.

7. Fundraising: Commercial programs marketed to schools to raise funds for school programs and activities, including door-to-door sales, affinity marketing programs, and similar ventures. [15]

8. Privatization: Management of schools or school programs by private for-profit corporations or other nonpublic entities.

As reflected in the number of media citations over the past twenty-five years, sponsored schools and commercialized classrooms have become the norm in the United States. Figure 2.1 below charts the number of citations for 1990 through 2006 for all eight categories of commercialism we tracked. [16]

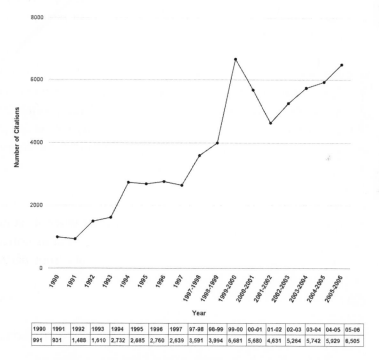

1990	1991	1992	1993	1994	1995	1996	1997	97-98	98-99	99-00	00-01	01-02	02-03	03-04	04-05	05-06
991	931	1,488	1,610	2,732	2,685	2,760	2,639	3,591	3,994	6,681	5,680	4,631	5,264	5,742	5,929	6,505

Figure 2.1. Combined Total Citations for All Presses and Activities.

Figure 2.2 compares the number of citations recorded for each of the eight categories for 1990–2006.

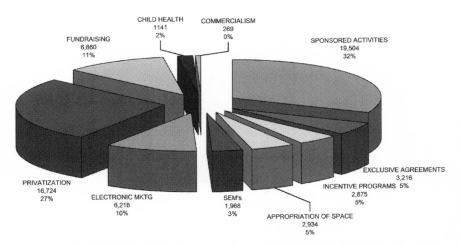

Figure 2.2. Combined Total Hits: Eight Categories of Commercialization, Four Presses, 1990–2006.

Tracking media citations provided us with a useful global picture of the growth of schoolhouse commercialism; however, using media references to track trends has several limitations. Press accounts are subject to the inconsistencies of editorial decision-making that are inherent in the mass media. Also, the more pervasive a practice or phenomenon becomes, the less "news" value it has and the less likely it is to surface in the media reports.

Practices that under official school district policy require school board action—the awarding of exclusive contracts to soft drink vendors or the decision to permit or to bar advertising—will elicit media coverage, while other activities, such as the use of particular commercially sponsored curricula in classrooms, crop up in reports only occasionally because day-to-day curriculum decisions, particularly when curriculum materials are supplied free by a marketing entity, tend to take place well out of sight of the daily press.

Search terms for categories of commercialism also necessarily change a bit year to year to take into account new marketers and marketing practices. Therefore, over time, the yearly changes in the number of citations within a category tracked became more and more suspect.

For these reasons, after 2006, we stopped reporting on trends based on the number of citations associated with commercializing activities and began to analyze the impacts of commercialism on children and schools.

The trends we observed from 1990 through 2006 in each category of commercialism we tracked are described below, along with specific examples of each type of commercializing activity.

Sponsorship of Programs and Activities

Sponsorship of athletic events appears to have helped legitimate sponsorship of programs and activities in schools. In 1984, for example, the Idaho High School Activities Association negotiated an agreement with the United Dairymen of Idaho that provided $37,000 for the travel expenses of students participating in boys and girls basketball tournaments.[17] By 1988 *Newsday* was accurately predicting that it was only a matter of time before "we see something like the 'Reebok/New York State High School Basketball Tournament,' the 'Nike/New York Scholastic Wrestling Championship,' or the 'Coca-Cola/New York Public School Track Meet.'"[18]

It soon became common for marketing firms to negotiate a wide variety of sports-related sponsorship agreements that funnel money to schools. The work of one such firm, School Properties, Inc., was described in a 1991 *Forbes* magazine article. The firm, based in Yorba Linda, California, was founded in 1987 to seek exclusive rights to sell sponsorships for regional and state championships in all sports. School Properties got 35 percent of the take the first year and 25 percent thereafter. In 1991 the firm negotiated a $2.8 million multiyear contract between Reebok and California Interscholastic Federation (CIF). The deal guaranteed that all California state play-off competitions and title events would be called the CIF/Reebok Championships.[19]

According to the *Sacramento Bee*, by 1993, 27 percent of CIF's 500-school Southern Section's $1.1 million budget came from corporate sponsorship, creating financial dependency and leaving the organization vulnerable to corporate decisions made on the basis of corporate, not school, priorities. CIF thus faced a financial crisis when Reebok announced in 1993 that it would not renew its contract because it wanted to focus on product-driven advertising.[20]

During the nineties, School Properties, Inc., also signed up Hardee's and First Security Bank for a sponsorship agreement in Utah, and Kraft, General Foods, and Burger King for one in Alaska. In the words of the *Forbes* article, ". . . you can thank [School Properties founder] Don Baird for bringing together big-time advertising and boondock jocks."

Some educators, such as Pinellas County, Florida, athletic director Bob Hosack, expressed concern. Hosack commented to the *St. Petersburg Times*, "It's a shame we have to do these things to raise money. But it's getting to a point where costs are so high [that] schools throughout the state and county are raising their own money. Just about anything they can think of that's legal is fair game."[21]

In California, some high schools rich in athletic talent came to be known simply as "shoe schools" because Nike, Reebok, Adidas, and others were lining up to give away products in hopes of courting future superstars. "The shoe companies are using the high school programs to increase their visibility, and that has created an uneven playing field," said Dean Crawley, a retired commissioner of the California Interscholastic Federation. "I would say there are probably eight to ten core schools that are sponsored by shoe companies like Nike in California. So to make things fair, they should create a league for those schools and call it a 'Shoe Division.'"[22] Athletic director Jim Perry of La Quinta (California) High School said shoes were even playing a role in school choice. "Open enrollment and shoe companies allow parents to shop their kids around for exposure and benefits, and that makes me sick."[23]

In the 1990s, sponsorship activities moved well beyond athletics. School districts and professional education organizations actively solicited sponsorships and sometimes formed consortia to do so.

Sponsorship is typically framed in terms of community goodwill and beneficence. For example, in 2005, when residents of Lacey's Spring, Alabama, opposed a new rock quarry in their community, they found that the quarry's owners, Rogers Group, Inc., of Nashville, Tennessee, had already secured community backing by agreeing to be a corporate sponsor for a local public elementary school.[24]

Although corporate branding programs are often attached to popular causes, a 2001 push by Cadbury Schweppes is more typical: to help market its Sour Patch Kids and Swedish Fish candies in the United States, the company distributed a half-million book covers with sample candies, targeting middle schools.[25]

In 1997, the Denver school district created a "Community Sponsorship of the Curriculum" program through which it invited local and national companies to support the district's education programs in return for advertising rights throughout the district. Sunkist, for example, sponsored Denver's Comprehensive Health Initiative. In return the company was given space for its "Just One—A Whole Day's Vitamin C" advertising campaign on school buses, scoreboards, and print material sent home with students.[26]

In 2004, NBC, Campbell's Soup, and Scholastic, Inc., teamed up to promote NBC's dramatic series *American Dreams* by sponsoring an essay contest for high school students that was coupled with a Scholastic curriculum on the essay topic, "How does your American dream compare to that of your parents?" Materials from the contest were distributed to 60,000 high schools and expected to reach 11 million students.[27] The program illustrates the seamlessness between marketing and popular entertainment; Campbell's soup products were to be "integrated into numerous episodes of the series," and a character in the show was to enter a similar essay contest.[28]

Still other scholarship programs yoke a brand name to a broader public policy discussion. In 2006, for example, Toyota awarded fifteen scholarships of $5,000 (Canadian) to Canadian students "who have demonstrated excellence in environmental community service"[29]—a subject that can be expected to serve the commercial and public policy interests of an automobile manufacturer in light of the industry's role in producing air pollution. Probably the most widespread of scholarship programs is the National Merit Scholarships, many of which carry the names of their corporate sponsors.[30]

In 2006 the American Automobile Association's national competition, the AAA Travel High School Challenge, brought together teenagers from around the country in team and individual competition to answer questions about world geography and travel, and included among its sponsors not only the automobile club but also airlines, hotels, a credit card company, and a chain nightclub. In a press release, AAA noted that the contest "was developed to build high school students' travel knowledge and geographic literacy, while creating awareness of career opportunities in the travel and tourism industry."[31]

Exclusive Agreements

The number of citations in the exclusive agreements category grew quickly between 1990–2006, perhaps as a reflection of corporate recognition that school-age children spend about a third of their money on food and beverages and that apparel spending has been a fast-growing category of the children's market.[32]

Food and Beverages Marketing in Schools

The classic example of exclusive agreements in schools is the "pouring rights" contract between a school or district and a soft drink bottler. In the late 1990s we found many stories that were routine accounts of school board meetings, usually in smaller communities, in which contracts between districts and soft drink bottlers were approved.[33] Over time an increasing number of articles examined controversies generated by such agreements.[34] Still later the media focus shifted again, to regulatory and legislative efforts to limit or bar the marketing, sale, or distribution of soft drinks and other foods of minimal nutritional value—so-called junk food—in schools.[35]

An August 2005 report from the Government Accountability Office (GAO) found that 75 percent of all high schools, 65 percent of middle schools, and 30 percent of elementary schools had some form of exclusive beverage-vending contract.[36]

Although beverage contracts have typically been portrayed as lucrative in the news (e.g., in 2005, *Newsweek* reported that soda and candy vending machines can produce returns to individual schools or districts of up to $75,000 a year),[37] research has not supported such claims. In 2005, the Portland-based Community Health Partnership (CHP), a public health advocacy group, found that the amount of money schools received ranged from $12 to $24 per student annually.[38] More recently, in 2014, Yvonne Terry-McElrath and her colleagues found schools' average per-student annual profit to be $1.75 for elementary schools, $1.54 for middle schools, and $4.18 for high schools.[39]

The growing backlash to its presence in schools was likely the cause for evolution in the soft drink industry's behavior with respect to its activities in schools. Between 2000 and 2006, thirty-four states created a state policy that, through legislation, regulation, or a combination of the two, required or recommended that schools adopt beverage standards.[40]

And in 2005, the Center for Science in the Public Interest (CSPI), a leading critic of the food and soft drink industries, along with lawyers who were veterans of the legal push against tobacco companies, announced plans to file a lawsuit in Massachusetts against Coke, Pepsi, and their local bottlers, seeking a ban on the sale and marketing of sodas in schools.[41]

By 2005–2006 the American Beverage Association (ABA) had begun to change its approach from outright opposition to regulation to promoting voluntary agreements. In May 2006, the industry announced a voluntary agreement, brokered by former president Bill Clinton, the American Heart Association, and Arkansas governor Mike Huckabee, to reduce the calories shipped for sale in schools. Under terms of the deal, beverage companies agreed to sell in elementary and middle schools only water, certain juices with no added sweeteners, and low-fat, regular, or flavored milk; and to limit portion sizes to eight ounces in elementary schools and ten ounces in middle schools. In high schools, the agreement permitted diet and unsweetened teas, diet sodas, so-called "fitness water," sports drinks, and light juice drinks, with portion sizes limited to twelve ounces.[42]

Importantly, the agreement imposed no limits on advertising on school property for banned products.[43] By agreeing to changes in which of their products they would sell in schools, the beverage companies preempted the suit, which would have addressed their marketing activities as well as their sales activities.[44] This has allowed them, in the years since the agreement was reached, to continue to focus—and focus others' attention—on the number of calories sold in schools rather than on the marketing done there.[45]

In 2014, after updates in USDA rulings on the nutritional value of food that can be sold in schools, the USDA is considering a rule to limit advertising in schools to only those foods that are eligible to be sold there (see chapter 4 for more discussion of this proposed rule).[46]

Athletic Apparel Companies and the School Market

In addition to the soft drink industry, the athletic wear industry, as we noted above, found a willing partner in schools during the 1990s. Having saturated the college market, manufacturers of athletic apparel, primarily Nike and Reebok, turned increasing attention to high school athletics, described by the *Sacramento Bee* as "one of the last untapped markets for corporations looking to tie themselves to a wholesome and marketable activity." According to Bill Paterson, author of the *Bee* article, another probable factor in Nike's decision to associate itself with high school athletics is the company's need to overcome the negative publicity associated with minority hiring, exploitation of foreign workers, and victimization of poor African-American children through its advertising practices.[47]

Athletic apparel agreements also involve sponsorship of some sort and are an opportunity that at least some educators seemed to welcome. Randy Quinn, executive director of the Colorado Association of School Boards, told the *Denver Post* in 1997: "It started on the university level. Nobody blinks an eye when Nike arranges for a contract with university football teams, or someone sponsors a scoreboard in university stadiums. The next logical progression in that movement would be the public schools. . . . Given the reality of economics and the scramble for dollars, it just seems to reflect reality."[48]

Incentive Programs

Corporate incentive programs are promoted to educators and parents as a source of income as well as aids to student motivation because they encourage desirable behavior, such as reading, by providing students with rewards (usually the sponsor's product or service) to either the school or to the children and their families or both.

The Campbell's Labels for Education Program has been around since 1973, and by 1998 had become a fixture in "tens of thousands of schools," according to the company.[49] In this program, schools can trade in labels from Campbell's products for a variety of equipment such as slide projectors, basketballs, film strips, computers—even a fifteen-passenger van. According to the *New York Times* in 1998, at 59 cents for a can of soup it would have taken $649,000 in soup sales to earn the van. The computer could have been had for $131,747.[50]

Instead of awarding schools with products, General Mills' Box Tops for Education program exchanges proofs of purchase for 10 cents each. Started in 1996, the program has grown over time by incorporating a variety of corporate partners.[51] The genius of the Box Tops incentive program is that it encourages parents and other adults to devise ways to encourage the children to collect as many box tops as possible.

In January 2013, its website shared tips on how some of its most successful coordinators raised money for their schools. The secret? Getting box tops in front of the children, teachers, and parents at all times, especially in the classroom.[52] One coordinator, for example, initiated a Box Tops Across America program, for which she sent every student home with a self-addressed envelope to send to a distant relative or friend with a note asking that person to collect box tops on behalf of the school. Then she created a U.S. map to display in the school hallway and pinned the cities and states as envelopes of box tops arrived.[53]

Another coordinator arranged for the classroom that collected the most box tops to win extra recess time, and created a "traveling Box Tops trophy . . . proudly displayed in the classroom." She involved teachers and encouraged each classroom to set—and meet—a Box Tops goal.[54]

Finally, a coordinator in Idaho offered this advice to others: "I'd recommend being consistent—consistently reminding students about Box Tops in the classrooms, consistently reminding parents about saving Box Tops. I'm a substitute teacher, so I'm popping into the classroom to remind kids to bring in their Box Tops every chance I get!"[55]

In advance of the 2008 elections, The UR Vote Counts program offered teen students an excuse to go to their local mall. It collected teens' votes there, enticing them with "the best discounts and offers available from our network of stores, restaurants, and partners via a monthly email delivered directly to U."[56] This program was marketed directly to social studies teachers via an e-mail to the member list of the National Council for the Social Studies.[57]

When incentive programs don't involve the provision of equipment or cash, they tend to say they promote learning. Perhaps the best example of a corporate-sponsored learning incentive program is Pizza Hut's BOOK IT! program. BOOK IT! has been around since 1985, and millions of children have participated.[58]

Students whose teachers are registered for this program are rewarded with a pizza if they meet the monthly reading goals established for them, and other prizes may also be awarded for class participation. As part of a 2004 promotion of BOOK IT!'s twentieth anniversary, the company awarded a South Carolina elementary school $20,000 as part of a contest in which students were enlisted to submit "a creative birthday wish" for the program's anniversary.[59] Pizza Hut gets its name associated with a worthy cause and an opportunity to promote its products to students and their families.

Other incentive programs include a similar reading promotion sponsored by the fast food chain Subway, grade-incentive programs sponsored by McDonald's and Denny's restaurants, and a reward program from Papa Joe's pizza restaurants that recognizes young people for their "acts of kindness."[60]

Appropriation of Space

Since virtually every public space in the United States, from bus stop benches to grocery carts, is already used for advertising, "clutter" is a major problem for marketers. Making an ad stand out is by no means easy. From this perspective, the attraction of schools and classrooms is obvious. Schools are filled with children who have money to spend, and they have historically been relatively ad-free. However, the situation changed dramatically between 1990 and 2006 as more and more marketing messages were directed to children in their schools.

In November 2005, for example, the Ypsilanti Public Schools in Michigan approved a policy permitting the sale of advertisements on school buses—making it possibly the first district in the state to do so, according to published reports (currently Arizona, California, Colorado, Florida, Indiana, Michigan, Minnesota, New Jersey, New Mexico, Nevada, Pennsylvania, Rhode Island, Tennessee, Texas, Utah, and Wisconsin allow advertising on the inside, outside, or both, of school buses).[61]

Shauli Zacks, a manager with Insight Media, the firm that contracted with the Ypsilanti school district to sell ad space, told the *South Bend Tribune* that preteens and teenagers "are power spenders" who were expected to spend nationwide some $51.8 billion over the course of a year. He added, "And for companies looking to build brand loyalty among kids, this is the perfect way to reach them."[62]

The sale of "naming rights" to finance new facilities—a novelty when we first began following commercial trends in schools[63]—became increasingly commonplace in the new century as schools and school districts awarded naming rights to corporate donors who gave money—tax-deductible to the corporation—for school buildings and maintenance.

In addition to such straightforward forms of appropriation of space, exclusive agreements are often also tied to appropriation of space, especially for exclusive beverage contracts that provide for branded scoreboards, coolers, and other equipment, and for branded vending machines, cans, and bottles.

Appropriating school space is an attractive strategy for marketers. However, not all corporations are willing to limit themselves to advertising on whatever surfaces schools have to offer. Many want to put their messages in the heart of schools' educational programs by sponsoring educational materials.

Sponsored Educational Materials

Sponsored educational materials have been around a long time. The magazine *Marketing Tools* traced corporate-sponsored educational materials as far back as 1890, when a paint company developed a handout on primary and secondary colors intended to be distributed in school art classes. The handout also contained a plug for the company's products. By 1929 the issue of sponsored content in schools was prominent enough for the National Education Association to empanel a committee (the Committee on Propaganda in the Schools) to study the matter.

Despite some occasionally harsh criticisms of the practice, sponsored educational materials have become a staple of marketers who want to put a corporate message in the school. In its 1995 publication *Captive Kids*, Consumers Union evaluated over one hundred of the sponsored materials provided by corporations, trade groups, and others and found the vast majority were highly commercialized propaganda or were educationally trivial, or both.

Sponsored materials are created with a marketing goal in mind and are therefore rarely, if ever, created with an enduring educational need in mind. As a result, the multitude of materials produced by and for corporations are hard to catalog because they very often have a short lifetime. There is no central clearinghouse that receives and catalogs them.

Sponsored materials may help a corporation or industry tell its "story" about a controversial issue; sell a product; or burnish its image as a good corporate citizen.

Examples of these sorts of programs have varied considerably. For instance, Highmark Blue Shield, a health insurer in Pennsylvania, passed out Wellness Homework Planners to elementary school students with "messages about health, nutrition, and physical activity."[64] BizWorld

Foundation, funded by a variety of corporate donors,[65] "provided curriculum to 3rd-8th grade teachers across the country . . . teaching entrepreneurship and business concepts in a real world context . . ."[66]

With the release of its film version of *The Lion, The Witch, and the Wardrobe* in late 2005, The Walt Disney Co. sent 250,000 "educational guides" to the film and the original story by C. S. Lewis to schools, hoping to get the book added to middle-school curriculums. "If we could get everybody in America to read the book, they might be excited about the movie," Disney senior vice president of publicity Dennis Rice told the *Chicago Tribune*.[67]

Scholastic, Inc.'s InSchool division has produced educational materials for such corporate sponsors as Brita, Disney, Microsoft, Nestlé, Playmobil, the American Egg Board, and Lexus.[68] In 2005, it worked with the cell phone company Firefly, distributing a curriculum on "communications inventions" to 75,000 teachers to help sell a cell phone tailored for eight- to twelve-year-olds to children and their parents.[69]

In 2011, Scholastic aroused controversy among environmental and other activists by producing sponsored educational materials for the American Coal Foundation's "The United States of Energy" fourth-grade curriculum, which emphasized the use and production of coal in many states.[70] As a result of this controversy, in July 2011, the company decided to halt distribution of the coal-related materials and to reduce (but not cease) its production and promotion of sponsored content.[71]

Video Placement Worldwide distributed company-sponsored videos on managing personal credit (by MasterCard), financial planning (by the Life and Health Insurance Foundation for Education), and the manufacturing operations of a candy company (by the Jelly Belly Candy Co.). Video Placement Worldwide shut down in 2011; however, a business that provides a similar service in 2015 is SchoolTube.[72]

In yet another example, Chase Bank commissioned a financial-literacy curriculum for second- and third-grade students for distribution in the 2006–2007 school year.[73] The curriculum was accompanied by a special piggy bank bearing the Chase logo. While a Chase spokeswoman described the program as "part of our philanthropy," the chief executive of the National Council on Economic Education warned that such programs typically are "tied to . . . marketing goals."[74] Regardless of whether a program such as this is presented as philanthropy, it promotes both the

Chase brand and the financial worldview that would lead potential customers to use the bank.

Although Chase discontinued that particular financial-literacy curriculum, the corporation still engages in promotions in schools. In 2012 it cosponsored a program run by musician will.i.am in Los Angeles, and in 2014 it worked with a Kent State student group to teach financial workshops for high school students that focused on spending and saving, opening and balancing checking and savings accounts, writing checks, depositing money, and creating and living within a budget.[75]

By 2006 it was common for sponsored materials to include some sort of audiovisual or electronic component. However, the continued development of electronic or digital marketing in schools merited a category of its own.

Electronic/Digital Marketing

Between 1998 and 2006 we tracked electronic marketing by following Channel One (television), Star Broadcasting (radio), and the Family Education Network (Internet/World Wide Web). In the 1990s, electronic marketing was dominated by Channel One, the Primedia-owned television service that provides television equipment to schools under the condition that teachers show a daily, mandatory twelve-minute news program that includes two minutes of commercials.[76] The vast majority of references in our 2005–2006 searches were to press releases distributed on behalf of Channel One itself; there were a handful of independently generated news articles about the company.[77]

Channel One still exists, reaching 5.5 million students daily without much fanfare.[78] Its commercial content peaked while it was owned by Alloy Marketing and Media from 2007 through 2012, but since Houghton Mifflin Harcourt purchased it in 2014, its commercial content is much reduced.[79]

The other primary example of electronic marketing from the early years is the cable television industry's Cable in the Classroom (CIC) program, which provided commercial-free programming licensed for rebroadcasting in schools.[80] Although not directly advertising commercial products, the program's executive director, Helen Soule, said in 2005 that it provides business benefits to the cable industry: it both indirectly markets cable products and promotes the industry to community regulators (who presumably can influence the terms under which cable franchises are granted).[81]

"Through CIC," Soule wrote, "cable has not only helped teachers and students, it has also realized business and public affairs benefits as schools purchase advanced services, as parents sign up for broadband at home and as policy makers understand the full range of what this industry is doing in communities across the country."[82]

Electronic marketing—which we now call "digital marketing"—developed rapidly in the first years of the new century.[83] Some programs followed Channel One's model of providing schools with equipment in exchange for the right to advertise to children. By mid-2001, for example, Network Next obtained signed contracts from five hundred high schools in which the schools agreed to display "discreet" advertising messages from sponsors such as H. J. Heinz Co., Walmart, and Bank of America as teachers delivered lectures to students.[84]

The deal called for NetworkNext to provide free mobile computer equipment to present Internet or PowerPoint presentations that would carry the advertising along with lecture content. The company announced a revenue goal of $250 million within five years.[85] (A news report noted, but did not elaborate on, the fact that the company was focusing its largesse on "the nation's wealthiest school districts."[86])

Sometimes digital marketing functions as "sponsored educational material" presented over the Internet. As early as 2001, Nuveen Investments, for instance, billed its website, Kid$ense, as helping children learn more about money. The site was promoted through elementary schools.[87]

In many other instances, the school serves as a portal by which students are encouraged to enter the digital marketplace. Children go online via educational sites or applications their teachers recommend in school, but once online, quickly expose themselves to sites that contain commercial content and/or that track their behavior for purposes of future marketing.[88] We will address digital marketing, which marketers recognize as the future of their field, in chapter 7.[89]

Fundraising

Fundraising is often done in conjunction with other types of commercialism, such as incentive programs (e.g., Box Tops for Education) or the provision of sponsored educational materials, events, or programs that ostensibly free up school or district funding for other needs ("ostensibly" because it is unlikely that a district would have chosen to fund field trips to car dealerships or pet stores, or an interscholastic "stock picking game" that promoted stock market investing, had those programs not been offered for free).[90] We began following fundraising as its own category in 1999–2000 because of the number of media citations that referenced fundraising as a distinct type of school-related marketing.

Restaurant-based fundraisers have been popular for a long time. Sometimes parents are encouraged to take the family out to eat so that the school can get a percentage of their bill. In McDonald's McTeacher's Nights, for example, teachers are recruited to work a second shift serving food to school families, again for a percentage of the bill.

In November 2001, teachers from 230 Southern California schools and from hundreds of other schools in the west spent part of a day working for McDonald's, with their schools taking 20 percent of the evening's sales in return. In December 2014, CBS news noted than in a recent investor conference call, McDonald's' U.S. president "told investors that the company will 'start with mom and we will be helping her to feel great about McDonald's—whether it's McTeacher's Nights, sponsoring kids sports, being a visible partner in local initiatives.'"[91]

Fundraising efforts abound. Many other restaurants run fundraisers that do not involve teachers but return a small percentage of the evenings' receipts to the school.[92] Students are regularly drafted to sell such popular products as cookie dough, candy, and wrapping paper to raise money for their schools or school clubs.[93]

A newer take on the traditional sales campaign removes children from the sales force and puts them back with their books: The commercialized "read-a-thon" offers children prizes for reading books. This is certainly an improvement over the other examples offered above, and improves also on Pizza Hut's BOOK IT! program in that it is not associated with branded products.[94] However, by offering children an extrinsic motivation for reading (winning prizes), a read-a-thon may actually reduce children's likelihood of developing an intrinsic love of reading.[95]

Privatization

A market potentially worth hundreds of billions of dollars established the "education industry" as something of a favorite among Wall Street investment advisors in the nineties. The "education industry" is diverse and includes firms that provide schools with supplies, perform services for schools, and own or operate preschools and postsecondary schools.

For investors, the desired model for the education industry is for-profit health care. As Kian Ghazi, an analyst for Lehman Brothers, a Wall Street investment firm, told the *American School Board Journal* in 1997, "The concept of making a buck off the dying and sick was outlandish 20 years ago. Making money off kids—that's the same kind of thing. So change is possible."

Between 1990 and 2006 we tracked only the segment of the education industry that manages K-12 schools for a profit. The privatization category is somewhat different from the other commercializing categories. We define privatization as the attempt to run public schools themselves for a profit. In the 1990s four firms dominated the industry: TesseracT (and its former name, Education Alternatives, Inc.), the Edison Project, Beacon Education Management (and its former name, Alternative Public Schools), and Advantage Schools, Inc. In 2009, because school privatization grew so much and because it differs from the other forms of commercialism in its relationships to advertising and marketing, we stopped following it as a type of commercialism in schools.[96]

SCHOOLHOUSE COMMERCIALIZING TRENDS—FROM 2006 TO 2014

As noted earlier, we stopped compiling media citations related to school commercialism in 2007. However, in the summer of 2014 we conducted searches of stories published by the top circulation dailies in the United States for citations to schoolhouse commercialism from January 1, 2011, through June 30, 2014, using search terms similar to those we had used in our earlier research.

In 2006, there were more articles about sponsored activities (32 percent) and privatization (27 percent) than any other category. Our 2014 searches produced few articles addressing school commercialism topics, with the majority of the stories taking up sponsored activities (30 percent) and fundraising (33 percent).[97] The focus on fundraising likely reflects the sorry state of school funding in the United States, especially since the economic downturn that began in 2008.

It is notable also that between 2011 and 2014, at least in the top circulation dailies, corporate activity in schools was not considered newsworthy. This may be because, by 2011, commercial projects in schools are assumed to be "business as usual."[98] Whether the newspapers are covering them or not, however, corporate marketing continues in schools.[99] For this reason, we turn our attention now to the potential effects of these marketing activities on the psychological and physical well-being of students and on the quality of the education they receive.

NOTES

1. Marshall, M. (1998, March 29). Gloria shoulda had a Coke and a smile. *Houston Chronicle*. Sec. A, p. 37, Two Star Edition.

2. Friddell, G. (1998, April 4). Student's act of cola defiance was refreshing. (Norfolk, VA) *Virginian-Pilot*. Sec. B, p. 1, Final Edition.

3. Choquette, K. K. (1998, March 26). Pepsi shirt 'joke' lands student in hot water. *USA Today*. Money sec., p. 1B.

4. Swoboda, F. (1998, March 27). For Pepsi folk, a joke on Coke (Neuilly-sur-Seine, France), *International Herald Tribune* (Washington Post Service), News sec., p. 1.

5. Davis, J. (1998, March 26). No Coke, Pepsi: Rebel without a pause. *Atlanta Constitution*. News sec., p. 1A, Constitution Edition.

6. Editorial. So what's next, Nike Elementary? (Baton Rouge, LA) *Advocate*, 29 March 1998, News sec., p. 16B.

7. Editorial. Pepsi shirt wasn't a huge crime. *Omaha World-Herald*, March 29, 1998, p. 20A.

8. Saunders, B. (1998, March 28). OK, class—line up, dress right, and salute the image (Raleigh, NC). *News and Observer*. p. A19, Final Edition.

9. Hiassen, C. (1998, March 31). Be true to your school . . . and its cola. Charleston (SC) *Gazette*, p. 4A.

10. Ross, C., & Kramer, L. (1997, November 17). Coke card promotion set for '98. *Advertising Age*. Retrieved January 15, 2015, from http://adage.com/article/news/coke-card-promotion-set-98/30940/.

11. Kennedy, B. (1998). School campuses no place to fight nation's cola wars. *Fort Worth Star-Telegram*, Metro sec., p. 1.

12. Beck, S. (1998, March 29). Cola joke hard to swallow. *South China Morning Post*. America sec., p. 11.

13. Beck, J. (1998, March 29). Selling our nation's schools to Madison Avenue. *Chicago Tribune*. Commentary sec., p. 19, Chicagoland Final Edition.

14. Usborne, D. (1998, March 29). Math and fizzics for the pupils of Dr Pepper (London). *Independent*. News sec., p. 21.

15. We began looking at this category in 1999–2000.

16. To examine the extent to which these types of commercial activity were present in schools, our methodology from 1998 through 2006 was as follows: We searched for mentions of them in the popular press and in the education, business, and marketing presses. The articles we found painted a picture of how students might experience, for example, a "sponsored program." By counting citations in each category each year and then comparing them to the citations we found in the same category in subsequent years, we were able to chart changes in the frequency with which each type of commercialism was mentioned.

17. Brewington, P. (1990, November 2). Budgetary shortfalls have schools courting corporations, parents. *USA Today*. Sports sec., p. 12C.

18. Herrmann, M. (1988, March 15). Get ready for sponsored sports. *Newsday*. Sports sec., p. 106, Nassau and Suffolk Edition.

19. Millman, J. (1991, February 4). High school hype. *Forbes*, p. 117.

20. Paterson, B. (1993, April 8). Corporate funding sometimes poor fit for high schools. *Sacramento Bee*. Neighbors sec., p. N10.

21. Cristodero, D. (1998, January 20). Schools find aid in ads, sponsorships. *St. Petersburg* (FL) *Times*. Sports sec., p. 1C.

22. Davidson, J., & Spears, S. (2001, March 15). Shoe-company influence strong at high school level. *Sacramento Bee*, p. C1. Retrieved July 2, 2014, from https://groups.google.com/forum/#!topic/rec.sport.basketball.women/PsRzQBd5ta0.

23. Davidson, J., & Spears, S. (2001, March 15). Shoe-company influence strong at high school level. *Sacramento Bee*, p. C1. Retrieved July 2, 2014, from https://groups.google.com/forum/#!topic/rec.sport.basketball.women/PsRzQBd5ta0.

24. Thomas, R. (2005, October 2). Proposed quarry prompts concerns. *Decatur* (AL) *Daily*. Distributed by Knight Ridder/Tribune News Service. Retrieved October 31, 2005, from LexisNexis Markets and Industry News Database.

25. Thompson, S. (2001, December 3). Cadbury's candy push. *Advertising Age*. Retrieved June 26, 2014, from http://adage.com/article/news/cadbury-s-candy-push/53205/.

26. King, P. (1997, April 14). On-sight insight: corporate sponsorships can serve a valuable purpose. *Nation's Restaurant News*, 16.

27. Schiller, G. (2004, September 10). Networks opt for events, brand tie-ins. *Shoot Magazine*. Retrieved July 23, 2014, from http://www.shootonline.com/node/31452.

28. Schiller, G. (2004, September 10). Networks opt for events, brand tie-ins. *Shoot Magazine.* Retrieved July 23, 2014, from http://www.shootonline.com/node/31452.

29. Government of Ontario, Canada (2006, April 20). Toyota Earth Day 2006 Scholarship winners recognized during Earth Week. Press release distributed by Canada NewsWire. Retrieved April 30, 2006, from the LexisNexis Business/Finance News Database. Toyota is still awarding these annual scholarships in honor of Earth Day. See Toyota (n.d.). Helping make every day an Earth Day. Retrieved July 22, 2014, from http://www.toyota.ca/cgi-bin/WebObjects/WWW.woa/wa/vp?vp=Home.Environ.EarthdayLanding&language=english.

30. See, for example, MacDonald, M. (2006, April 27). Corporate dollars for merit scholars. *Atlanta Journal-Constitution,* 7JH.

31. AAA Travel (2006, May 15). Travel challenge champ wins $25,000 scholarship. Press release distributed by Business Wire. Retrieved May 31, 2006, from LexisNexis Business/Finance News Database.

32. McNeal, J. U. (1998, April). Tapping the three kids' markets. *American Demographics,* 37–41.

33. Molnar, A. (1996). *Giving Kids the Business: The Commercialization of America's Schools.* Boulder: Westview Press; Molnar, A. (1998). *Sponsored Schools and Commercialized Classrooms: Tracking Schoolhouse Commercializing Trends.* Milwaukee: Center for the Analysis of Commercialism in Education, University of Wisconsin-Milwaukee. Retrieved January 15, 2015, from http://nepc.colorado.edu/publication/sponsored-schools-and-commercialized-classrooms; Molnar, A. (1999). *Cashing in on Kids: Second Annual Report on Trends in Schoolhouse Commercialism.* Milwaukee: Center for the Analysis of Commercialism in Education, University of Wisconsin- Milwaukee. Retrieved January 15, 2015, from http://nepc.colorado.edu/publication/cashing-kids; Molnar, A., & Morales, J. (2000). *Commercialism@School.com. Third Annual Report on Trends in Schoolhouse Commercialism.* Milwaukee: Center for the Analysis of Commercialism in Education, University of Wisconsin-Milwaukee. Retrieved January 15, 2015, from http://nepc.colorado.edu/publication/commercialismschoolcom.

34. Molnar, A. (1999). *Cashing in on Kids: Second Annual Report on Trends in Schoolhouse Commercialism.* Milwaukee: Center for the Analysis of Commercialism in Education, University of Wisconsin- Milwaukee. Retrieved January 15, 2015, from http://nepc.colorado.edu/publication/cashing-kids; Molnar, A., & Morales, J. (2000). *Commercialism@School.com. Third Annual Report on Trends in Schoolhouse Commercialism.* Milwaukee: Center for the Analysis of Commercialism in Education, University of Wisconsin-Milwaukee. Retrieved January 15, 2015, from http://nepc.colorado.edu/publication/commercialismschoolcom; Molnar, A., & Reaves, J. A. (2001). *Buy Me! Buy*

Me! Fourth Annual Report on Trends in Schoolhouse Commercialism. Tempe, AZ: Education Policy Studies Laboratory, Arizona State University. Retrieved January 15, 2015, from http://nepc.colorado.edu/publication/buy-me-buy-me-0.

35. Molnar, A. (2002). *What's in a Name? The Corporate Branding of America's Schools. The Fifth Annual Report on Trends in Schoolhouse Commercialism*. Tempe, AZ: Education Policy Studies Laboratory, Arizona State University. Retrieved January 15, 2015, from http://nepc.colorado.edu/publication/whats-a-name-the-corporate-branding-americas-schools; Molnar, A. (2003, October). *No Child Left Unsold: The Sixth Annual Report on Schoolhouse Commercialism Trends, 2002–2003*. Tempe, AZ: Education Policy Studies Laboratory, Arizona State University. Retrieved January 15, 2015, from http://nepc.colorado.edu/publication/no-student-left-unsold; Molnar, A. (2004). *Virtually Everywhere: Marketing to Children in America's Schools: The Seventh Annual Report on Trends in Schoolhouse Commercialism, 2003–2004*. Tempe, AZ: Education Policy Studies Laboratory, Arizona State University. Retrieved January 15, 2015, from http://nepc.colorado.edu/publication/virtually-everywhere-marketing-children-americas-schools; Molnar, A., and Garcia, D. (2005). *Empty Calories: Commercializing Activities in America's Schools: The Eighth Annual Report on Trends in Schoolhouse Commercialism, 2004–2005*. Tempe, AZ: Education Policy Studies Laboratory, Arizona State University. Retrieved January 15, 2015, from http://nepc.colorado.edu/publication/empty-calories-commercializing-activities-americas-schools.

36. Government Accountability Office (2005, August 8). *School Meal Programs: Competitive Foods are Widely Available and Generate Substantial Revenues for Schools*. Washington, DC: Author. Retrieved August 18, 2006, from http://www.gao.gov/new.items/d05563.pdf. See also Warner, M. (2005, December 7). Lines are drawn for big suit over sodas. *New York Times*. Retrieved January 15, 2015, from http://www.nytimes.com/2005/12/07/business/07soda.html?pagewanted=all&_r=0.

37. Tyre, P., & Stavely-O'Carroll, S. (2005, August 8). How to fix school lunch. *Newsweek*, p. 50. Retrieved January 15, 2015, from http://www.newsweek.com/how-fix-school-lunch-117759.

38. Pinson, N. (2005, April 14). *School Soda Contracts: A Sample Review of Contracts in Oregon Public School Districts, 2004*. Portland, OR: Community Health Partnership, p. 2. See also Warner, M. (2005, December 7). Lines are drawn for big suit over sodas. *New York Times*. Retrieved January 15, 2015, from http://www.nytimes.com/2005/12/07/business/07soda.html?pagewanted=all&_r=0.

39. Terry-McElrath, Y. M., Turner, L., Sandoval, A., Johnson, L. D., & Chaloupka, F. J. (2014). Commercialism in US elementary and secondary school

nutrition environments: Trends from 2007–2012. *JAMA-Pediatrics, 168*(3): 234–42.

40. Mello, M. M., Pomeranz, J., & Moran, P. (2008, April). The interplay of public health law and industry self-regulation: The case of sugar-sweetened beverage sales in schools. *American Journal of Public Health, 98*(4): 595–604. Retrieved December 6, 2014, from http://www.ncbi.nlm.nih.gov/pmc/articles/ PMC2376983/.

41. Warner, M. (2005, December 7). Lines are drawn for big suit over sodas. *New York Times*. Retrieved January 15, 2015, from http://www.nytimes.com/ 2005/12/07/business/07soda.html?pagewanted=all&_r=0.

42. *Memorandum of Understanding* (2006). Washington, DC: American Beverage Association. Retrieved July 14, 2014, from http://www.ameribev.org/files/ 336_MOU%20Final%20%28signed%29.pdf; Wilbert, C., Lee, E., & Ho, D. (2006, May 4). Beverage industry tightens policy. *Atlanta Journal and Constitution,* A1.

43. Wilbert, C., Lee, E., & Ho, D. (2006, May 4). Beverage industry tightens policy. *Atlanta Journal and Constitution,* A1; Lokeman, R. C. (2006, May 8). Turning back the flood of soft drinks at schools. *Kansas City Star*. Distributed by Knight Ridder/Tribune News Service. Retrieved May 31, 2006, from LexisNexis Popular Press Database.

44. Wootan, M. (2014, December 7). Personal communication (e-mail) with Faith Boninger.

45. American Beverage Association (2014). School beverage guidelines. Author. Retrieved December 11, 2014, from http://www.ameribev.org/nutrition-science/school-beverage-guidelines/. For another example of the focus on calories sold rather than on marketing, see the Healthy Weight Commitment Foundation: Healthy Weight Commitment Foundation (n.d.). Fighting obesity by balancing calories in with calories out. Author. Retrieved December 15, 2014, from http://www.healthyweightcommit.org/about/overview/.

46. U.S. Department of Agriculture, Food and Nutrition Service (2014, February 25). 7 CFR Parts 210 and 220, RIN 0584-AE25. Retrieved February 26, 2014, from https://s3.amazonaws.com/public-inspection.federalregister.gov/ 2014-04100.pdf.

47. Paterson, B. (1993, April 8). Corporate funding sometimes poor fit for high schools. *Sacramento Bee*. Neighbors sec., p. N10.

48. Bingham, J. (1997, August 20). Corporate deals boost school aims in Jeffco. *Denver Post*, Denver sec., p. B1, Second Edition.

49. CSC Brands LP (n.d.). Labels for education frequently asked questions. Retrieved May 15, 1998, from www.campbellsoup.com.

50. Hays, C. L. (1998, April 12). First lessons in the power of money. *New York Times*. sec. 3, p. 1. Retrieved January 15, 2015, from http://www.nytimes.com/1998/04/12/business/first-lessons-in-the-power-of-money.html.

51. General Mills (2013). About Box Tops. Retrieved January 22, 2013, from http://www.boxtops4education.com/learn/whyjoin.aspx/. The Avery Dennison Corporation ran a program in 2011 in conjunction with Box Tops for Education called Avery Gives Back to Schools. The top five schools at the end of the promotion won $10,000 worth of Avery school supplies, 10,000 Bonus Box Tops coupons, and $1,000 worth of gift cards. Twenty-five runner-up schools won 5,000 Bonus Box Tops coupons. Avery Dennison Corporation (2011). Avery Gives Back to Schools. Retrieved September 9, 2011, from http://givebacktoschools.avery.com/schools/index.

52. General Mills (2013, January 1). With bicycle safety top of mind, kindergarteners get head start to a great year. Retrieved January 22, 2013, from http://www.boxtops4education.com/Article.aspx/With-Bicycle-Safety-Top-of-Mind--Kindergarteners-Get-Head-Start-to-a-Great-Year/1716/.

53. General Mills (2012, June 27). Box Tops' own McQueen finishes with a flourish. Retrieved January 22, 2013, from http://www.boxtops4education.com/Article.aspx/Box-Tops-Own-McQueen-Finishes-With-a-Flourish/1696/.

54. General Mills (2012, June 1). Box Tops pixie makes magic. Author. Retrieved January 22, 2013, from http://www.boxtops4education.com/Article.aspx/Box-Tops-Pixie-Makes-Magic/1692/.

55. General Mills (2012, June 1). This Box Tops coordinator is consistent—and persistent! Retrieved January 22, 2013, from http://www.boxtops4education.com/Article.aspx/This-Box-Tops-Coordinator-is-Consistent---and-Persistent--/1689/.

56. General Growth Properties, Inc. (2008). UR votes count. Retrieved September 23, 2008, from http://www.urvotescount.com/index.php?option=com_content&view=article&id=93&Itemid=129.

57. Whitson, T. (2008, September 23). Personal communication (e-mail) with Alex Molnar.

58. Pizza Hut, Inc. (2014). Book it! Celebrating 30 years. Retrieved July 22, 2014, from http://www.bookitprogram.com/.

59. Pizza Hut, Inc. (2004, November 16). In celebration of its 20-year anniversary, Pizza Hut BOOK IT! program awards winning elementary classroom with $20,000. Press release for Pizza Hut distributed by Business Wire, Inc.

60. Taylor, V. (2004, December 9). Whipping up success. *Tampa Bay Times*. Retrieved July 23, 2014, from http://www.sptimes.com/2004/12/09/Hernando/Whipping_up_success.shtml.

61. Campaign for a Commercial-Free Childhood (n.d.). 2012 School Bus Ad Action Center. Author. Retrieved March 7, 2014, from http://www.

commercialfreechildhood.org/action/2012-school-bus-ad-action-center; Campaign for a Commercial-Free Childhood (n.d.). 2013 School Bus Ad Action Center. Author. Retrieved March 7, 2014, from http://www.commercialfreechildhood.org/action/2013schoolbusads; Southbendtribune.com (2005, November 20). Michigan school district allowing ads in buses. Author. Retrieved July 1, 2014, from http://articles.southbendtribune.com/2005-11-20/news/27009991_1_ad-space-school-buses-teens.

62. Southbendtribune.com (2005, November 20). Michigan school district allowing ads in buses. Author. Retrieved July 1, 2014, from http://articles.southbendtribune.com/2005-11-20/news/27009991_1_ad-space-school-buses-teens.

63. Molnar, A. (2002). *What's in a Name? The Corporate Branding of America's Schools: The Fifth Annual Report on Trends in Schoolhouse Commercialism, Year 2001–2002.* Tempe, AZ: Commercialism in Education Research Unit, Education Policy Studies Laboratory, Arizona State University. Retrieved January 15, 2015, from http://nepc.colorado.edu/publication/whats-a-name-the-corporate-branding-americas-schools.

64. Highmark Blue Shield to cover select services to prevent and treat obesity (2005, October 31). *PR Newswire.* Retrieved January 15, 2015, from http://www.prnewswire.com/news-releases/highmark-blue-shield-to-cover-select-services-to-prevent-and-treat-obesity-55677457.html.

65. See Bizworld.org's sponsorship page. Retrieved August 29, 2006, from http://www.bizworld.org/sponsors.html.

66. Bizworld Foundation announces benefit luncheon featuring Marc Benioff . . . (2005, December 13). Press release distributed by Market Wire for BizWorld Foundation. Retrieved December 31, 2005, from LexisNexis Markets and Industry News Database.

67. Caro, M. (2005, November 20). Chronicling 'Narnia.' *Chicago Tribune,* Sec. 7, pp, 1, 14. Retrieved January 15, 2015, from http://articles.chicagotribune.com/2005-11-20/news/0511200453_1_white-witch-narnia-wardrobe.

68. Lewin, T. (2011, July 31). Children's publisher backing off its corporate ties. *New York Times.* Retrieved August 2, 2011, from http://www.nytimes.com/2011/08/01/education/01scholastic.html; Scholastic, Inc. (2011). Lexus Eco Challenge. Retrieved November 2, 2011, from http://www.scholastic.com/lexus; Scholastic, Inc. (2011). Freebie Corner. Retrieved November 2, 2011, from http://www.scholastic.com/freebiecorner.

69. Spethman, B. (2006, January 1). It's for you. *Promo,* p. 16.

70. Alma Hale Paty's post presents a coal industry perspective on the partnership between the American Coal Foundation and Scholastic. Paty, A. H. (2010, November 30). American Coal Foundation and Scholastic, Inc.: Partnering for

energy education. Retrieved May 6, 2011, from http://www.coalblog.org/?p= 1590.

71. Lewin, T. (2011, July 31). Children's publisher backing off its corporate ties. *New York Times*. Retrieved August 2, 2011, from http://www.nytimes.com/ 2011/08/01/education/01scholastic.html?_r=1; Scholastic, Inc. (2011, May 13). Statement from Scholastic on "The United States of Energy." Retrieved May 17, 2011, from http://oomscholasticblog.com/2011/05/statement-from-scholastic-on-the-united-states-of-energy.html.

72. A to Z Teacher Stuff (2011, November 2). Video Placement Worldwide closing their doors. Author. Retrieved July 2, 2014, from http://forums. atozteacherstuff.com/showthread.php?t=152881; SchoolTube, Inc. (2012). SchoolTube Channels for Sponsors and Partners. Retrieved December 8, 2014, from http://www.schooltube.com/info/channels/.

73. Kish, M. (2006, May 15). Banks enroll to help educators. *Indianapolis Business Journal 27*(10), 21.

74. Kish, M. (2006, May 15). Banks enroll to help educators. *Indianapolis Business Journal 27*(10), 21.

75. Fox Business (2012, December 19). Singer will.i.am sets eye on financial literacy. Author. Retrieved December 15, 2014, from http://video.foxbusiness. com/v/2046167481001/singer-william-sets-eye-on-financial-literacy/?#sp= show-clips. Vindy.com (2014, February 2). KSU student groups, Chase Bank offer financial-literacy program. Retrieved December 15, 2014, from http:// www.vindy.com/news/2014/feb/02/ksu-student-groups-chase-bank-offer-fina/.

76. Channel One celebrates 15 years of journalistic excellence . . . (2005, October 4). Press release distributed by Business Wire for Channel One. Retrieved October 31, 2005, from LexisNexis Markets and Industry News Database.

77. See, for example, Henricks, J. (2005, November 17). Behold the power of advertising. *Dallas Morning News*, 10B.

78. Indication of how Channel One has become accepted is that in June 2012, it announced a collaboration with partners Promethean and the National PTA to create a Parent Connection program to deliver daily Channel One News broadcasts shown in the classroom directly to parents' mobile phones, to encourage parents and children to talk about the broadcasts. In July 2012, the Campaign for a Commercial-Free Childhood (CCFC) called on state education departments to study Channel One—particularly for hypersexualizing content associated with its website —and to encourage school districts to stop using it until their reviews of it were complete. Promethean (2012, June 26). Promethean and Channel One News announce *The Parent Connection*. Author. Retrieved August 1, 2013, from http://www1.prometheanworld.com/dutch/server.php?show=ConWebDoc. 18432; Campaign for a Commercial-Free Childhood (2012, July 30). CCFC asks

states to study Channel One News; Letter outlines concerns, urges review of controversial in-school advertiser. Author. Retrieved August 30, 2013, from http://www.commercialfreechildhood.org/ccfc-asks-states-study-channel-one-news-letter-outlines-concerns-urges-review-controversial-school.

79. The company switched hands many times. When Alloy owned it, it developed the website to link to its several other websites geared toward high school students. It also routinely ran interview segments with celebrities that were virtually product placements for movies and television shows. In 2014, publisher Houghton Mifflin Harcourt bought the company and reduced its commercial tone. The daily broadcast still contains two minutes of commercials, but the company is also selling a version of the program without commercials. Our perusal of several days of programming found no product placements as news segments, and the website no longer promotes hypersexualized content. Golin, J. (2014, November 13). Personal communication (e-mail) with Faith Boninger.

80. Rebranded as Cable Impacts, the program "highlights the positive use of broadband in education and commitment to the teaching of 21st century digital skills and citizenship." Offerings include sponsored educational materials and educational games and activities. National Cable & Telecommunications Association (n.d.). Education. Author. Retrieved December 8, 2014, from https://www.ncta.com/cableimpacts/work/573. Cable Impacts (n.d.). Teaching Digital Citizenship. Author. Retrieved December 8, 2014, from http://www.teachinctrl.org/; Cable Impacts Foundation (n.d.). Educational Games and Activities. Author. Retrieved December 8, 2014, from http://www.cableplays.org/; Jensen, E. (2006, May 22). Cable initiative a hit in classrooms. *Television Week*, 28.

81. Soule, H. (2005, August 8). Cable teaches media smarts—and helps its bottom line. *CableFax's Cable World 17* (15). Retrieved August 31, 2004, from LexisNexis Markets and Industry News Database.

82. Soule, H. (2005, August 8). Cable teaches media smarts—and helps its bottom line. *CableFax's Cable World 17* (15). Retrieved August 31, 2005, from LexisNexis Markets and Industry News Database.

83. In 2009 we followed common usage trends and began referring to "digital marketing" instead of "electronic marketing."

84. Lindeman, T. (2001, July 11). Point Breeze, Pa., Internet company signs up high schools. *Pittsburgh Post-Gazette.* Retrieved January 15, 2015, from http://www.highbeam.com/doc/1G1-76454984.html.

85. Lindeman, T. (2001, July 11). Point Breeze, Pa., Internet company signs up high schools. *Pittsburgh Post-Gazette.* Retrieved January 15, 2015, from http://www.highbeam.com/doc/1G1-76454984.html.

86. Lindeman, T. (2001, July 11). Point Breeze, Pa., Internet company signs up high schools. *Pittsburgh Post-Gazette.* Retrieved January 15, 2015, from http://www.highbeam.com/doc/1G1-76454984.html.

87. New Jersey Hills Media Group. (2001, January 24). Primer in capitalism offered to young Randolph students. Author. Retrieved June 26, 2014, from http://newjerseyhills.com/primer-in-capitalism-offered-to-young-randolph-students/article_d926fb8f-bcef-596e-bd55-2b3a1b82857a.html?mode=jqm.

88. Molnar, A., Boninger, F., Wilkinson, G., & Fogarty, J. (2009). *Click: The Twelfth Annual Report on Schoolhouse Commercialism Trends: 2008–2009.* Boulder and Tempe: Education and the Public Interest Center & Commercialism in Education Research Unit. Retrieved December 8, 2014, from http://nepc. colorado.edu/publication/schoolhouse-commercialism-2009.

89. Bernoff, J. (2009, July 20). Advertising will change forever: Digital spending will nearly double in 5 years, but ad budgets won't. *Advertising Age.* Retrieved July 20, 2009, from http://adage.com/digitalnext/article?article_id= 138023 [subscription required]; Dumenco, S. (2013, August 5). Never mind Publicis Omnicom. Are Google and Facebook too damn big? Retrieved August 13, 2013, from http://adage.com/article/the-media-guy/mind-publicis-omnicom-google-facebook-big/243478/ [subscription required]; Davis, J. (2013, August 19). Personal communication (telephone) with Faith Boninger.

90. Borja, R. R. (2004, October 6). New breed of retail field trips emerging. *Education Week, 24*(6), pp. 1, 14. Retrieved September 16, 2005, from http:// secure.edweek.org/ew/ewstory.cfm?slug=06retail.h24; Security Analysts of San Francisco holds annual fund drive to promote financial literacy (2004, October 6). Press release distributed for Security Analysts of San Francisco by PR News-wire.

91. Picchi, A. (2014, December 11). Why McDonald's says it wants "to be in the schools." *CBS News.* Retrieved December 13, 2014, from http://www. cbsnews.com/news/why-mcdonalds-says-it-wants-to-be-in-the-schools/.

92. Scholastica Travel (n.d.). 20 chain restaurants with fundraising opportu-nities for school trips. Author. Retrieved December 8, 2014, from http://www. scholasticatravel.com/2012/08/06/20-chain-restaurants-with-fundraising-opportunities-for-school-trips/.

93. For an example of a company that caters to school and other nonprofit organizations, see Best Fundraising Ideas in America (2014). Easy Fundraising Ideas. Retrieved December 8, 2014, from http://www.easy-fundraising-ideas. com/.

94. Read-a-Thon (n.d.). Reader online store. Author. Retrieved December 15, 2014, from http://www.read-a-thon.com/sample-store/.

95. Bem, D. (1972). Self-perception theory. In L. Berkowitz (ed.), *Advances in Experimental Social Psychology* (vol. 6). New York: Academic Press.

96. We did, however, continue to address privatization in a series of research briefs that examines educational management organizations. See http://nepc.

colorado.edu/ceru/annual-report-education-management-organizations for briefs beginning in 1999.

97. Our current search did not examine privatization.

98. Hunter, B. (2013, May 15). Personal communication (telephone) with Faith Boninger.

99. Ben Ishai, E. (2012, February). School commercialism: High cost, low revenues. *Public Citizen*. Retrieved December 8, 2014, from http://www. commercialalert.org/PDFs/SchoolCommercialismReport_PC.pdf; Molnar, A., Garcia, D. R., Boninger, F., & Merrill, B. (2006, January 1). *A National Survey of the Types and Extent of the Marketing of Foods of Minimal Nutritional Value in Schools*. Commercialism in Education Research Unit, Arizona State University. Retrieved December 8, 2014, from http://nepc.colorado.edu/publication/national-survey-types-and-extent-marketing-foods-minimal-nutritional-value-schools.

3

THREATS TO CHILDREN'S PSYCHOLOGICAL WELL-BEING

Since 2011, our research has focused on understanding whether and to what extent corporate commercializing activities in schools pose threats to children's well-being. While it has become common to think of marketing activities and advertising as largely benign, and to argue that they are an acceptable way for schools to earn extra dollars and to constructively engage with the business community, our analysis of the available evidence suggests that corporate commercializing activities pose serious threats to children's well-being.

Before discussing the specific threats these corporate activities pose, we think it will be helpful to first review how advertising and marketing influences people's opinions and behaviors. In other words, to explore how it works.

BACKGROUND: HOW ADVERTISING WORKS

People Think Advertising Does Not Affect Them

Despite powerful evidence that advertising and marketing shape attitudes and influence purchasing decisions and behavior, children and adults commonly feel that they are immune to the influence of marketing.[1] Some people even identify with the interests of marketers. For example, focus groups to access mothers' attitudes toward marketing to children in school have found that mothers exempted food marketers from responsibility for reducing the amount of marketing done in schools while accepting that profit is the marketers' bottom line.[2]

The available evidence suggests to us that "under the radar," marketing and advertising not only persuade people to buy more, but also convince them that they can derive identity, fulfillment, and self-expression through purchases of goods and services.[3] This all but invisible underlying value message is embedded in every product promotion and helps anchor it as a powerful and largely unchallenged assumption of our culture.[4]

Research on persuasion processes provides evidence that marketing does "collateral damage" to children on its way to influencing their purchase behaviors.[5] Until recently, analyses of how children respond to advertising have primarily explored the question of what level of cognitive development enables children to understand persuasive intent and by implication, at least theoretically, to resist direct marketing attempts.[6] These analyses assumed that if children could recognize advertising as an attempt to persuade them, and if they could actively argue against it, the advertising was "fair." If children could not recognize persuasive intent and formulate counterarguments, then the advertising was "not fair."

This was the basis of the American Psychological Association's 2004 recommendation to restrict advertising to children under the ages of seven to eight.[7] Research to that point suggested that younger children perceive ads as factual and neither recognize nor defend against persuasive intent. This approach, however, assumes that the process by which advertising works is always a fully conscious one, and that it is therefore subject to conscious control. Several lines of subsequent research, however, suggest that even when children (or adolescents, or adults) are cognitively able to recognize persuasive intent, advertising often still influences them.[8]

Getting Around Cognitive Resistance

Peripheral Persuasion

Since the mid-1970s, psychologists have distinguished between advertising seeking to persuade via direct argument and advertising using more peripheral (or heuristic) strategies. These include, for example, promoting a good mood and liking for an ad or product by provoking laughter, or evoking trust in a product by showcasing a popular spokesperson—or simply saturating a target audience with repeated exposure to an ad. Such peripheral effects are not logical and often influence people without their awareness.[9]

Narrative Persuasion

Because peripheral strategies may be undermined if the audience is aware of and actively argues against a persuasive message, advertisers are interested in undermining such resistance. Research focusing on "narrative persuasion" demonstrates that when people are transported into a story (as in a movie, a book, or video game) and are exposed to persuasive attempts in the context of that story, they tend not to counterargue those attempts—and are effectively persuaded.[10] Research findings are consistent with predictions that persuasion through transportation into a story is likely to be persistent over time, resistant to change, and predictive of behavior.[11]

To maximize this kind of persuasion, the media company Relativity, which runs film and TV studios and has divisions representing fashion and sports talent, created, for example, a branded entertainment arm, called Madvine, in early 2014. In August 2014, Madvine celebrated a multiyear, exclusive deal with global liquor marketer Pernod Ricard that, among other opportunities, gives the marketer access to at least one upcoming film "at script level," according to Madvine's CEO—meaning that the brand has a "seat at the table with the director."[12]

Implicit Persuasion

Some advertising bypasses cognitive processing completely by activating automatic behavioral scripts, associations, or emotions. In 2004, the market research company Harris Interactive advised its clients that children's affinity for brands is made on an emotional (noncognitive) level and that as children get older they seek rational support for choices they have already made on an emotional basis.[13]

Research backs up their claim: For example, children as young as two years old recognize brand logos on product packages,[14] and children as young as three years old not only recognize brands but also use them in socially meaningful ways.[15] They judge their peers as popular or unpopular, or fun or boring, because of the brands they use, and they draw inferences about other children based on the brands of food those children eat.[16]

Food products dominate advertising and marketing to children in and out of school.[17] Such advertising may very well be made all the more potent because, as Jennifer Harris and her colleagues have suggested, humans may automatically respond to food cues in their environment.[18]

Whether or not humans are "hardwired" to respond to food cues, reviews of research on food marketing to children find that advertising influences children's food preferences, purchasing, and consumption—with or without their conscious awareness.[19]

Research on school food environments, in particular, found that student snack food purchases were significantly associated with the number of snack machines in school.[20] Similarly, a 2009 National Bureau of Economic Research (NBER) study of ninth-grade children found that a fast food restaurant within a tenth of a mile of their school was associated with a 5.2 percent increase in obesity rates.[21]

Recent research suggests that the very presence of snack machines and fast food restaurants may encourage students to eat by serving as cues to snack.[22] Jennifer Harris and her colleagues let children ages seven to eleven eat a snack while watching a cartoon that contained advertising either for food or for other products. Those children who saw food advertising ate 45 percent more of the snack. In a follow-up experiment, adult participants who were exposed to "fun" snack food advertising ate more snack foods than participants who were exposed to other advertising.[23]

It is especially interesting that in these experiments food advertising increased consumption of food products other than the ones being advertised—a finding consistent with the view that the underlying message of all advertising is to reinforce the values of consumption.[24] It is also notable that the reported effects on consumption were not related to reported hunger or other conscious influences, suggesting that automatic responses like this may be especially pernicious and difficult to defend against.[25]

Embedded Advertising

The current cutting-edge approach to marketing is "embedded advertising." In its original context in television and film, embedded advertising included both "product placement" (products appearing as props) and "product integration" (products being mentioned in the dialogue or the plot of a program).[26] Considered the future of marketing, embedded advertising in dialogue and plot has skyrocketed in the United States and internationally.[27] Although popular with marketers, the approach has come under attack for several reasons, among them the perceived unfairness of advertising to viewers without their awareness and the abuse of the creative process as writers are required to organize story lines around products.[28]

Embedded advertising may be cutting edge, but it is hardly new. Early efforts included placements in silent films and a 1950s diamond marketing strategy disguised as newspaper articles about celebrity engagements.[29] In addition to ubiquitous product placements in movies and television, embedded advertising is associated with "branded entertainment," a marketing approach that blends advertising and entertainment in the form of live consumer events or the placement of products into the content of selected media,[30] and with "native advertising," which is the increasingly popular practice of businesses sponsoring the publication of articles in the print and digital press.[31]

Researchers at PQ Media observed that branded entertainment strategies have "evolved at a frenetic pace" in the past decade because they do, in fact, work.[32] Similarly, spending on native advertising has skyrocketed as advertisers realize its utility.[33]

Social media marketing research firm Socintel360 predicts that marketers will spend $4.3 billion on native advertising in 2015, up 34 percent from $3.2 billion spent in 2014. They expect spending to reach $8.8 billion by 2018. A primary explanation for the success of this type of marketing is that it engages its targets more than traditional advertising does.[34]

Branded entertainment blurs the distinction between advertising and content and promotes the development of an interactive immersive relationship between marketers and consumers, particularly children. It allows consumers to personally interact with brands and build emotional connections with them. These emotional connections, in turn, lead consumers to be more aware of those brands with which they develop an interactive relationship, to hold more positive attitudes toward them, and to be more likely to buy their products.[35]

School-based advertising is inherently embedded. When brands are associated with or made central to activities, lessons, or special programs, or when they appear as the name of a sponsored sports field or the school itself, they are embedded into the school context.[36] In other words, the advertising message has "gone native." The examples below illustrate that school marketing is often subtle, because, once in a school, companies do not have to be obvious in order to create a presence or influence student opinion. In fact, their efforts are likely to be more successful if they can fly under the radar.[37] It is not surprising, therefore, that corporations package enticements as money, equipment, or prizes in exchange for access to students as a benefit to schools. Nor is it surprising that environmental concerns (including recycling, conservation, and reduced energy use) and healthy lifestyles (including sports, food, and cookery) are also popular avenues of approach for corporate marketers.[38]

Research on the "sleeper effect" in psychology demonstrates the efficacy of embedded advertising even if the children learn later that they were the targets of a persuasive attempt. Persuasive material that is processed normally by the brain (i.e., without being identified as persuasive) "gets in" such that even if the biased nature of the material is later disclosed, and the children actively reject the message, in a short time the original persuasion reasserts itself.[39]

EMBEDDED ADVERTISING IN SCHOOLS

To illustrate the nature and scope of advertising embedded in schools, we provide below an example of school-based marketing for each of the categories of school commercialism discussed in chapter 2.

Sponsored Programs and Activities

From 2009 to 2012, the DASH+ Contest for high school students offered high school teams the chance to design and pitch an automobile dashboard concept.[40] The grand prize, a trip to Detroit, included a Ford River Rouge Factory Tour, in which student winners were shown the final assembly process for Ford F-150 trucks.[41] The website, contest, and related materials were sponsored by Progressive Automotive, Discovery Education, the U.S. Department of Energy, and the X-Prize Foundation. Sponsors' logos were prominent on the website's page headings and on materials.

Exclusive Agreements

In 2010 the Wisconsin Interscholastic Athletic Association (WIAA) signed an exclusive agreement with When We Were Young Productions to stream high school sporting events over the Internet. Local newspapers sued the WIAA (unsuccessfully), recognizing that by losing the right to broadcast games, they were losing "eyeballs" (business and potential advertising revenue).[42] Although students watching the streamed games may not care which site they use, the vendors' embedded presence is valuable to them.

Sponsored Educational Materials

The oil company BP has been active internationally in creating curriculum materials designed to promote its "green" credentials. In the United States, it was one of several corporate and other partners who wrote California's environmental curriculum in 2010.[43] In the United Kingdom, BP's extensive education website offers all manner of educational resources for schools on science, geography, environmental studies, citizenship, engineering, and enterprise, among other topics. According to the company, the website embodies its "responsibility to ensure that our educational resources reflect our focus on energy, environment, leadership and business skills."[44]

In addition to these sponsored educational materials offered to British schoolteachers, BP conducts workshops on earth science for schoolchildren in the Natural History Museum.[45] In all of these efforts, the company presents itself and the world in the ways it would like children to see them. No blinking lights or sirens—or even a disclaimer that says, "This is advertising"—accompany any of it; the company's worldview simply permeates its efforts.

Incentive Programs

The Sunny Delight Beverages Company timed its second annual SunnyD Book Spree in 2010 for the August–November back-to-school season. Schools collecting and submitting the most SunnyD proofs-of-purchase (or simply index cards with a "proof" notation) won up to $2,000 worth of company-selected books. All schools that sent in twenty proofs received twenty books.[46] A television advertising campaign supported the promotion, and the brand website encouraged parents to create supporting Facebook groups, to post signs in local sites like supermarkets and libraries, and to bring SunnyD products to classroom and other student parties.[47]

Fundraising

In 2009, the Houston Independent School District encouraged families to enroll in Power for Schools. The program asked families to register with a participating energy provider, which in turn makes a donation to the school district for each family that opts into the program.[48]

Appropriation of Space

Frostproof Elementary School in Polk County, Florida, asked local businesses to sponsor classrooms in exchange for ads on the school marquee. Rogers and Walker Gun Shop, for example, received marquee space in 2010 for donating $300 to two classrooms.[49]

Digital Marketing

Digital marketing weaves around and through other forms of marketing, both in and outside of schools.[50] Program details and sponsored educational materials for Fuel Our Future Now (described above) were featured online, and high school sporting events are streamed online through the Wisconsin Interscholastic Athletic Association's (WIAA's) exclusive agreement with When We Were Young Productions.

A digital presence for marketing initiatives is a powerful marketing tool because children spend a lot of time, much of it unsupervised, on the Internet; they can voluntarily access marketing sites; the time they spend on marketing sites can be almost unlimited; and much digital marketing is interactive and therefore engaging. Unlike passively ingested thirty-second commercials that could easily be missed during a snack or bathroom break, digital marketing actively engages its targets in brand-related activity over a protracted period of time. It's always there.

In-school efforts can nudge students toward Internet-based marketing outside of school.[51] Google, for example, introduces students to its Internet environment by engaging schools in "1:1 programs" by which students are each provided with Google Chromebooks equipped with Google Apps for Education, which provides filtered e-mail, online documents, website creation, streaming media, and other applications.[52] Moreover, it allows users to collaborate in real time through "cloud computing," using online software and Google for data storage and management.

In Oregon, which began using the service statewide in April 2010, Department of Education spokeswoman Susanne Smith said, "This is a way for students to prepare for the workplace by using workplace technology in the classroom"[53] —that is, to prepare for using Google technology in the workplace.[54]

HOW ADVERTISING THREATENS CHILDREN'S WELL-BEING

Children are now exposed to hundreds, if not thousands, of ads daily.[55] Indeed, the ubiquity of ads often serves as a rationale for further exposure. When considering whether to allow a particular advertising program in a school district, many parents, administrators, and policy makers argue, in effect, "Well, what's the harm? Children see so many ads anyway; what harm is there in one more, especially when allowing it will help us pay for needed programs?" In other words, if there's no harm, then there's no need to restrict advertising in schools.

In contrast, workers in other youth-related fields tend to consider rampant advertising harmful to children.[56] Even marketers express concerns. A 2004 Harris Interactive poll of 878 individuals working in the youth marketing industry (primarily youth marketing, advertising and public relations, and media) found that only 30 percent of respondents thought children were "well-equipped to deal with the current media and advertising environment." Only 24 percent thought the industry was "policing itself sufficiently in terms of advertising appropriately to children," just 28 percent thought that current ratings systems are effective, and 80 percent favored regulating how companies use information they collect from young people.[57]

However, the same respondents thought it appropriate to advertise to children several years before the age that they thought those children could actually make intelligent decisions as consumers. They no doubt understood how vital it is to the marketing industry to familiarize young children with brands—in other words, to "brand" them.

Threats to Psychological Well-Being

A substantial body of research supports the conclusion that advertising poses a threat to children's psychological health.[58] Children exposed to advertising, for example, tend to have values and engage in activities consistent with materialism, demonstrate heightened insecurity about themselves and their place in the social world, and have a distorted understanding of gender roles.[59] Advertising not only persuades children to want and buy more, but it also promotes the idea that they can derive identity, fulfillment, self-expression, and confidence through what they buy.[60]

Heightened Insecurity

Psychologist Helga Dittmar and her colleagues have studied the effects of consumer culture on children and the development of what they call "the new materialism." They define new materialism as a person not simply being interested in things or valuing possessions, but rather attempting to find happiness "through money and material goods."[61] They point out that children, through their immersion in consumer culture, internalize the twin ideals emphasized by that culture: the "good life" and the "body perfect." Other research by Dittmar finds that this internalization creates insecurities in children about themselves in general and about their bodies in particular.[62] These insecurities grow out of the discrepancies between children's real bodies and lives and the idealized images they see around them—in toys, television shows, music videos, and advertisements.[63] Researchers report that girls as young as five years old report wanting a thinner body.[64] Ironically, with increasing rates of childhood obesity (often associated with the marketing of so-called "junk food") these "real-ideal discrepancies" have become ever more extreme.

Dittmar reasons that consumer culture creates vulnerability in children by causing them to feel far away from their ideal and to feel bad about this gap, and then exploits the vulnerability it creates by presenting solutions (products) that purportedly can repair children's identity deficits and negative emotions—which, of course, they cannot. Consider, for example, Old Spice's award-winning 2008–2009 Swagger ad campaign. It consisted of advertisements featuring football and rap stars explaining that Old Spice transformed them from super-nerds to super-cool stars—implying, of course, that the product can do the same for any boy who buys it.[65] Other products are similarly promoted: Anthony's Body Essentials come in such variations as Energy, Strength, Spirit, and Courage, and Abercrombie & Fitch sells a popular cologne called Fierce.[66]

Dittmar found that the effects on children are both psychological and behavioral: lower self-esteem, more dissatisfaction, more eating disorders, and more compulsive shopping.[67] Most vulnerable are children who feel the most pressure to conform to their peer culture. In one set of studies published in 2008, children who felt more pressure to conform both scored higher on a materialism scale and were more likely to believe that peers would reject a fictional character who didn't get a new pair of popular athletic shoes.[68]

Distorted Gender Socialization

The marketing of body products to children leads to early and disturbing effects on children's gender socialization. According to media researcher Sut Jhally, boys and girls learn from marketing messages that "hypersexuality" is normal and appropriate, and that sexuality is a commodity that can and should be bought.[69] Spending patterns demonstrate the effectiveness of these messages.

In 2007, the market research company Packaged Facts estimated that spending on hair care, skin care, and color cosmetics products by and for preteens and teenagers reached $7 billion (retail); the company predicted that amount would rise to $8.5 billion by 2012.[70] Self-care brands have increased sales to boys in the ten- to fourteen-year-old age range through such "underground" marketing techniques as tie-ins on social networking and Internet gaming sites, interactive websites, and giveaways in school health education classes.

A 2010 *New York Times* article reports that Tag has a page on Facebook. Axe has an avatar in Pain, a PlayStation game. Swagger sponsors Xbox team competitions. Dial for Men offers advice from "sexperts." Brands create downloadable apps, have lengthy "advergames" on their websites, and urge fans to text friends with coy messages about the products. They make commercials just for YouTube, which is, in turn, filled with commercials made by boys themselves.[71]

More evidence of the effectiveness of this advertising comes from Axe's "Wake-Up Service" advertising campaign. First introduced in Japan in 2007, it landed on the short list for the 2010 international Warc Prize for effective advertising.[72] The campaign—which led to an increase in repeat Axe purchases of over 65 percent—gets to young men first thing in the morning by enlisting them to subscribe to a daily "wake-up call" on their cell phones from a young woman whispering, "Don't forget to spray Axe today."[73]

Psychologist and author Lyn Mikel Brown claims that products such as Axe preach an extreme, singular definition of masculinity at a time in their development when boys are grappling uneasily with identity. She suggests that these products "cultivate anxiety in boys at younger and younger ages about what it means to man up, to be the kind of boy they're told girls will want and other boys will respect. They're playing with the failure to be that kind of guy, to be heterosexual even."[74]

Displaced Values and Activities

Consumer culture can preempt the development of other interests that may be more functional for children. Psychologist Allen Kanner notes that when people believe they need material goods to be happy, they devote much of their time to such materially oriented activities as making money, worrying about making money, looking at advertisements, fantasizing about what they will buy, and shopping. This undermines their ability to understand and to satisfy nonmaterial needs, such as enjoying family and friends, engaging in creative and artistic endeavors, or developing spiritual practices.[75]

This displacement is likely more serious for children than for adults: when consumer-oriented activity displaces unstructured, child-directed creative play, it is at the expense of characteristics such as creative thinking and spirituality.[76] Consumer culture may not only make children unhappy by highlighting their distance from an idealized life and body as noted above, but it may also prevent them from cultivating interests and practices that would lay the foundation for a satisfying adult life. This conclusion is consistent with correlations found between higher materialistic values and higher rates of anxiety, depression, psychological distress, chronic physical symptoms, and lower self-esteem.[77] In teenagers, higher materialistic values also correlate with increased smoking, drinking, drug use, weapon carrying, vandalism, and truancy.[78]

Exploitation of Adolescents' Psychological Vulnerabilities

The exploitation of psychological vulnerabilities by advertisers has a potent effect on teenagers. Recent research has found that developmentally, teenagers have reduced ability to control impulsive behaviors and to resist immediate gratification. This increases their susceptibility to peer influence and image advertising.[79] Not surprisingly, adolescents are vulnerable to ads that target their identity-formation processes.[80] Their reduced ability to control impulsive behaviors, to resist immediate gratification, and to seek self-identity increases their susceptibility to peer influence and image advertising.[81] Thus, the general characteristic of advertising—the creation and amplification of insecurities and then, literally, the sale of a "solution" for those insecurities in the form of a product—has an especially powerful impact on adolescents.

Traditionally, it has been considered "fair" to market to teenagers because they are old enough to recognize and evaluate the persuasive intention of an advertisement.[82] This may be true to the extent that teenagers certainly can recognize an advertisement's persuasive intent and so fully discount it in the context of a highly logical assessment of the product involved; but the weight of the available research evidence suggests that people of all ages are subject to strategies that inhibit or bypass such a logical evaluation of the advertisement and product, and that all children and especially adolescents are vulnerable because of the characteristics associated with their intellectual and emotional development.

For these reasons, Jennifer Harris and her colleagues at Yale University have argued that industry self-regulatory programs that restrict advertising to children until age twelve should change to encompass children until at least age fourteen.[83]

Digital advertising, in particular, is well suited to exploit teens' developmental challenges.[84] On the web, for example, a purchase is only a click away from any advertisement, making impulsive purchases easier than they have ever been. Digital marketing strategies (addressed in detail in chapter 7) that collect data about users in order to match advertising to their computer use histories and other personal information are used to further exploit the vulnerabilities of adolescents through highly targeted marketing.[85]

For example, "like" features on social media sites that allow users to click a button to endorse an item ensure that teen users are regularly informed of their peers' brand preferences. Facebook pioneered the "like" feature, but other sites, such as Instagram, Pinterest, and Twitter, work similarly.

Although Facebook users can "like" anything (including their friends' statuses, groups, and brands), Facebook and marketers have united to make sure that brands are easy to "like": brand websites now contain buttons that visitors can click to post their opinions about the brand to their Facebook friends.[86] In addition, Facebook appropriates users' names and other data to create "social ads," and many sites offer buyers the opportunity to announce online purchases to their friends on Facebook.[87] Teens see, then, a continuous stream of products that their friends like and buy. Other social media sites are on parallel paths toward turning information collected about their users into money.[88]

At Nielsen's Consumer 360 conference in June 2010, Facebook executive Sheryl Sandberg claimed that a research study had found that people who receive product recommendations from their friends are 400 percent more likely to buy that product, and that compared with products not recommended by friends, friend-recommended products are associated with 68 percent better product recognition and 200 percent greater memory of brand messaging.[89]

Something that Sandberg did not mention in her 2010 talk is that the continual reminders that teens see on social media about their friends' desires signal to them over and over that consumption leads to happiness and satisfaction, the central assumption of consumer culture.

This latent message of consumer culture is especially effective because it is invisible and assumed, and therefore seldom questioned. In this chapter we have discussed this assumption's negative impact on children's psychological well-being. In chapter 4 we explore how it may also threaten their physical health, primarily by influencing the amount and nature of the foods they choose to consume.

NOTES

1. Davison, W. P. (1996). The third-person effect revisited. *International Journal of Public Opinion Research, 8*(2), 113–19. Retrieved September 28,

2010, from http://ijpor.oxfordjournals.org.ezproxy1.lib.asu.edu/content/8/2/113. full.pdf+html; Kilbourne, J. (2006). Jesus is a brand of jeans. *New Internationalist,* September, 10–12. Retrieved June 25, 2010, from http://www.newint.org/ features/2006/09/01/culture/. For an argument that people have little insight into their cognitive processes in any case, see Nisbett, R. E., and Wilson, T. D. (1977). Telling more than we can know: Verbal reports on mental processes. *Psychological Review, 84,* 231–59. Retrieved March 31, 2010, from http://www. lps.uci.edu/~johnsonk/philpsych/readings/nisbett.pdf; Nisbett, R. E., & Wilson, T. D. (1977). The halo effect: Evidence for unconscious alteration of judgments. *Journal of Personality and Social Psychology, 35,* 250–56. Retrieved March 31, 2010, from http://osil.psy.ua.edu/672readings/T6-SocCog2/haloeffect.pdf; Shavitt, S., Lowrey, P., & Haefner, J. (1998, July 1). Public attitudes toward advertising: More favorable than you might think. *Journal of Advertising Research, 38,* 7–22; Wilson, T. D., & Bar-Anan, Y. (2008). The unseen mind. *Science, 321,* 1046–47. Retrieved June 23, 2010, from http://www.sciencemag.org.ezproxy1. lib.asu.edu/cgi/reprint/321/5892/1046.pdf.

2. KRC Research (2014, June 11). Findings from focus groups among mothers on food and beverage marketing to children (Webinar). Author.

3. Kilbourne, J. (2006). Jesus is a brand of jeans. *New Internationalist,* September, 10–12. Retrieved June 25, 2010, from http://www.newint.org/features/ 2006/09/01/culture/. See also Jhally, S., & Barr, W. (n.d.). Advertising, cultural criticism, and pedagogy: An interview with Sut Jhally (conducted by William O'Barr). Retrieved November 23, 2010, from http://www.sutjhally.com/articles/ advertisingcultura/.

4. Cultural observers long have noted that propaganda is most effective when it goes unnoted. See, for instance, Pratkanis, A., & Aronson, E. (2001). *Age of Propaganda: The Everyday Use and Abuse of Persuasion.* New York: Holt Paperbacks, 87; McNay, L. (1994). *Foucault: A Critical Introduction.* Cambridge: Polity, 94–95; Kilbourne, J. (2006). Jesus is a brand of jeans. *New Internationalist,* September 10–12. Retrieved June 25, 2010, from http://www.newint. org/features/2006/09/01/culture/.

5. Harris, J. L., Bargh, J. A., & Brownell, K. D. (2009). Priming effects of television food advertising on eating behavior. *Health Psychology, 28*(4), 404–13. Retrieved August 25, 2014, from http://www.yaleruddcenter.org/ resources/upload/docs/what/advertising/primingeffectstvfoodads.pdf; Harris, J. L., Brownell, K. D., & Bargh, J. A. (2009). The food marketing defense model: Integrating psychological research to protect youth and inform public policy, 230. *Social Issues and Policy Review, 3*(1), 211–74. Retrieved April 1, 2010, from http://www.yaleruddcenter.org/resources/upload/docs/what/advertising/ FoodMarketingDefenseModelSIPR12.09.pdf; Nairn, A., & Fine, C. (2008). Who's messing with my mind? The implications of dual-process models for the

ethics of advertising to children. *International Journal of Advertising, 27*(3), 447–70.

6. See Harris, J. L., Brownell, K. D., & Bargh, J. A. (2009). The food marketing defense model: Integrating psychological research to protect youth and inform public policy, 230. *Social Issues and Policy Review, 3*(1), 211–74. Retrieved April 1, 2010, from http://www.yaleruddcenter.org/resources/upload/docs/what/advertising/FoodMarketingDefenseModelSIPR12.09.pdf.

7. Wilcox, B., Kunkel, D., Cantor, J., Dowrick, P., Linn, S., & Palmer, E. (2004). *Report of the APA Task Force on Advertising and Children.* Washington, DC: American Psychological Association. Retrieved March 31, 2010, from http://www.chawisconsin.org/Obesity/O2ChildAds.pdf; "Fairness" is a basis of the self-regulatory guidelines of the Children's Advertising Review Unit. See Children's Advertising Review Unit (2009). *Self-Regulatory Program for Children's Advertising*, 3. Retrieved June 24, 2010, from http://www.caru.org/guidelines/guidelines.pdf.

8. Graff, S., Kunkel, D., & Mermin, S. E. (2012, February). Government can regulate food advertising to children because cognitive research shows that it is inherently misleading. *Health Affairs, 31*(2), 392–98; Harris, J. A., Heard, A., & Schwartz, M. B. (2014). *Older but Still Vulnerable: All Children Need Protection from Unhealthy Food Marketing.* Yale Rudd Center for Food Policy and Obesity. Retrieved November 24, 2014, from http://www.yaleruddcenter.org/resources/upload/docs/what/reports/Protecting_Older_Children_3.14.pdf.

9. Eagly, A. E., & Chaiken, S. (1983). Process theories of attitude formation and change: The elaboration likelihood model and the heuristic systematic models. In A. E. Eagly & S. Chaiken (eds.), *The Psychology of Attitudes.* Fort Worth, TX: Harcourt Brace Jovanovich, 305–25; Mallinckrodt, V., & Mizerski, D. (2007). The effects of playing an advergame on young children's perceptions, preferences and request. *Journal of Advertising, 36*, 87–100; Ellis, A. W., Holmes, S. J., & Wright, R. L. (2009). Age of acquisition and the recognition of brand names: On the importance of being early. *Journal of Consumer Psychology, 20*(1), 43–52; Nairn, A., & Fine, C. (2008). Who's messing with my mind? The implications of dual-process models for the ethics of advertising to children. *International Journal of Advertising*, 27(3), 447–70; Petty, R. E., & Cacioppo, J. T. (1986). *Communication and Persuasion: Central and Peripheral Routes to Attitude Change.* New York: Springer; Tellis, G. J. (2004). *Effective Advertising: Understanding When, How, and Why Advertising Works.* Thousand Oaks, CA: Sage. For an argument that people have little insight into their cognitive processes, see Nisbett, R. E., & Wilson, T.D. (1977). Telling more than we can know: Verbal reports on mental processes. *Psychological Review, 84*, 231–59. Retrieved March 31, 2010, from http://www.lps.uci.edu/~johnsonk/philpsych/readings/nisbett.pdf; Nisbett, R. E., & Wilson, T. D. (1977). The halo effect:

Evidence for unconscious alteration of judgments. *Journal of Personality and Social Psychology, 35*, 250–56. Retrieved March 31, 2010, from http://osil.psy. ua.edu/672readings/T6-SocCog2/haloeffect.pdf; Wilson, T. D., & Bar-Anan, Y. (2008). The unseen mind. *Science, 321*, 1046–47. Retrieved June 23, 2010, from http://www.sciencemag.org.ezproxy1.lib.asu.edu/cgi/reprint/321/5892/1046.pdf.

10. Green, M. C., Garst, J., & Brock, T. C. (2004). The power of fiction: Determinants and boundaries. In L. J. Shrum (ed.), *The Psychology of Entertainment Media: Blurring the Lines between Entertainment and Persuasion*. Mahwah, NJ: Erlbaum, 161–76; Green, M. C., & Brock, T. C. (2002). In the mind's eye: Transportation-imagery model of narrative persuasion. In M. C. Green, J. J. Strange, and T. C. Brock (eds.), *Narrative Impact: Social and Cognitive Foundations*. Mahwah, NJ: Erlbaum, 315–41.

11. Appel, M., & Richter, T. (2007). Persuasive effects of fictional narratives increase over time. *Media Psychology, 10*(1), 113–34; Green, M. C., Garst, J., & Brock, T. C. (2004). The power of fiction: Determinants and boundaries. In L. J. Shrum (ed.), *The Psychology of Entertainment Media: Blurring the Lines between Entertainment and Persuasion*. Mahwah, NJ: Erlbaum, 161–76; Williams, J. H., Green, M. C., Houston, T. K, & Allison, J. J. (2011). Stories to communicate risks about tobacco: Development of a brief scale to measure transportation into a video story. *Health Education Journal, 70*(2), 184–91.

12. The film was still "at script level" when the deal was signed, so it does not have a name yet. Its working title is "Untitled Armored Car Project" and stars Zach Galifianakis, Owen Wilson, and Kristen Wiig. Schultz, E. J. (2014, August 21). Why You Will See Kahlua in Upcoming Zach Galifianakis Flick. *Advertising Age*. Retrieved August 21, 2014, from http://adage.com/article/media/kahlua-upcoming-zach-galifianakis-flick/294654/?utm_source=daily_email&utm_medium=newsletter&utm_campaign=adage&ttl=1409177551 [subscription required].

13. Harris Interactive (2004). Trends & tudes, 3(11). Cited in Harris, J. L., Brownell, K. D., & Bargh, J. A. (2009). The food marketing defense model: Integrating psychological research to protect youth and inform public policy, 230. *Social Issues and Policy Review, 3*(1), 211–74. Retrieved April 1, 2010, from http://www.yaleruddcenter.org/resources/upload/docs/what/advertising/FoodMarketingDefenseModelSIPR12.09.pdf. See also research on "peripheral" persuasion processes: Eagy, A. E., & Chaiken, S. (1983). Process theories of attitude formation and change: The elaboration likelihood model and the heuristic systematic models. In A. E. Eagly & S. Chaiken (eds.), *The Psychology of Attitudes*. Fort Worth, TX: Harcourt Brace Jovanovich, 305–25; Petty, R. E., & Cacioppo, J. T. (1986). *Communication and Persuasion: Central and Peripheral Routes to Attitude Change*. New York: Springer; Tellis, G. J. (2004). *Effective*

Advertising: Understanding When, How, and Why Advertising Works. Thousand Oaks, CA: Sage.

14. Valkenburg, P. M., & Buijzen, M. (2005). Identifying determinants of young children's brand awareness: Television, parents, and peers. *Journal of Applied Developmental Psychology, 26*(4), 456–68.

15. McAlister, A. R., & Cornwell, T. B. (2010). Children's brand symbolism understanding: Links to theory of mind and executive functioning. *Psychology and Marketing, 27*(3), 203–28. Retrieved June 23, 2010, from http://www3. interscience.wiley.com.ezproxy1.lib.asu.edu/cgi-bin/fulltext/123279991/ PDFSTART. See also Ellis, A. W., Holmes, S. J., & Wright, R. L. (2010). Age of acquisition and the recognition of brand names: On the importance of being early. *Journal of Consumer Psychology, 20*(1), 43–52.

16. McAlister, A. R., & Cornwell, T. B. (2010). Children's brand symbolism understanding: Links to theory of mind and executive functioning. *Psychology and Marketing, 27*(3), 203–28. Retrieved June 23, 2010, from http://www3. interscience.wiley.com.ezproxy1.lib.asu.edu/cgi-bin/fulltext/123279991/ PDFSTART; Roberto, C. A., Baik, J., Harris, J. L, & Brownell, K. D. (2010). Influence of licensed characters on children's taste and snack preferences. *Pediatrics, 126*(1), 88–93. Retrieved June 24, 2010, from http://www. yaleruddcenter.org/resources/upload/docs/what/advertising/LicensedCharacters_ Pediatrics_7.10.pdf.

17. Chester, J., & Montgomery, K. (2007, May). Interactive food and beverage marketing: Targeting children and youth in the digital age. Berkeley, CA: Public Health Institute. Retrieved August 19, 2009, from http://digitalads.org/ documents/digiMarketingFull.pdf; Federal Trade Commission (2008, July). *Marketing Food to Children and Adolescents: A Review of Industry Expenditures, Activities, and Self-Regulation.* Washington, DC: Author. Retrieved August 26, 2008, from http://www.ftc.gov/os/2008/07/P064504foodmktingreport. pdf.

18. Harris, J. L., Bargh, J. A., & Brownell, K. D., (2009). Priming effects of television food advertising on eating behavior. *Health Psychology, 28*(4), 404–13. Retrieved January 12, 2015, from http://www.yaleruddcenter.org/ resources/upload/docs/what/advertising/primingeffectstvfoodads.pdf.

19. Harris, J. L., Brownell, K. D., & Bargh, J. A. (2009). The food marketing defense model: Integrating psychological research to protect youth and inform public policy (p. 217); *Social Issues and Policy Review, 3*(1), 211–74. Retrieved April 1, 2010, from http://www.yaleruddcenter.org/resources/upload/docs/what/ advertising/FoodMarketingDefenseModelSIPR12.09.pdf; Institute of Medicine (IOM). (2006). *Food Marketing to Children and Youth: Threat or Opportunity?* Washington, DC: National Academies Press; Stead, M., McDermott, L., & Hastings, G. (2007). Towards evidence-based marketing: The case of childhood

obesity. *Marketing Theory, 7*(4), 379–406. Retrieved August 18, 2009, from http://mtq.sagepub.com/cgi/content/abstract/7/4/379?ck=nck; Story, M., & French, S. (2004). Food advertising and marketing directed at children and adolescents in the U.S. *International Journal of Behavior, Nutrition, and Physical Activity, 1*(3). Retrieved April 1, 2010, from http://www.ijbnpa.org/content/pdf/ 1479-5868-1-3.pdf; Strack, F., & Deutsch, R. (2004). Reflective and impulsive determinants of social behavior. *Personality and Social Psychology Review, 8*(3), 220–47. Retrieved June 23, 2010, from http://psr.sagepub.com.ezproxy1. lib.asu.edu/cgi/reprint/8/3/220; Wilson, T. D., & Bar-Anan, Y. (2008). The unseen mind. *Science, 321*, 1046–47. Retrieved June 23, 2010, from http://www. sciencemag.org.ezproxy1.lib.asu.edu/cgi/reprint/321/5892/1046.pdf.

20. Neumark-Sztainer, D., French, S. A., Hannan, P. J., Story, M., & Fulkerson, J. A. (2005). School lunch and snacking patterns among high school students: Associations with school food environment and policies. *International Journal of Behavioral Nutrition and Physical Activity* [serial online]. 2005; 2:14. Retrieved August 18, 2009, from www.ijbnpa.org/content/2/1/14.

21. Rabin, R. C. (2009, March 26). Proximity to fast food a factor in student obesity. *New York Times*. Retrieved March 26, 2009, from http://www.nytimes. com/2009/03/26/health/nutrition/26obese.html; Johnson, D. B., Bruemmer, B., Lund, A. E., Evens, C. C., & Mar, C. M. (2009). Impact of school district sugar-sweetened beverage policies on student beverage exposure and consumption in middle schools. *Journal of Adolescent Health, 45*, S30–S37.

22. See also Kessler, D. (2009). *The End of Overeating: Taking Control of the Insatiable American Appetite*. New York: Rodale; Miley, M. (2008, October 21). Anti-smoking warnings make you want to smoke, claims study. *Advertising Age*. Retrieved April 1, 2010, from http://adage.com/article?article_id=131905 [subscription required]; Chou, S., Rashad, I., & Grossman, M. (2008). Fast-food restaurant advertising on television and its influence on childhood obesity. *Journal of Law and Economics, 51*(4). Retrieved April 22, 2009, from http://www. nber.org/digest/aug06/w11879.html.

23. Harris, J. L., Bargh, J. A., & Brownell, K. D. (2009). Priming effects of television food advertising on eating behavior. *Health Psychology, 28*(4), 404–13. Retrieved August 25, 2014, from http://www.yaleruddcenter.org/ resources/upload/docs/what/advertising/primingeffectstvfoodads.pdf.

24. Harris, J. L., Bargh, J. A., & Brownell, K. D. (2009). Priming effects of television food advertising on eating behavior. *Health Psychology, 28*(4), 404–13. Retrieved August 25, 2014, from http://www.yaleruddcenter.org/ resources/upload/docs/what/advertising/primingeffectstvfoodads.pdf; Jhally, S., & Barr, W. (n.d.). Advertising, cultural criticism, and pedagogy: An interview with Sut Jhally (conducted by William O'Barr). Retrieved November 23, 2010, from http://www.sutjhally.com/articles/advertisingcultura/.

25. Harris, J. L., Brownell, K. D., & Bargh, J. A. (2009). The food marketing defense model: Integrating psychological research to protect youth and inform public policy. *Social Issues and Policy Review, 3*(1), 211–71. Retrieved March 31, 2010, from http://www.yaleruddcenter.org/resources/upload/docs/what/advertising/FoodMarketingDefenseModelSIPR12.09.pdf; Bargh, J. A., & Ferguson, M. J. (2000). Beyond behaviorism: The automaticity of higher mental processes. *Psychological Bulletin, 126*, 925–45; Dijksterhuis, A., Smith, P. K., van Baaren, R. B., & Wigboldus, D. H. J. (2005). The unconscious consumer: Effects of environment on consumer behavior. *Journal of Consumer Psychology, 15*(3), 193–202. See also Goodall, C. E. (2009). *Automatic Attitude Activation: Studies of Processing and Effects of Alcohol Advertisements and Public Service Announcements* (Doctoral dissertation, Ohio State University, 2009). Retrieved September 28, 2010, from http://etd.ohiolink.edu/send-pdf.cgi/Goodall%20Catherine%20E.pdf?osu1242256246.

26. Oxenford, D. D., Braverman, B., & Tomlinson, J. W. (2008, July). FCC initiates embedded advertising and sponsorship identification rulemaking proceeding. *Davis Wright Tremaine LLP*. Retrieved March 9, 2010, from http://www.dwt.com/LearningCenter/Advisories?find=21206.

27. PQ Media (2010, June). *PQ Media Global Branded Entertainment Marketing Forecast 2010–2014*. Stamford, CT: Author; Hampp, A. (2010, June 29). Product placement dipped last year for the first time. *Adage.com-Madison+Vine*. Retrieved June 29, 2010, from http://adage.com/madisonandvine/article?article_id=144720 (subscription required); Hudson, S., Hudson, D., & Peloza, J. (2007). Meet the parents: A parents' perspective on product placement in children's films. *Journal of Business Ethics, 80*, 289–304 (citing PQ Media [2005, March], *Product Placement Spending in Media 2005*. PQ Media LLC); Smit, E., van Reijmersdal, E., & Neijens, P. (2009). Today's practice of brand placement and the industry behind it. *International Journal of Advertising, 28*(5), 761–82; Marx, W. (2007). PQ Media Market Analysis finds global product placement spending grew 37 percent in 2006. Retrieved March 11, 2010, from http://www.prwebdirect.com/releases/2007/3/prweb511540.htm.

28. Department for Culture, Media and Sport (2010). *Consultation on Product Placement on Television Summary of Responses.* London: DCMS; Department for Children, Schools and Families & Department for Culture, Media and Sport (2009). *Impact of the Commercial World on Children's Wellbeing. Report of an Independent Assessment.* (DCSF-00669-2009) (p. 89). Nottingham: DCSF Publications; Markey, E. J., & Waxman, H. A. (2007, September 26). Letter to Kevin J. Martin, chairman of the Federal Communications Commission. Retrieved July 7, 2008, from http://markey.house.gov/docs/telecomm/Letter%20with%20Waxman%20to%20FCC%20re%20product%20placement.pdf; Writers Guild of America, West, and Writers Guild of America, East (2005,

November 14). *Are You SELLING to Me? Stealth Advertising in the Entertainment Industry*. Author. Retrieved September 18, 2008, from http://www.wga.org/uploadedFiles/news_and_events/press_release/2005/white_paper.pdf.

29. Epstein, E. J. (1982). Have you ever tried to sell a diamond? *Atlantic Online*. Retrieved September 20, 2010, from http://www.theatlantic.com/past/docs/issues/82feb/8202diamond1.htm.

30. PQ Media (2010, June). *PQ Media Global Branded Entertainment Marketing Forecast 2010–2014*. Stamford, CT: Author, 9.

31. Contently (2014, July 9). Study: Sponsored content has a trust problem. Author. Retrieved November 4, 2014, from http://contently.com/strategist/2014/07/09/study-sponsored-content-has-a-trust-problem-2/; Sebastian, M. (2014, August 6). Native-ad slayer John Oliver visits native-ad seller Hearst and explains his hit piece. *Advertising Age*. Retrieved November 4, 2014, from http://adage.com/article/media/john-oliver-lampooned-native-advertising/294480/; HuffPost Partner Studio (2014, August 26). 8 myths about native advertising that are almost entirely untrue. *Huffington Post*. Retrieved November 4, 2014, from http://www.huffingtonpost.com/2014/09/04/native-advertising-myths_n_5708709.html.

32. PQ Media (2010, June). *PQ Media Global Branded Entertainment Marketing Forecast 2010–2014*. Stamford, CT: Author, 12.

33. Sebastian, M. (2014, November 3). Media companies strike gold with sponsored content. *Advertising Age*. Retrieved November 24, 2014, from http://adage.com/article/media/media-companies-strike-gold-sponsored-content/295679/?utm_source=daily_email&utm_medium=newsletter&utm_campaign=adage&ttl=1415577938 [subscription required]; Sebastian, M. (2014, November 21). Native ad spending to jump despite marketer reservations. *Advertising Age*. Retrieved November 24, 2014, from http://adage.com/article/digital/native-ad-spending-jumps-marketers-reservations/295956/?utm_source=digital_email&utm_medium=newsletter&utm_campaign=adage&ttl=1417191984 [subscription required]; SocIntel360 (2014, September 1). Why native advertising is a boon for publishers, marketers, and users. Author. Retrieved November 24, 2014, from http://www.socintel360.com/why-native-advertising-is-a-boon-for-publishers-marketers-and-users/133/.

34. PQ Media (2010, June). *PQ Media Global Branded Entertainment Marketing Forecast 2010–2014*. Stamford, CT: Author, 17; Sebastian, M. (2014, November 21). Native ad spending to jump despite marketer reservations. *Advertising Age*. Retrieved November 24, 2014, from http://adage.com/article/digital/native-ad-spending-jumps-marketers-reservations/295956/?utm_source=digital_email&utm_medium=newsletter&utm_campaign=adage&ttl=1417191984 [subscription required].

35. PQ Media (2010, June). *PQ Media Global Branded Entertainment Marketing Forecast 2010–2014.* Stamford, CT: Author, 9.

36. Dixon's Academy in England is named for the electrical retailer that sponsors it.

37. Petty, R. E., & Cacioppo, J. T. (1986). *Communication and persuasion: Central and peripheral routes to attitude change.* New York: Springer.

38. For examples, see Fiori, L. (2009, October 20). Schools going green to get more of the green. *Journal Times* (Racine, WI). Retrieved October 23, 2009, from http://www.journaltimes.com/news/local/education/article_5159e14a-bcd7-11de-a37f-001cc4c03286.html; Neff, J. (2010, September 6). Growth market as progressive schools push green agenda. *Advertising Age.* Retrieved October 19, 2010, from http://adage.com/article?article_id=145741 [subscription required]; Tapping into a new generation (2010, March 8). *Wall Street Journal.* Retrieved March 8, 2010, from http://online.wsj.com/article/SB10001424052748704187204575101372029189644.html?mod=WSJ_hpp_MIDDLENexttoWhatsNewsSecond.

39. Petty, R. E., & Cacioppo, J. T. (1977). Forewarning, cognitive responding, and resistance to persuasion. *Journal of Personality and Social Psychology, 35*(9), 645–55.

40. Blanco, S. (2009, February 3). Auto X Prize, DOE launch Fuel Our Future student website. Retrieved August 25, 2014, from http://green.autoblog.com/2009/02/03/auto-x-prize-doe-launch-fuel-our-future-student-website/; Discovery Education (2010). Fuel Our Future Now. Retrieved June 9, 2010, from http://fuelourfuturenow.com/.

41. Discovery Education (2010). Fuel Our Future Now: Prizes. Retrieved July 7, 2010, from http://www.fuelourfuturenow.com/contest/prizes.cfm.

42. Treleven, E. (2010, June 4). Judge rules in favor of WIAA in webcasting of sports events. *Wisconsin State Journal.* Retrieved June 24, 2010, from http://host.madison.com/wsj/news/local/article_21b2de10-8684-5290-a22a-453d8306fe4d.html.

43. Daysog, R. (2010, September 7). BP aids state's school content. *Sacramento Bee.* Retrieved September 7, 2010, from http://www.sacbee.com/2010/09/07/3009448/bp-aids-statesschool-content.html.

44. BP (2010). About BP Educational Service. Author. Retrieved September 1, 2010, from http://www.bp.com/sectiongenericarticle.do?categoryId=8041&contentId=7035835.

45. BP (2010). Natural History Museum. Author. Retrieved June 11, 2010, from http://www.bp.com/sectiongenericarticle.do?categoryId=9019518&contentId=7036187.

46. Sunny Delight Beverages Company (2010). SunnyD® book spree offer & sweepstakes official rules. Retrieved August 10, 2010, from http://www.sunnyd.com/contest-martina-mcbride-book-spree/Participate.aspx.

47. Sunny Delight Beverages Company (2010). Choose your book spree kit. Retrieved August 10, 2010, from http://www.sunnyd.com/contest-martina-mcbride-book-spree/Participate.aspx.

48. Power For Schools (2009, September 30). School fundraising: watts it all about? (press release). Retrieved June 17, 2010, from https://www.powerforschools.org/powerforschools/en/PressRelease.html.

49. Levitz, J., & Simon, S. (2010, June 14). A school prays for help. *Wall Street Journal Online*. Retrieved June 16, 2010, from http://online.wsj.com/article/SB10001424052748704875604575280422614633564.html.

50. Chester, J., & Montgomery, K. (2007, May). Interactive food and beverage marketing: Targeting children and youth in the digital age. Berkeley, CA: Public Health Institute. Retrieved August 19, 2009, from http://digitalads.org/documents/digiMarketingFull.pdf.

51. Molnar, A., Boninger, F., Wilkinson, G., & Fogarty, J. (2008). *Click: The Twelfth Annual Report on Schoolhouse Commercialism Trends: 2008–2009.* Tempe, AZ: Commercialism in Education Research Unit, Education Policy Studies Laboratory, Arizona State University. Retrieved August 25, 2009, from http://www.epicpolicy.org/publication/schoolhouse-commercialism-2009.

52. Google (n.d.). Discover a better way of learning. Retrieved November 3, 2014, from https://www.google.com/work/apps/education/.

53. The Associated Press (2010, April 29). Oregon offers Google apps program to schools. *Education Week*. Retrieved May 2, 2010, from http://www.edweek.org/ew/articles/2010/04/28/350531ororegonschoolsgoogle_ap.html?utm_source=fb&utm_medium=rss&utm_campaign=mrss [no longer available].

54. Molnar, A., Boninger, F., Wilkinson, G., & Fogarty, J. (2008). *Click: The Twelfth Annual Report on Schoolhouse Commercialism Trends: 2008–2009.* Tempe, AZ: Commercialism in Education Research Unit, Education Policy Studies Laboratory, Arizona State University. Retrieved January 15, 2015, from http://nepc.colorado.edu/publication/schoolhouse-commercialism-2009; Learmonth, M. (2010, September 6). What big brands are spending on Google. *Advertising Age*. Retrieved September 7, 2010, from http://adage.com/digital/article?article_id=145720 [subscription required].

55. American Academy of Pediatrics (2006, December). Policy statement: Children, adolescents, and advertising. *Pediatrics, 118*(6), 2563–69. Retrieved August 23, 2010, from http://pediatrics.aappublications.org/cgi/reprint/118/6/2563.

56. York, E. B. (2008, November 19). NIH: Banning fast food ads will make kids less fat. *Advertising Age*. Retrieved March 26, 2009, from http://adage.com/

article?article_id=132718 (subscription required); Geraci, J. C. (2004). What do youth marketers think about selling to kids? *Advertising & Marketing to Children, April–June 2004*, 11–17 (pp. 14–15). Retrieved September 7, 2010, from http://www.cruxresearch.com/downloads/selling-to-kids-0404.pdf; Nixon, B. (2004). Advertising and marketing to children—everybody's business. *Advertising & Marketing to Children*, April–June 2004, 19–25. Retrieved March 8, 2010, from http://www.emeraldinsight.com.ezproxy1.lib.asu.edu/journals.htm?issn=1747-3616&volume=5&issue=3.

57. Geraci, J. C. (2004). What do youth marketers think about selling to kids? *Advertising & Marketing to Children, April–June 2004*, 11–17 (14–15). Retrieved September 7, 2010, from http://www.cruxresearch.com/downloads/selling-to-kids-0404.pdf.

58. For a review, see Molnar, A., Boninger, F., Wilkinson, G., Fogarty, J., & Geary, S. (2010). *Effectively Embedded: Schools and the Machinery of Modern Marketing—The Thirteenth Annual Report on Schoolhouse Commercializing Trends: 2009–2010*. Boulder, CO: National Education Policy Center. Retrieved January 15, 2015, from http://nepc.colorado.edu/publication/Schoolhouse-commercialism-2010.

59. Dittmar, H. (ed.) (2008). *Consumer Culture, Identity and Well-Being: The Search for the 'Good Life' and the 'Body Perfect.'* Hove, England, and New York: Psychology Press, Taylor and Francis Group, chapters 6, 7, 8; Hanley, P. (2010, January 26). Consumer culture saturates kids' lives. *Star-Phoenix*. Retrieved February 1, 2010, from http://www.thestarphoenix.com/technology/Consumer+culture+saturates+kids+lives/2484487/story.html [no longer available]; Hoffman, J. (2010, January 29). Masculinity in a spray can. *New York Times*. Retrieved February 1, 2010, from http://www.nytimes.com/2010/01/31/fashion/31smell.html; Jhally, S. (2005). Advertising as social communication (online course; part three: Advertising and Social Issues). Retrieved July 22, 2009, from http://www.comm287.com/partthree/; Kasser, T. (2002). *The High Price of Materialism*. Cambridge, MA: MIT Press; Schor, J. B. (2004). *Born to Buy*. New York, Scribner.

60. Kilbourne, J. (2006). Jesus is a brand of jeans. *New Internationalist,* September, 10–12. Retrieved June 25, 2010, from http://www.newint.org/features/2006/09/01/culture/. See also Jhally, S. & Barr, W. (n.d.). *Advertising, cultural criticism, and pedagogy: An interview with Sut Jhally* (conducted by William O'Barr). Retrieved November 23, 2010, from http://www.sutjhally.com/articles/advertisingcultura/.

61. Dittmar, H. (2008). *Consumer Culture, Identity and Well-Being: The Search for the 'Good Life' and the 'Body Perfect.'* Hove, England, and New York: Psychology Press, Taylor and Francis Group, 218.

62. Dittmar, H. (ed.) (2008). *Consumer Culture, Identity and Well-Being: The Search for the 'Good Life' and the 'Body Perfect.'* Hove, England, and New York: Psychology Press, Taylor and Francis Group, chapters 6, 7, 8. For anecdotal evidence that young boys are also susceptible, see Hoffman, J. (2010, January 29). Masculinity in a spray can. *New York Times.* Retrieved February 1, 2010, from http://www.nytimes.com/2010/01/31/fashion/31smell.html.

63. Dittmar, H. (ed.) (2008). *Consumer Culture, Identity and Well-Being: The Search for the 'Good Life' and the 'Body Perfect.'* Hove, England, and New York: Psychology Press, Taylor and Francis Group, 210; Bell, B. T., Lawson, R., & Dittmar, H. (2007). The impact of music videos on adolescent girls' body dissatisfaction. *Body Image, 4*(2) 137–45. Cited in Dittmar, Helga (ed.) (2008). *Consumer Culture, Identity and Well-Being: The Search for the 'Good Life' and the 'Body Perfect.'* Hove, England, and New York: Psychology Press, Taylor and Francis Group, 210.

64. Lowes, J., & Tiggerman, M. (2003). Body dissatisfaction, dieting awareness, and the impact of parental influence on young children. *British Journal of Health Psychology, 8*, 135–47.

65. Terrazas, B. (2008, August 26). Old Spice Swagger—LL Cool J and Brian Urlacher. *Everything's Better with Brentter: An Advertising Blog* by Brent Terrazas (blog). Retrieved June 28, 2010, from http://www.brentter.com/old-spice-swagger-ll-cool-j-and-brian-urlacher/; O'Neill, M. (2010, July 22). How Old Spice Swaggerized Their Brand and Men Everywhere. *Social Times.* Retrieved November 3, 2014, from http://socialtimes.com/how-old-spice-swaggerized-their-brand-and-men-everywhere_b18042; Brian Urlacher Old Spice Swagger Commercial (2008). Retrieved June 28, 2010, from http://www.youtube.com/watch?v=kNUCsUUaevk.

66. Hoffman, J. (2010, January 29). Masculinity in a spray can. *New York Times.* Retrieved February 1, 2010, from http://www.nytimes.com/2010/01/31/fashion/31smell.html.

67. Dittmar, H. (ed.) (2008). *Consumer Culture, Identity and Well-Being: The Search for the 'Good lLife' and the 'Body Perfect.'* Hove, England, and New York: Psychology Press, Taylor and Francis Group, 216.

68. Dittmar, H. (ed.) (2008). *Consumer Culture, Identity and Well-Being: The Search for the 'Good Life' and the 'Body Perfect.'* Hove, England, and New York: Psychology Press, Taylor and Francis Group, 193.

69. Jhally, S. (2005). Advertising as social communication (online course; part three: Advertising and Social Issues). Retrieved July 22, 2009, from http://www.comm287.com/partthree/.

70. Packaged Facts (2007, December 1). Teen and tween grooming products: The U.S. market. Author. Retrieved June 29, 2010, from http://www.packagedfacts.com/Teen-Tween-Grooming-1535802/.

71. Hoffman, J. (2010, January 29). Masculinity in a spray can. *New York Times*. Retrieved February 1, 2010, from http://www.nytimes.com/2010/01/31/fashion/31smell.html; Old Spice's "Make an Old Spice Swagger Commercial" ran in the summer of 2009: Make an Old Spice Swagger Commercial (website). Retrieved June 28, 2010, from http://www.oldspice.com/swaggerize-your-wallet/challenge/12/Make-an-Old-Spice-Swagger-Commercial/.

72. Reitgazi, F., & Hoban, S. (2010). APG Creative Strategy Awards—Axe 'wake-up service' by BBH Singapore. Campaignmonitor.com. Retrieved August 25, 2014, from http://www.campaignlive.co.uk/news/926148/; The Warc Prize for Ideas and Evidence: Shortlist. Retrieved August 25, 2014, from http://warcprize.warc.com/shortlist.aspx.

73. Axe Wake-Up Service, Inc. (website). Retrieved June 28, 2010, from http://202.218.121.130/2008/axewakeupservice/en/; Hoffman, Jan (2010, January 29). Masculinity in a spray can. *New York Times*. Retrieved February 1, 2010, from http://www.nytimes.com/2010/01/31/fashion/31smell.html.

74. Brown, L. M., cited in Hoffman, J. (2010, January 29). Masculinity in a spray can. *New York Times*. Retrieved February 1, 2010, from http://www.nytimes.com/2010/01/31/fashion/31smell.html. For commentary on hypersexuality in boys, see also: Jhally, S. (2005). Advertising as social communication (online course; part three: Advertising and Social Issues). Retrieved July 22, 2009, from http://www.comm287.com/partthree/.

75. Kanner, A. D. (2007, June 8). The corporatized child (p. 3). Paper presented at the Psychology-Ecology-Sustainability Conference, Lewis and Clark University, Portland, OR. See also: Jhally, S., & Barr, W. (n.d.). Advertising, cultural criticism, and pedagogy: an interview with Sut Jhally (conducted by William O'Barr). Retrieved November 23, 2010, from http://www.sutjhally.com/articles/advertisingcultura/.

76. Hanley, P. (2010, January 26). Consumer culture saturates kids' lives. *Star-Phoenix*. Retrieved February 1, 2010, from http://www.thestarphoenix.com/technology/Consumer+culture+saturates+kids+lives/2484487/story.html [no longer available].

77. Schor, J. B. (2004). *Born to Buy*. New York, Scribner.

78. Kasser, T. (2002). *The High Price of Materialism*. Cambridge, MA: MIT Press.

79. Montgomery, K. C., & Chester, J. (2009). Interactive food and beverage marketing: Targeting adolescents in the digital age. *Journal of Adolescent Health, 45*, S18–S29; Giedd, J. N. (2008). The teen brain: Insights from neuroimaging. *Journal of Adolescent Health, 42*, 335–43. Retrieved October 15, 2010, from http://download.journals.elsevierhealth.com/pdfs/journals/1054-139X/PIIS1054139X0800075X.pdf?refuid=S1054-139X(09)00149-9&refissn=1054-139X&mis=.pdf; Pechmann, C., Levine, L., Loughlin, S., & Leslie, F. (2005).

Impulsive and self-conscious: Adolescents' vulnerability to advertising and promotion. *Journal of Public Policy Marketing, 24,* 202–21; Steinberg, L. (2008). A social neuroscience perspective on adolescent risktaking. *Development Review, 28,* 78–106.

80. Montgomery, K. C., & Chester, J. (2009). Interactive food and beverage marketing: Targeting adolescents in the digital age. *Journal of Adolescent Health, 45,* S18–S29; Harris, J. L., Brownell, K. D., & Bargh, J. A. (2009). The food marketing defense model: Integrating psychological research to protect youth and inform public policy (p. 212). *Social Issues and Policy Review, 3*(1), 211–74. Retrieved March 31, 2010, from http://www.yaleruddcenter.org/resources/upload/docs/what/advertising/FoodMarketingDefenseModelSIPR12.09.pdf.

81. For simplicity's sake we include "adolescents" in with "children," but adolescents are even more susceptible than younger children to the psychological harms caused by advertising because of the sensitivities associated with their developmental stage. Self-regulation guidelines for advertisers have only very recently begun to recognize adolescents' susceptibility; and up until now adolescents have been grouped with adults. For research on adolescents, see Food Marketing Workgroup (2011, July). Re: Interagency Working Group on Food Marketed to Children: General Comments and Proposed Marketing Definitions: FTC Project No. P094513 (Comment on Marketing Definitions) (pp. 10–13). Retrieved September 9, 2011, from http://www.ftc.gov/os/comments/foodmarketedchildren/07843-80010.pdf/; Montgomery, K. C., & Chester, J. (2009). Interactive food and beverage marketing: Targeting adolescents in the digital age. *Journal of Adolescent Health, 45,* S18–S29; Giedd, J. N. (2008). The teen brain: Insights from neuroimaging. *Journal of Adolescent Health, 42,* 335–43. Retrieved October 15, 2010, from http://download.journals.elsevierhealth.com/pdfs/journals/1054-139X/PIIS1054139X0800075X.pdf?refuid=S1054-139X(09)00149-9&refissn=1054-139X&mis=.pdf/; Pechmann, C., Levine, L., Loughlin S., & Leslie, F. (2005). Impulsive and self-conscious: Adolescents' vulnerability to advertising and promotion. *Journal of Public Policy Marketing, 24,* 202–21; Steinberg, L. (2008). A social neuroscience perspective on adolescent risk-taking. *Development Review, 28,* 78–106.

82. Wilcox, B., Kunkel, D., Cantor, J., Dowrick, P., Linn, S., & Palmer, E. (2004). *Report of the APA Task Force on Advertising and Children.* Washington, DC: American Psychological Association. Retrieved March 31, 2010, from http://www.chawisconsin.org/Obesity/O2ChildAds.pdf. "Fairness" is a basis of the self-regulatory guidelines of the Children's Advertising Review Unit: Children's Advertising Review Unit (2009). Self-regulatory program for children's advertising (p. 3). Retrieved June 24, 2010, from http://www.caru.org/guidelines/guidelines.pdf.

83. Harris, J. L., Heard, A., & Schwartz, M. (2014, January). Older but still vulnerable: All children need protection from unhealthy food marketing. Yale Rudd Center for Food Policy and Obesity. Retrieved November 3, 2014, from http://www.yaleruddcenter.org/resources/upload/docs/what/reports/Protecting_ Older_Children_3.14.pdf.

84. Montgomery, K. C., & Chester, J. (2009). Interactive food and beverage marketing: Targeting adolescents in the digital age. *Journal of Adolescent Health, 45,* S18–S29.

85. Chester, J., & Montgomery, K. (2007, May). Interactive food and beverage marketing: Targeting children and youth in the digital age. Berkeley, CA: Public Health Institute. Retrieved August 19, 2009, from http://digitalads.org/ documents/digiMarketingFull.pdf; Chester, J., & Montgomery, K. (2008). Digital marketing to youth: An emerging threat. *Consumer Policy Review, 18*(6). Retrieved August 21, 2009, from http://digitalads.org/reports.php.

86. Patel, K. (2010, September 20). How your likes are turning Facebook into the 'loyalty card of the internet.' *Advertising Age.* Retrieved September 28, 2010, from http://adage.com/digital/article?article_id=145982 [subscription required]; Warc (2010, August 3). Facebook seeks to extend online influence. Author. Retrieved August 10, 2010, from http://www.warc.com/News/7DiM.asp.

87. Bloomberg News and Ad Age staff (2013, August 29). Facebook seeks to clarify how it uses member data for ads. *Advertising Age.* Retrieved August 21, 2014, from http://adage.com/article/digital/facebook-seeks-clarify-member-data-ads/243912/ [subscription required]; Facebook (2014). Facebook Ads. Author. Retrieved November 4, 2014, from https://www.facebook.com/settings?tab= ads&section=social&view.

88. Delo, C. (2014, April 11). Why it's hard to be a brand on Instagram. *Advertising Age.* Retrieved August 21, 2014, from http://adage.com/article/ digital/hard-a-brand-instagram/292607/ [subscription required].

89. We were unsuccessful in our search to find the actual study. Sandberg is quoted in this article: Carr, A. (2010, June 17). Facebook COO Sheryl Sandberg is embracing the end of email, here's why. *Fast Company* (website). Retrieved June 25, 2010, from http://www.fastcompany.com/1660619/facebook-coo-sheryl-sandberg-on-the-end-of-e-mail-branding-in-social-networks.

4

THREATS TO CHILDREN'S PHYSICAL WELL-BEING

Thus far we have argued that irrespective of the particular product or service advertised, commercial marketing transmits the underlying value message that happiness can be purchased and that the way to the good life is through consumerism. Of course, every advertisement also promotes a particular product, service, and/or point of view that may pose its own particular threats to children's well-being. Advertisements for beauty products, for example, as we mentioned in chapter 3, may threaten children's body image and sexual identity.[1]

It is foods and beverages, however, especially those of little or no nutritional value, that are by far the most heavily marketed products in schools. In other words, exactly the types of foods implicated in the rapid increase in childhood obesity and metabolic syndrome are the foods most likely to be marketed in schools. For this reason, the most significant health threat associated with advertising in school has to do with the preponderance of advertising for food products, and the potential relationship of this advertising to obesity, metabolic syndrome, and the host of illnesses associated with them.[2]

OBESITY

In the United States, childhood obesity has almost tripled since 1980. The percentage of obese six- to eleven-year-olds increased from 7 percent in

1980 to nearly 20 percent in 2008, while in the same time period the percentage of obese twelve- to nineteen-year-olds increased from 5 percent to 18 percent.[3]

The United States is not the only country with a childhood obesity problem. Worldwide, between 1980 and 2013, the prevalence of overweight or obese children and adolescents increased by nearly 50 percent between 1980 and 2013.[4] In 2013, more than 22 percent of girls and nearly 24 percent of boys living in developed countries, and approximately 13 percent of both girls and boys living in developing countries, were overweight or obese.[5]

Pediatric studies warn that obesity poses a significant threat to children's long-term health.[6] Among these threats are elevated cholesterol levels, higher blood pressure, coronary plaque formation, greater likelihood of type 2 diabetes, several types of cancer, bone and joint problems, sleep apnea, gout, gallstones, and a shorter life expectancy.[7]

The list of medical implications continues to grow. Type 2 diabetes, for example, progresses more rapidly in children than it does in adults, and typical treatment fails to slow it.[8] Consequently, obese children are at risk for complications such as heart disease, eye problems, nerve damage, amputations, and kidney failure much earlier in life than people who become diabetic as adults.[9] In addition, a 2014 study found an association between type 2 diabetes and subsequent cognitive decline.[10]

Researchers have also identified psychosocial problems associated with obesity.[11] Children as young as three begin stereotyping fat as "bad," and overweight children are less accepted by their peers and more socially isolated.[12] The more overweight children are, the more they are teased by their peers. Such teasing has been found to lead to depression, anxiety, lower self-esteem, poor body image, and suicidal thoughts.[13] Teasing also makes overweight children more likely to binge-eat and to be reluctant to engage in the physical activity that they need to become healthier.[14]

BACKGROUND: ADVERTISING FOOD TO CHILDREN

Although there is no direct evidence tying any specific advertising campaign or food to obesity,[15] a strong body of evidence makes the case that advertising and marketing do influence children's food preferences and eating behavior.[16] So also do the huge sums of industry money spent on advertising, marketing, and lobbying to prevent or to weaken any possible restriction on marketing to children.[17] As Margo Wootan, director of nutrition policy at the Center for Science in the Public Interest, explained in an episode of *The Knife and Fork Show*, "Food marketing affects what children want to eat, what they're willing to eat, what they do eat . . . [and] helps to shape what kids think of as food . . ."[18]

Wootan's claim is consistent with the research. It finds that food advertising influences which foods children prefer (both immediately and over time), what they ask their parents to buy, and even how much they eat in a sitting.[19]

While it is true that most foods of minimal nutritional value, or foods high in fat, sugar, or salt, may be safely eaten in small quantities, it is also true that marketing is designed to convince its targets to like and want more of the product being marketed. In schools, as elsewhere, food marketing focuses on selling products that are unhealthy when consumed to excess. When it is successful, therefore, it influences children's eating habits in a direction that contributes to obesity and the many health problems associated with it.[20]

Huge sums of money are spent on food and beverage marketing to children, both in and out of schools. To examine just how much is spent, and on what kind of marketing, the Federal Trade Commission (FTC) published illuminating reports in 2008 and in 2012.[21]

Since the FTC has the legal authority to subpoena and collect information from corporations that these companies, the commission's reports provide especially important baseline information that helps us understand the impact of the voluntary self-regulation introduced by the food and beverage industry in 2006. The industry launched two new self-regulation regimes in 2006, and the FTC's 2008 report examines 2006 industry spending, before the self-regulation guidelines were implemented. The 2012 FTC report examines 2009 industry spending, after self-regulation had begun. Thus the two FTC reports allow us to make a rough assessment of the impact of self-regulation on the companies' spending on marketing to children.

Spending on Food Advertising to Children

The data in the 2008 and 2012 FTC reports suggest that the total amount of money spent on advertising food and beverages to children, both in and out of schools, decreased between 2006 and 2009. However, to some extent this reduction in spending may reflect, at least in part, a shift to less expensive, but more effective, alternative media advertising (e.g., digital and mobile media, viral advertising campaigns).[22]

The forty-eight major national food and beverage marketers studied in the 2012 FTC report spent nearly $149 million marketing their products in schools ($37 million less than reported in the 2008 report). About 93 percent ($82.3 million) of this $149 million was for the marketing of carbonated beverages, with $55.9 million spent on marketing juice and other noncarbonated beverages, mostly to teens.[23] Of the total $149 million spent in schools, $31.3 million was directed at children younger than thirteen.[24]

According to the FTC, the data it collected on food and beverage marketing may underestimate in-school marketing of food products because much of the sales in schools of quick-service restaurant foods is done by local or regional franchisees under contract to the school, and data were not collected on expenditures by these franchisees.[25]

Counter-marketing

In 2008, the FTC recommended that the food corporations it studied expand their efforts to educate children and teens about the importance of healthy eating and exercise, especially among minority populations.[26] No doubt the FTC recommendation was well-intentioned; however, these education efforts, called counter-marketing, are themselves in practice often little more than a form of stealth advertising—just another way for companies to put their brand names in front of children in school.

So-called counter-marketing is also likely to reflect and promote the corporation's self-serving perspective on health, as when Coca-Cola heavily emphasizes the role of exercise in combating obesity.[27]

Counter-marketing practices are also problematic because they tend to shift the onus of responsibility from corporations to children. Instead of calling on marketers to eliminate or significantly curtail their marketing programs, they call on children to resist corporate efforts to promote the consumption of foods of little or no nutritional value, and if they fall prey

to those marketing messages to blame themselves for choosing to consume excessive amounts of the high-calorie/low-nutritional-value food
marketed to them. In our view, asking the industry to "counter-market"
against its financial interests seems a little like hiring an assassin to be
your bodyguard.

Several companies reported to the FTC on their school-based counter-
marketing efforts to teach children about nutrition and physical activity.[28]
These included dissemination of materials for teachers to use, partnership
with the Afterschool Alliance to create a tool kit for students participating
in after-school programs across the United States, and a multimedia campaign to promote the benefits of drinking milk that included in-school
posters, a teen-targeted website, print advertising, and other promotional
programs.[29]

Research sponsored by the companies and reported to the FTC
showed modest, if any, effect of their counter-marketing programs on the
adoption of healthy behaviors. In contrast, one marketer submitted "consumption research" that indicated increased sales partly as a result of its
counter-marketing promotional techniques.[30] In addition to promoting a
given "better for you" product offered by a brand, counter-marketing
campaigns promote the brand itself, including its flagship products, many
of which are not "better for you."[31]

Government Regulation versus Self-Regulation

Since 2006 some food companies have policed their own efforts to restrict advertising to children. The Children's Food and Beverage Advertising Initiative (CFBAI), established by the Better Business Bureau in
2006, now has seventeen member corporations: Burger King Corporation; Campbell Soup Company; The Coca-Cola Company; ConAgra
Foods, Inc.; The Dannon Company, Inc.; Ferrero USA, Inc.; General
Mills, Inc.; The Hershey Company; Kellogg Company; Kraft Foods
Group, Inc.; Mars, Inc.; McDonald's USA, LLC; Mondelēz Global, LLC;
Nestlé USA; PepsiCo, Inc.; Post Foods, LLC; and Unilever United States.

According to data compiled by the FTC, CFBAI member corporations
accounted for 89 percent of 2009 spending on marketing food and beverage products to children and adolescents.[32] In 2014, the advertising trade
publication *Advertising Age* named all but three of them in its list of 100

Largest Global Marketers, based on the amount of money they spent on measured advertising in 2013.[33]

The CFBAI has worked to improve the nutritional quality of foods advertised to children below age twelve. As of December 31, 2013, CFBAI's participants use "category-specific uniform nutrition criteria" rather than their own, weaker, company-specific criteria to determine which foods are allowed in child-directed advertising (advertising primarily directed to children under age twelve). This change required companies to reformulate many of their products to meet the new criteria. CFBAI director Elaine Kolish explained in a January 2014 press release that "while not every recipe for every food advertised to children in 2013 was able to be changed to meet the new criteria, those foods will not be advertised to children until they do."[34]

Further, CFBAI also expanded the range of marketing activities that it covers to reflect the evolution of marketing practice toward digital strategies. The initiative now covers, for example, advergames, advertising on video games and movie DVDs, mobile media (including cell phones), apps used in mobile media, and word-of-mouth marketing.

Margo Wootan, of the Center for Science in the Public Interest, notes that policies by CFBAI-participating companies are more detailed than those of companies that do not participate in the initiative. For example, CFBAI pledges specify for which media the companies are limiting marketing of unhealthy food, and how they define whether those media are directed toward children. CFBAI's nutrition standards are clear and explained through a detailed report.[35]

Companies that do not belong to CFBAI, if they address food marketing at all, tend to be vague about the details, making it unclear to parents and advocates what the company has really agreed to do (i.e., which media are covered and how they define "child-directed advertising").[36]

The FTC noted, however, that despite this meaningful expansion in the CFBAI's efforts, it still does not cover several marketing strategies that food companies' own research shows are effective in reaching children (e.g., product packaging, in-store promotion, and using licensed characters from popular children's movies and television shows).[37]

With respect to advertising in schools in particular, the CFBAI reported "excellent" compliance on the part of member companies with their commitments not to advertise branded foods and beverages.[38] However, the CFBAI's restrictions do not cover middle and high schools at all and in elementary schools, do not cover such activities as fundraising and other donations to schools, adult-directed marketing, public service messaging, and materials that identify products offered for sale in schools (such as menus and placards used in conjunction with food displays). [39] In addition, franchisees, independent distributors, and local bottlers for CFBAI member companies do not always adhere to the member companies' pledge commitments. [40]

In addition to CFBAI, beverage companies have focused their efforts on reducing the calorie count of the beverages sold in schools, in conjunction with the American Beverage Association and Alliance for a Healthier Generation. [41] While it is possible that this approach may influence children to purchase lower-calorie drinks, it still allows marketing the brand. Moreover, marketing the brand in school inevitably highlights the continued availability of the full-calorie main product line outside of school. [42]

Although public health advocates such as the Center for Science in the Public Interest and other members of the Food Marketing Workgroup laud the CFBAI for what it has accomplished, they point to the weaknesses detailed above when they call for public policy to supplement self-regulation. [43] Industry points to its accomplishments to argue that legislated regulation would be superfluous, at best. [44] Nevertheless, Congress and regulatory agencies have debated several school food marketing-related issues in recent years.

In 2009 Congress mandated an Interagency Working Group (IWG) composed of the Agriculture Department, Centers for Disease Control and Prevention, Federal Trade Commission, and Food and Drug Administration to develop voluntary guidelines for food marketing to children. As the process progressed, and in the face of heavy lobbying against the IWG guidelines by the food industry, Congress demanded information the IWG could not provide, such as cost-benefit analysis data indicating how many food-industry and marketing-related jobs would be lost because of the guidelines. By May 2012, after the IWG had released proposed voluntary guidelines and had received public comment, it became evident that no final guidelines were going to be released. [45]

In January 2012, the United States Department of Agriculture (USDA) released new nutrition standards that limit the calories, salt, and sugar content of food served as a school meal. [46] In June 2013, the USDA finalized rules for competitive foods (foods not included in the National

School Lunch Program), sold in such locations as cafeterias, school stores, and vending machines in schools, effective fall 2014.[47] These rules limit the calories, salt, and sugar content of foods sold in schools via "à la carte" sales in school cafeterias or other venues, including vending machines, school stores, and snack bars.

In a rule it proposed in February 2014, the USDA recognized that a product's presence in a school setting effectively advertises it and thus encourages students to purchase it. The rule is intended to strengthen school wellness policies by requiring schools to implement marketing policies for food and beverages consistent with the competitive food nutrition standards.[48]

As written, the proposed new rule has significant loopholes. It allows schools to continue to advertise food products of little or no nutritional value after school hours, and to continue to advertise products that meet the nutrition standards, such as diet sodas, all day. It does not require removal of advertising on "durable equipment," such as scoreboards, nor does it address the use of sponsored educational materials.[49]

Bruce Hunter, former associate executive director for advocacy and policy of AASA, the School Superintendents Association, pointed out another problem with the USDA's new rules: underfunding. By providing less than half the funding districts need to provide the healthier food, he argues, the USDA rules may increase the likelihood that districts will turn to corporate advertising and sponsorships to make up the shortfall.[50]

While the regulatory efforts may over time improve the nutritional value of food and beverage products sold in schools, then, they are structured in such a way that they reinforce commercialism as a normal and legitimate part of the school environment.

NUTRITIONAL THREATS TO CHILDREN'S PHYSICAL WELL-BEING

Nonnutritious Food Is Heavily Marketed via Sales in Schools

Selling specific products is the most obvious way that foods are advertised in schools—embedding brand promotion in the food for sale. In a 2004 report, the U.S. Government Accountability Office (GAO) estimated that nearly nine out of ten schools offered so-called competitive foods (that is, foods not included in the National School Lunch Program) in à la carte cafeteria lines, vending machines, and school stores.[51]

Many, if not most, of the foods and beverages advertised in schools are so low in nutritional value they have been labeled foods of "minimal nutritional value" by the USDA, or "junk food" in everyday language. Some foods, such as French fries or ice cream, have nutritional value but also are high in fat, sugar, and/or salt and should be eaten in moderation.

The extent to which marketing for a given food product in school presents a threat to a child's health is tied to the nutritional value both of the particular food promoted and of the other foods sold by the same brand. This is because any advertisement for a particular offering in a brand's collection of products advertises both the product and the brand.[52] *New York Times* reporter Michael Moss's exposé of food industry marketing found that food companies readily create healthy product "extensions" to address consumers' particular health concerns, knowing that they will benefit from sales of the new items, from goodwill engendered by their effort, and also, oftentimes, from increased sales of the main product line generated by the brand extensions.[53]

So, for instance, Domino's sells "Smart Slice" pizza in schools. Smart Slice pizza both meets federal regulations for competitive foods and helps market the Domino's brand to students.[54] In this way marketing for a particular nutritionally sound restaurant food offering such as some of the products sold by Chick-fil-A, McDonald's, or Panda Express, still promotes restaurant brands that feature many unhealthy options.

Brands take particular advantage of this phenomenon when they sell "copycat foods" in schools. These foods meet USDA Smart Snacks requirements for competitive foods that can be sold in schools, but they are marketed using the same brand names, product names, and spokespeople as their less-healthy counterparts sold outside of schools.[55]

If a child likes a copycat product in school, when she looks for it in a supermarket or convenience store, she will switch over to the less-healthy alternative available there. A few of the copycat foods sold in school in the 2014–2015 school year are Cheetos Flamin' Hot Puffs Reduced Fat, Doritos Reduced Fat Nacho Cheese, Smartfood Reduced Fat White Cheddar Flavored Popcorn, Pepperidge Farm Goldfish made with Whole Grain Pretzels, and the Domino's Smart Slice mentioned above.[56]

Food sales in schools involve multiple categories of advertising, including appropriation of space, exclusive agreements with marketers, and fundraising. School space is appropriated when company logos appear on vending machines, cans, cups, wrappers, and so forth, both at the original point of purchase and throughout the school as students carry products with them. According to the GAO, high schools and middle schools have more competitive foods than elementary schools (and, as we mentioned earlier, food marketing in middle and high schools is not limited by the CFBAI[57]).

Food advertising via vending machine and school stores is widespread, and other spaces that may be branded include scoreboards, rooftops, bulletin boards, walls, textbooks, and school buses. A 2008 study of schools in Montgomery County, Maryland, found that all of its high schools, half of its middle schools, and a quarter of its elementary schools had school stores, most of which (80 percent) sold foods and beverages. The high schools housed an average of twenty-one vending machines each.[58]

Similarly, a 2006 study of twenty California high schools found that all but one of the schools surveyed contained vending machines, mostly located in high-traffic areas, for a total of 276 vending machines across the nineteen schools.[59] And our own 2006 survey of school administrators found that two-thirds of schools nationwide had marketing for foods of minimal nutritional value or foods high in fat or sugar (in a context in which over 80 percent had some kind of corporate marketing more generally).[60]

Significantly, a 2012 study of Maine high schools found that despite a 2007 law prohibiting both the sale and advertising of foods of minimal nutritional value, 85 percent of the high schools allowed such advertising. On average, twenty-eight different noncompliant foods were advertised in each school, with brand names seen most frequently in yearbooks and on scoreboards, posters, and vending machines. Brands were also advertised in school media and on paper products, sports equipment, athletic uniforms, and other school equipment and supplies.[61]

Exclusive agreements, especially for drinks, determine which brands students see in school. When beverage companies, in conjunction with the Alliance for a Healthier Generation, began in 2006 to reduce sales of high-calorie sweetened soft drinks in schools, they did reduce the number of beverage calories consumed in school.[62] However, schools with soft drink vending contracts continue to advertise products more acceptable to critics because they have some nutritional value (juice) or are low calorie (diet soda or branded water).[63] These products, of course, also carry brand-marketing messages that promote the brands' other, often less nutritional, products.[64]

A school or district with a Pepsi contract advertises Pepsi products such as Tropicana, Gatorade, and Diet Pepsi. One with a Coca-Cola contract advertises Coca-Cola products such as Minute Maid, Powerade, Dasani water, and Diet Coke. In Madawaska, Maine, the middle/high school, for example, has vending machines that sell Powerade and Dasani water during the school day. After school, Coke, Diet Coke, and Sprite are also sold at the canteen.[65]

The high schools in Flagstaff, Arizona, suggest the value of branded vending machines. In these schools, Pepsi-branded vending machines are functional only after hours, but they sit in school space, like billboards, during the school day as well. During the day, other vending machines sell water.[66] According to a district administrator, Flagstaff schools have seen a significant drop in drink sales since Arizona implemented strict school food guidelines. Even with less income, he posited, students' exposure to the brand is worth the cost to the company of maintaining the vending contract.[67]

Food Propaganda Is Often Disguised as Educational Material

Sponsorship of educational programs and materials is another form of embedded advertising. Although a case has been made for distinguishing between sponsorship and advertising,[68] we find this argument unconvincing because the benefits of advertising routinely accrue to sponsorships. Unless a corporation anonymously donates the money for a sponsored program, at the very least it gets public credit for providing something to the school. It is also common for sponsorships to provide programs or materials that enhance its agenda among schoolchildren.

According to marketing firm Education Funding Partners, the "cause marketing" involved in activities such as sponsoring a classroom "is about leveraging a charitable brand to increase sales, support product positioning or differentiate from competitors." It is "the intersection of philanthropy and marketing."[69]

Corporations can seem philanthropic when they provide "sponsored educational materials." These materials used to be called, more accurately in our view, propaganda.[70] They can be colorful and engaging, and may even align with state and now Common Core standards, but they also tend to present a worldview wholly consistent with that of the sponsor.

For example, in 2009 the Healthy Weight Commitment Foundation began its work to promote "ways to help people achieve a healthy weight through energy balance—calories in and calories out."[71] The Healthy Weight Commitment Foundation is a "CEO-led organization," a coalition of "more than 275 retailers, food and beverage manufacturers, restaurants, sporting goods and insurance companies, trade associations, nongovernmental organizations (NGOs), and professional sports organizations."[72]

According to the organization, its school program, Together Counts, is used by over 15 million students across the country. Together Counts provides a school curriculum for children in grades K-5, Energy Balance 101 (Healthy Schools. Healthy Kids). The curriculum, described as aligned with Common Core guidelines, "focuses on the balance of calories in and calories out," a mantra of the food and beverage industry that has been explicitly questioned by nutritional experts.[73]

Since children, especially young children, tend to believe what their teachers tell them, when a corporation's perspective is presented in school without any attribution to a source other than the teacher, they are very unlikely to question its validity.

Another example of propaganda disguised as educational material is SchoolTube, a program for schools that purports to provide "The Best Videos from Students and Teachers Everywhere." In addition to teachers and students, however, sponsors can create channels on this platform. To sponsors, channels are described as "a designated page on School-Tube.com to convey your messages through the power of video."[74]

Sponsors can brand their channel with a banner that links back to their website. More than that, they are assured that SchoolTube is approved in 90 percent of schools, endorsed by top associations, and unlike most social networks and video sharing sites that are blocked by schools' firewalls, is one of the few universally accepted web platforms in all schools.[75]

When we looked on SchoolTube for videos related to nutrition, we found several videos posted by the American Meat Institute that promote the perspective of the meat industry. The videos feature academic experts in an effort to "debunk the myths" that may cause viewers to eliminate meat from their diet. One addresses the "myth" that Americans eat too much meat and that meat's saturated fat content leads to heart disease. Another addresses the "myth" that grass-fed beef is safer than "beef from cattle finished on corn and grains," and yet another shows what beef processing looks like "when it's done right."[76]

These meat industry videos may be valid as argument in a debate with nutritionists who are concerned about the nutritional value of meat, but they are biased in favor of the meat industry, and without being placed in the context of a lesson by the teacher, amount to propaganda.

Digital Advertising Used to Market Foods in Schools

As we have previously noted, the marketing and advertising industries believe their future lies in digital marketing strategies.[77] Digital marketing via computers, video game consoles, handheld game players, and cellular telephones, is now ubiquitous. And food companies are leading the way in digital messaging, especially to teens.[78] Digital media are exceptionally well matched to both support and manipulate teens as they struggle with the developmental challenges of adolescence: they provide teens with opportunity for self-expression, identity exploration, and social interaction, and they facilitate mobility and independence.

Notably, the vast majority of digital advertising to teens and all children takes place outside school walls. Schools enter the picture when they expose children to digital marketing media and messages and, perhaps equally important, when they reinforce those messages.

Advertisers now view schools as a valuable portal to digital advertising. And educators encourage students to be connected as education increasingly moves online. Not only do schools typically require students to do Internet-based research (not at all unreasonable) and teachers recommend homework-help or other interesting educational sites (also not unreasonable), but many districts and even states (e.g., Alabama, Florida, Michigan, and New Mexico) have implemented requirements for students to take virtual courses.[79] All of these push children to spend more time online and increase the likelihood of their exposure to online advertising.[80]

On the face of it, children spending time online for educational purposes may not seem problematic, even if they do see more ads. Our concern here is that the Internet in general is not primarily or even necessarily an educational environment; rather, it is often an environment designed to meet the needs of marketers. Educators, in sending children into this environment, need to socialize them with respect to how to use it and how to interpret what they see there. In other words, they need to help children become critical framers of the information they find online. If they do not, simply sending them online is just offering them as targets for more marketing (and in this case, marketing that does not meet any district policies that may be in effect for in-school marketing).

Schools also reinforce digital marketing that children see outside of school by exposing them to those same products and brands in school. For example, beverage pouring rights agreements with schools reinforce powerful online marketing programs such as My Coke Rewards, a crown jewel of the Coca-Cola Company.

Coca-Cola is certainly one of the most successful digital marketers in the world, as evidenced by its social media success: of 10.6 billion total social media brand impressions generated by the Top 100 brands in July 2012, 1.4 billion were generated by Coca-Cola (not even counting those impressions generated by Sprite, a Coca-Cola brand that came in eighth place).[81]

Digital users of all ages are responsible for Coke's vast number of impressions, but Carol Kruse, the executive responsible for developing the popular My Coke Rewards loyalty program, acknowledged that, "We're especially targeting a teen or young adult audience. They're always on their mobile phones and they spend an inordinate amount of time on the Internet."[82]

My Coke Rewards launched in 2006 and is still active, with fifteen brands and the option for participants to donate their points to participating schools.[83] Participants create online accounts at MyCokeRewards.com so that they can enter PIN codes printed on bottle caps and cartons to redeem rewards.

In their analysis of the specific techniques used to target teens via My Coke Rewards, the Center for Digital Democracy and the Berkeley Media Studies group point to the following: creating immersive environments that keep users engaging with the site (i.e., with the brand); infiltrating social networks such as Facebook and Twitter; sending news alerts, rewards info, sweepstakes opportunities, bonus points, and other exclusives via location-based and mobile marketing; collecting personal data both from participants themselves and from others whose profiles suggest that they would be likely to be interested in the program; and studying the subconscious in order to try to trigger it.[84]

With each visit to the My Coke Rewards site, participants "supply demographic and psychographic details" that allow Coke's marketing team to "identify consumers across brands and experiences, and learn when and how to connect with them"—by, for instance, personalizing the look and messaging of a particular web page, e-mail, or mobile content, or by sending an exclusive offer.[85] Coca-Cola and other food corporations (e.g., Frito-Lay, McDonald's, PepsiCo) pioneered and have mastered these strategies that are now widely used by countless companies on the Internet, where encouraging consumer "engagement" with brands is the prime marketing goal.[86]

My Coke Rewards is part of a "360-degree" marketing strategy designed to engage with young people over and over, wherever they are and whatever they are doing—browsing cyberspace, watching television, or engaging in an offline activity.[87] When Coca-Cola brands are present in school (in the form of actual branded products, branded but inactive vending machines, or signs on playground fences), the school's implied approval of the brands reinforces the relationship with students that the corporation works so hard to construct. The financial value of in-school marketing was made obvious by the furor that erupted among bottlers when a company executive suggested—before My Coke Rewards even existed—that the company remove itself from schools.[88]

Marketing Subverts Healthy Eating Messages

Programs such as My Coke Rewards show how sophisticated marketers' targeting of children has become. Marketing now permeates and defines children's experience in their play outside of school, their work inside the school, and in their home life. Children's physical health is threatened not only by the fact—demonstrated so well by Coca-Cola's success—that food marketers lead the industry in engaging children, but also by food marketers' special presence in schools. Ironically, as we have already noted, even as their classes teach children to avoid foods that are unhealthy for them when consumed to excess, the marketing environment in many schools teaches them just the opposite and in a more consistent and compelling way.

NOTES

1. Gunter, B. (2014). *Media and the Sexualization of Childhood*. New York: Routledge, 51.

2. Institute of Medicine. (2006). *Food Marketing to Children and Youth: Threat or Opportunity?* Washington, DC: The National Academies Press. Retrieved January 31, 2013, from http://www.nap.edu/books/0309097134/html/.

3. Centers for Disease Control and Prevention (2011, September 15). Childhood obesity facts. Author. Retrieved April 30, 2011, from http://www.cdc.gov/healthyyouth/obesity/facts.htm/. Notably, data published in 2012 suggest the first decreases in childhood obesity in decades—in several U.S. cities that have had obesity reduction policies in place for a number of years. Tavernise, S. (2012, December 10). Obesity in young is seen as falling in several cities. *New York Times*. Retrieved February 14, 2013, from http://www.nytimes.com/2012/12/11/health/childhood-obesity-drops-in-new-york-and-philadelphia.html/.

4. Ng, M., et al. (2014, August 30). Global, regional, and national prevalence of overweight and obesity in children and adults during 1980–2013: A systematic analysis for the Global Burden of Disease Study 2013. *Lancet, 384* (9945), 766–81. Retrieved September 20, 2014, from http://www.thelancet.com/journals/lancet/article/PIIS0140-6736(14)60460-8/abstract.

5. Ng, M., et al. (2014, August 30). Global, regional, and national prevalence of overweight and obesity in children and adults during 1980–2013: A systematic analysis for the Global Burden of Disease Study 2013. *Lancet, 384* (9945), 766–781. Retrieved September 20, 2014, from http://www.thelancet.com/journals/lancet/article/PIIS0140-6736(14)60460-8/abstract.

6. Committee on Communications, American Academy of Pediatrics (2006). Children, adolescents, and advertising. *Pediatrics*. Retrieved January 31, 2013, from http://pediatrics.aappublications.org/content/118/6/2563.full.pdf+html/; Glickman, D., Parker, L., Sim, L. J., Del Valle Cook, H., & Miller, E. A. (eds.) (2012, May). *Accelerating Progress in Obesity Prevention: Solving the Weight of the Nation*. Washington, DC: Institute of Medicine of the National Academies. Retrieved January 30, 2013, from http://books.nap.edu/openbook.php?record_id=13275/; Tompson, T., Benz, J., Agiesta, J., Brewer, K. H., Bye, L., Reimer, R., & Junius, D. (2013, January). Obesity in the United States: Public Perceptions. Associated Press and NORC Center for Public Affairs Research. Retrieved January 30, 2013, from http://www.apnorc.org/projects/Pages/Obesity-in-the-United-States.aspx/.

7. Centers for Disease Control and Prevention (2012). Child obesity facts. Atlanta, GA: Author. Retrieved February 5, 2013, from http://www.cdc.gov/healthyyouth/obesity/facts.htm/; Fontaine, K. R, Redden, C. T., Wang C., Westfall A. O., & Allison, D. B. (2003). Years of life lost due to obesity. *Journal of*

the American Medical Association, 289, 187–93. Retrieved April 30, 2012, from http://www.permanente.net/homepage/kaiser/pdf/19391.pdf/; Koebnick, C., Smith, N., Black, M. H., Porter, A. H., Richie, B. A., Hudson, S., Gililland, D., Jacobsen, S. J., & Longstreth, G. F. (2012). Pediatric obesity and gallstone disease. *Journal of Pediatric Gastroenterology and Nutrition, 55*(3), 328–33; Musemeche, C. (2012, April 25). Childhood obesity leads to unnecessary surgeries. *New York Times.* Retrieved February 11, 2013, from http://parenting.blogs. nytimes.com/2012/04/25/childhood-obesity-leads-to-unnecessary-surgeries/; Huge rise in gout cases (2012, October 6). Nursingtimes.net. Retrieved March 7, 2013, from http://www.nursingtimes.net/nursing-practice/clinical-zones/ rheumatology/huge-rise-in-gout-cases/5050304.article/; Stanford Hospital and Clinics (2013). Health effects of obesity. Stanford, CA: Author. Retrieved February 5, 2013, from http://stanfordhospital.org/clinicsmedServices/COE/ surgicalServices/generalSurgery/bariatricsurgery/obesity/effects.html/; Sturm, R., & Wells, K. B. (2001). Does obesity contribute as much to morbidity as poverty or smoking? *Public Health, 115*: 229–35. Retrieved April 30, 2012, from http://www.rand.org/pubs/reprints/RP952.html/.

8. Grady, D. (2012, April 29). Obesity-linked diabetes in children resists treatment. *New York Times.* Retrieved February 11, 2013, from http://www. nytimes.com/2012/04/30/health/research/obesity-and-type-2-diabetes-cases-take-toll-on-children.html/; Today Study Group (2012, June 14). A clinical trial to maintain glycemic control in youth with type 2 diabetes. *New England Journal of Medicine; 366,* 2247–56. Retrieved February 11, 2013, from http://www.nejm. org/doi/full/10.1056/NEJMoa1109333/.

9. Grady, D. (2012, April 29). Obesity-linked diabetes in children resists treatment. *New York Times.* Retrieved February 11, 2013, from http://www. nytimes.com/2012/04/30/health/research/obesity-and-type-2-diabetes-cases-take-toll-on-children.html/; MacNeil/Lehrer Productions (2012, June 6). Study: Standard treatment ineffective for kids with obesity-linked diabetes. *PBS Newshour.* Retrieved June 12, 2012, from http://www.pbs.org/newshour/bb/health/ jan-june12/diabetes_06-06.html/; Today Study Group (2012, June 14). A clinical trial to maintain glycemic control in youth with type 2 diabetes. *New England Journal of Medicine, 366,* 2247–56. Retrieved February 11, 2013, from http:// www.nejm.org/doi/full/10.1056/NEJMoa1109333/.

10. Rawlings, A. M., Sharrett, A. R., Schneider, A. L. C., Coresh, J., Albert, M., Couper, D., Griswold, M., Gottesman, R. F., Wagenknecht, L. E., Windham, B. G., & Selvin, E. (2014). Diabetes in midlife and cognitive change over 20 years: A cohort study. *Annals of Internal Medicine, 161*(11), 785–93. Retrieved December 10, 2014, from http://annals.org/article.aspx?articleid=1983393.

11. Brownell, K. D., Schwartz, M. B., Puhl, R. M., Henderson, K. E., & Harris, J. L. (2009). The need for bold action to prevent adolescent obesity.

Journal of Adolescent Health, 45, S8–S17. Retrieved January 30, 2013, from http://www.jahonline.org/article/S1054-139X(09)00107-4/; Stanford Hospital and Clinics (2013). Health effects of obesity. Stanford, CA: Author. Retrieved February 5, 2013, from http://stanfordhospital.org/clinicsmedServices/COE/surgicalServices/generalSurgery/bariatricsurgery/obesity/effects.html/; Storch, E. A., Milsom, V. A., DeBraganza, N., Lewin, A. B., Geffken, G. R., & Silverstein, J. H. (2007). Peer victimization, psychosocial adjustment, and physical activity in overweight and at-risk-for-overweight youth. *Journal of Pediatric Psychology, 32*(1), 80–89. Retrieved February 4, 2013, from http://jpepsy.oxfordjournals.org/content/32/1/80/.

12. Cramer, P., & Steinwert, T. (1998, July–September). Thin is good, fat is bad: How early does it begin? *Journal of Applied Developmental Psychology, 19*(3), 429–51; Zeller, M. H., Reiter-Purtill, J., & Ramey, C. (2008, April). Negative peer perceptions of obese children in the classroom environment. *Obesity, 16*(4), 755–62.

13. Puhl, R. M., Peterson, J. L., & Luedicke, J. (2012, January). Weight-based victimization: Bullying experiences of weight loss treatment-seeking youth. *Pediatrics, 131*(1), e1–e9. Retrieved January 31, 2013, from http://www.yaleruddcenter.org/resources/upload/docs/what/bias/Bullying_Experiences_of_Weight_Loss_Treatment_Pediatrics_12.12.pdf/.

14. Faith, M. S., Leone, M. A., Ayers, T. S., Heo, M., & Pietrobelli, A. (2002, August). Weight criticism during physical activity, coping skills, and reported physical activity in children. *Pediatrics, 110*(2), e23. Retrieved February 4, 2013, from http://pediatrics.aappublications.org/content/110/2/e23/; Storch, E. A., Milsom, V. A., DeBraganza, N., Lewin, A. B., Geffken, G. R., & Silverstein, J. H. (2007). Peer victimization, psychosocial adjustment, and physical activity in overweight and at-risk-for-overweight youth. *Journal of Pediatric Psychology, 32*(1), 80–89. Retrieved February 4, 2013, from http://jpepsy.oxfordjournals.org/content/32/1/80/.

15. Washington Legal Foundation (2011, September 25). Five questions for . . . CFBAI's Elaine Kolish on self regulation of advertising. *Legal Pulse.* Retrieved February 12, 2013, from http://wlflegalpulse.com/2011/09/15/five-questions-for-cfbais-elaine-kolish-on-self-regulation-of-advertising/.

16. Committee on Communications (2006). Children, adolescents, and advertising. *Pediatrics, 118*(6), 2563–69. Retrieved January 31, 2013, from http://pediatrics.aappublications.org/content/118/6/2563.full.pdf+html/; Harris, J. L., Brownell, K. D., & Bargh, J. A. (2009). The Food Marketing Defense Model: Integrating psychological research to protect youth and inform public policy. *Social Issues and Policy Review, 3*(9), 211–71. Retrieved January 31, 2013, from http://yaleruddcenter.org/resources/upload/docs/what/advertising/FoodMarketingDefenseModelSIPR12.09.pdf/; Hastings, G., McDermott, L., An-

gus, K., Stead, M., & Thomson, S. (2006). The extent, nature and effects of food promotion to children: A review of the evidence. Geneva: World Health Organization. Retrieved January 31, 2013, from http://www.who.int/dietphysicalactivity/publications/Hastings_paper_marketing.pdf/; Institute of Medicine (2006). *Food Marketing to Children and Youth: Threat or Opportunity?* Washington, DC: The National Academies Press. Retrieved January 31, 2013, from http://www.nap.edu/books/0309097134/html/.

17. Federal Trade Commission (2012, December). *A Review of Food Marketing to Children and Adolescents: Follow-Up Report* (p. ES-1). Washington, DC: Author. Retrieved December 1, 2014, from http://www.ftc.gov/opa/2012/12/foodmarketing.shtm/; Wilson, D., & Rogers, J. (2012, April 27). Special Report: How Washington went soft on childhood obesity. *Reuters.* Retrieved January 29, 2013, from http://www.reuters.com/article/2012/04/27/us-usa-foodlobby-idUSBRE83Q0ED20120427/.

18. Wootan, M. (2012). Interviewed on *The Knife and Fork Show* (Season 1, Episode 1; quotation at 5:07). Retrieved November 27, 2012, from http://www.youtube.com/watch?v=STtUmjKfRt4&feature=plcp/. (*The Knife and Fork Show* is an Internet video program produced by the website *Food Chemical News* [http://www.agra-net.com/portal2/fcn/home.jsp?template=showcmsnewsletter&pubid=ag096].)

19. Harris, J. L., Brownell, K. D., & Bargh, J. A. (2009). The Food Marketing Defense Model: Integrating psychological research to protect youth and inform public policy. *Social Issues and Policy Review, 3*(9), 211–71. Retrieved January 31, 2013, from http://yaleruddcenter.org/resources/upload/docs/what/advertising/FoodMarketingDefenseModelSIPR12.09.pdf/; Harris, J. L., Bargh, J. A., & Brownell, K. D. (2009). Priming effects of television food advertising on eating behavior. *Health Psychology, 28*(4), 404–13. Retrieved January 31, 2013, from http://www.yale.edu/acmelab/articles/Harris_Bargh_Brownell_Health_Psych.pdf/; Hastings, G., McDermott, L., Angus, K., Stead, M., & Thomson, S. (2006). The extent, nature and effects of food promotion to children: A review of the evidence. Geneva: World Health Organization. Retrieved January 31, 2013, from http://www.who.int/dietphysicalactivity/publications/Hastings_paper_marketing.pdf/; Institute of Medicine. (2006). *Food Marketing to Children and Youth: Threat or Opportunity?* Washington, DC: The National Academies Press. Retrieved January 31, 2013, from http://www.nap.edu/books/0309097134/html/.

20. Moss, M. (2013). *Salt Fat Sugar: How the Food Giants Hooked Us.* New York: Random House.

21. The Federal Trade Commission subpoenaed forty-four companies marketing food and beverages to children in the United States for its 2008 report, and forty-eight such companies for its 2012 report. Federal Trade Commission (2008, July). Marketing food to children and adolescents: A review of industry

expenditures, activities, and self-regulation. Washington, DC: Author. Retrieved August 26, 2008, from http://www.ftc.gov/os/2008/07/ P064504foodmktingreport.pdf; Federal Trade Commission (2012, December). A review of food marketing to children and adolescents: Follow-up report (p. ES-1). Washington, DC: Author. Retrieved December 1, 2014, from http://www.ftc. gov/opa/2012/12/foodmarketing.shtm/.

22. Federal Trade Commission (2012, December). A review of food marketing to children and adolescents: Follow-up report (p. ES-1). Washington, DC: Author. Retrieved December 10, 2014, from http://www.ftc.gov/opa/2012/12/ foodmarketing.shtm/; PQ Media (2010, June) *PQ Media Global Branded Entertainment Marketing Forecast 2010–2014*. Stamford, CT: Author, 12.

23. Federal Trade Commission (2012, December). A review of food marketing to children and adolescents: Follow-up report (p. 23). Washington, DC: Author. Retrieved December 10, 2014, from http://www.ftc.gov/opa/2012/12/ foodmarketing.shtm/.

24. Federal Trade Commission (2012, December). A review of food marketing to children and adolescents: Follow-up report (p. 23). Washington, DC: Author. Retrieved December 10, 2014, from http://www.ftc.gov/opa/2012/12/ foodmarketing.shtm/.

25. Federal Trade Commission (2012, December). A review of food marketing to children and adolescents: Follow-up report (pp. 3–4). Washington, DC: Author. Retrieved December 10, 2014, from http://www.ftc.gov/opa/2012/12/ foodmarketing.shtm/.

26. Federal Trade Commission (2012, December). A review of food marketing to children and adolescents: Follow-up report (pp. 96–99). Washington, DC: Author. Retrieved December 10, 2014, from http://www.ftc.gov/opa/2012/12/ foodmarketing.shtm/.

27. Journey Staff (2012, January 1). Enjoy an active, healthy lifestyle through physical activity and nutrition. *Coca-Cola Journey*. Retrieved March 7, 2013, from http://www.coca-colacompany.com/stories/physical-activity/; Coca-Cola Company (2012, November). Our position on obesity, including well-being facts. Atlanta, GA: Author. Retrieved March 7, 2013, from http://assets.coca-colacompany.com/c2/a7/2f6eab904c7cbf3fcbc0646bd988/ Our%20Position%20on%20Obesity.pdf/.

28. Federal Trade Commission (2012, December). A review of food marketing to children and adolescents: Follow-up report (p. ES-1). Washington, DC: Author. Retrieved December 11, 2014, from http://www.ftc.gov/opa/2012/12/ foodmarketing.shtm/.

29. The FTC did not report which companies reported these activities. Federal Trade Commission (2012, December). A review of food marketing to children

and adolescents: Follow-up report (p. ES-1). Washington, DC: Author. Retrieved December 1, 2014, from http://www.ftc.gov/opa/2012/12/foodmarketing.shtm/.

30. Federal Trade Commission (2012, December). A review of food marketing to children and adolescents: Follow-up report (p. 99). Washington, DC: Author. Retrieved December 1, 2014, from http://www.ftc.gov/opa/2012/12/foodmarketing.shtm/.

31. Moss, M. (2013). *Salt Fat Sugar: How the Food Giants Hooked Us*. New York: Random House.

32. Federal Trade Commission (2012, December). A review of food marketing to children and adolescents: Follow-up report (p. 56). Washington, DC: Author. Retrieved December 1, 2014, from http://www.ftc.gov/opa/2012/12/foodmarketing.shtm/.

33. Only Con-Agra Foods, Inc., Kraft Foods Group, Inc., and Post Foods, LLC, were not among the one hundred top-spending marketers in 2014. *Advertising Age* (2014, December 8). 100 Largest Global Marketers. Author. Retrieved December 10, 2014, from http://adage.com/datacenter/globalmarketers2014#708 [subscription required].

34. Council of Better Business Bureaus (2014, January 17). CFBAI celebrates new year with new uniform nutrition criteria for child-directed advertising. Author. Retrieved December 1, 2014, from http://www.bbb.org/council/news-events/news-releases/2014/01/cfbai-celebrates-new-year-with-new-uniform-nutrition-criteria-for-child-directed-advertising/.

35. Wootan, M. (2014, December 5). Personal communication (e-mail) with Faith Boninger.

36. Wootan, M. (2014, December 5). Personal communication (e-mail) with Faith Boninger.

37. Federal Trade Commission (2012, December). A review of food marketing to children and adolescents: Follow-up report (p. ES-14). Washington, DC: Author. Retrieved December 1, 2014, from http://www.ftc.gov/opa/2012/12/foodmarketing.shtm/.

38. Children's Food and Beverage Advertising Initiative (2012, December). The Food and Beverage Advertising Initiative: A report on compliance and progress during 2011 (p. 13). Better Business Bureau. Retrieved January 31, 2013, from http://www.bbb.org/us/storage/16/documents/cfbai/CFBAI%20Report%20on%20Compliance%20and%20Progress%20During%202011.pdf/.

39. Children's Food and Beverage Advertising Initiative (2012, December). The Food and Beverage Advertising Initiative: A report on compliance and progress during 2011 (p. 15). Better Business Bureau. Retrieved January 31, 2013, from http://www.bbb.org/us/storage/16/documents/cfbai/

CFBAI%20Report%20on%20Compliance%20and%20Progress%20During%20
2011.pdf/.

40. Federal Trade Commission (2012, December). A review of food marketing to children and adolescents: Follow-up report (p. ES-13). Washington, DC:
Author. Retrieved December 1, 2014, from http://www.ftc.gov/opa/2012/12/
foodmarketing.shtm/.

41. American Beverage Association (2010, March 8). Alliance school beverage guidelines: Final report. Retrieved January 9, 2013, from http://www.
ameribev.org/nutrition--science/school-beverage-guidelines/; Wescott, R. F.,
Fitzpatrick, B. M., & Phillips, E. (2012, October). Industry self-regulation to
improve student health: Quantifying changes in beverage shipments to schools.
American Journal of Public Health, 102(10), 1928–35.

42. Moss, M. (2013). *Salt Fat Sugar: How the Food Giants Hooked Us*. New
York: Random House; Kanner, A. (2008, November). Now, class, a word from
our sponsors . . . *Builder/Designer*. Retrieved December 10, 2014, from http://
commercialfreechildhood.org/sites/default/files/kanner_nowclassaword.pdf.

43. Food Marketing Workgroup (2012). Policy. Author. Retrieved December
10, 2014, from http://www.foodmarketing.org/policy/.

44. Food Marketing Workgroup (2012). Policy recommendations to strength-
en self-regulation. Author. Retrieved December 1, 2014, from http://www.
foodmarketing.org/policy/policy-recommendations-to-strengthen-self-
regulation/; Lammi, G. (2012, March 8). "It's time to move on," FTC chairman
says about "voluntary" food ad guidelines. *Legal Pulse*, Washington Legal Foundation. Retrieved February 11, 2013, from http://wlflegalpulse.com/2012/03/08/
its-time-to-move-on-ftc-chairman-says-about-voluntary-food-ad-guidelines/;
Washington Legal Foundation (2011, September 25). Five questions for . . .
CFBAI's Elaine Kolish on self-regulation of advertising. *Legal Pulse*. Retrieved
February 12, 2013, from http://wlflegalpulse.com/2011/09/15/five-questions-for-
cfbais-elaine-kolish-on-self-regulation-of-advertising/.

45. The Interagency Working Group consisted of the Agriculture Department,
Centers for Disease Control and Prevention, Federal Trade Commission, and
Food and Drug Administration; Bachman, K. (2012, August 4). Industry group:
Feds would muzzle advertising of popular foods. *AdWeek*. Retrieved January 29,
2013, from http://www.adweek.com/news/advertising-branding/industry-group-
feds-would-muzzle-advertising-popular-foods-133878/; Schultz, E. J. (2012,
May 7). FTC attempt to limit food marketing to kids loses steam. *Advertising
Age*. Retrieved January 29, 2013, from http://adage.com/article/news/ftc-
attempt-limit-food-marketing-kids-loses-steam/234583/ [subscription required];
Watzman, N. (2012, May 1). Congressional letter writing campaign helps torpe-
do voluntary food marketing guidelines for kids. *Sunlight Foundation Reporting
Group*. Washington, DC: The Sunlight Foundation. Retrieved January 29, 2013,

from http://reporting.sunlightfoundation.com/2012/congressional_letter_writing_campaign/; Wilson, D., & Roberts, J. (2012, April 27). Special Report: How Washington went soft on childhood obesity. *Reuters*. Retrieved January 29, 2013, from http://www.reuters.com/article/2012/04/27/us-usa-foodlobby-idUSBRE83Q0ED20120427/.

46. Hellmich, N. (2012, January 25). Government requires more fruits, veggies for school lunches. *USA Today*. Retrieved April 6, 2013, from http://yourlife.usatoday.com/fitness-food/diet-nutrition/story/2012-01-25/Government-requires-more-fruits-veggies-for-school-lunches/52779404/1/.

47. Shah, N. (2013, June 27). Rules for school vending machines, snacks unveiled. *Education Week*. Retrieved June 27, 2013, from http://blogs.edweek.org/edweek/rulesforengagement/2013/06/rules_for_school_vending_machines_snacks_unveiled.html?cmp=ENL-EU-NEWS2.

48. U.S. Department of Agriculture, Food and Nutrition Service (2014, February 25). 7 CFR Parts 210 and 220, RIN 0584-AE25. Retrieved February 26, 2014, from https://s3.amazonaws.com/public-inspection.federalregister.gov/2014-04100.pdf; Harrington, E. (2014, February 25). Michelle Obama pushing ban on junk food advertising in schools. *Washington Free Beacon*. Retrieved February 26, 2014, from http://freebeacon.com/michelle-obama-pushing-ban-on-junk-food-advertising-in-schools/.

49. U.S. Department of Agriculture, Food and Nutrition Service (2014, February 25). 7 CFR Parts 210 and 220, RIN 0584-AE25 (pp. 24–25). Retrieved February 26, 2014, from https://s3.amazonaws.com/public-inspection.federalregister.gov/2014-04100.pdf.

50. Hunter, B. (2014, November 26). Personal communication (e-mail) with Faith Boninger.

51. United States Government Accountability Office. (2004). Report to congressional requesters: Competitive foods are available in many schools; actions taken to restrict them differ by state and locality (GAO-04-673). Washington, DC: Author. Retrieved January 7, 2013, from http://www.gao.gov/new.items/d05563.pdf/.

52. Moss, M. (2014, June 10). The Domino's Smart Slice goes to school. *New York Times*. Retrieved November 5, 2014, from http://www.nytimes.com/2014/06/11/dining/the-dominos-smart-slice-goes-to-school.html?_r=0.

53. Moss, M. (2013). *Salt Fat Sugar: How the Food Giants Hooked Us*. New York: Random House.

54. Moss, M. (2014, June 10). The Domino's Smart Slice goes to school. *New York Times*. Retrieved November 5, 2014, from http://www.nytimes.com/2014/06/11/dining/the-dominos-smart-slice-goes-to-school.html?_r=0.

55. Wilking, C. (2014, May). Copycat snacks in schools. *Public Health Advocacy Institute*. Retrieved November 5, 2014, from http://www.phaionline.org/wp-content/uploads/2014/05/PHAI-Copy-Cat-Snacks-Issue-Brief-FINAL.pdf.

56. Wilking, C. (2014, May). Copycat snacks in schools. *Public Health Advocacy Institute*. Retrieved November 5, 2014, from http://www.phaionline.org/wp-content/uploads/2014/05/PHAI-Copy-Cat-Snacks-Issue-Brief-FINAL.pdf.

57. Children's Food and Beverage Advertising Initiative (2012, December). The Food and Beverage Advertising Initiative: A report on compliance and progress during 2011 (p. 15). Better Business Bureau. Retrieved January 31, 2013, from http://www.bbb.org/us/storage/16/documents/cfbai/CFBAI%20Report%20on%20Compliance%20and%20Progress%20During%202011.pdf/. United States Government Accountability Office (2004). Report to congressional requesters: competitive foods are available in many schools; Actions taken to restrict them differ by state and locality (GAO-04-673). Washington, DC: Author. Retrieved January 7, 2013, from http://www.gao.gov/new.items/d05563.pdf/.

58. Batada, A., & Wootan, M. G. (2008). Food and beverage marketing survey: Montgomery County Public Schools. *Center for Science in the Public Interest*. Retrieved April 30, 2012, from http://cspinet.org/nutritionpolicy/MCPS_foodmarketing_report2008.pdf/.

59. Craypo, L., Francisco, S. S., Boyle, M., & Samuels, S. (2006). Food and beverage marketing on California high school campuses survey: Findings and recommendations. California Project Lean. Retrieved January 9, 2013, from http://www.californiaprojectlean.org/docuserfiles//SchoolMarketingReport2006.pdf/.

60. Molnar, A., Garcia, D. R., Boninger, F., & Merrill, B. (2006, January 1). A national survey of the types and extent of the marketing of foods of minimal nutritional value in schools. Commercialism in Education Research Unit, Arizona State University. Retrieved December 1, 2014, from http://nepc.colorado.edu/publication/national-survey-types-and-extent-marketing-foods-minimal-nutritional-value-schools.

61. Polacsek, M., O'Roarke, K., O'Brien, L., Blum, J. W., & Donahue, S. (2012, March–April). Examining compliance with a statewide law banning junk food and beverage marketing in Maine schools. *Public Health Reports*, 127, 216–23. Retrieved January 28, 2013, from http://www.une.edu/news/2012/upload/PHRarticle-Marketing-Polacsek.pdf/. All schools had marketing of foods low in nutrition, but some of that marketing was actually compliant with the law because the law itself was so weak (banning only marketing of Foods of Minimal Nutritional Value). Polacsek, M. (2013, February 13). Personal communication (e-mail) with Faith Boninger.

62. American Beverage Association (2010, March 8). Alliance school beverage guidelines: Final report. Retrieved January 9, 2013, from http://www.ameribev.org/nutrition-science/school-beverage-guidelines/; Wescott, R. F., Fitzpatrick, B. M., & Phillips, E. (2012, October). Industry self-regulation to improve student health: Quantifying changes in beverage shipments to schools. *American Journal of Public Health, 102*(10), 1928–35.

63. A 2011 national study of 152 schools found that 83 percent of schools had vending machines, with soft drinks the most common item found in them. Rovner, A. J., Nansel, T. R., Wang, J., & Ianotti, R. J. (2011). Food sold in school vending machines is associated with overall student dietary intake. *Journal of Adolescent Health, 48*(1), 13–19.

64. Kanner, A. (2008, November). Now, class, a word from our sponsors . . . *Builder/Designer*. Retrieved December 10, 2014, from http://commercialfreechildhood.org/sites/default/files/kanner_nowclassaword.pdf.

65. Deschenes, K. (2013, January 16). Personal communication (telephone) with Faith Boninger.

66. Kuhn, B. (2013, January 15). Personal communication (telephone) with Faith Boninger.

67. Kuhn, B. (2013, January 15). Personal communication (telephone) with Faith Boninger.

68. Los Angeles Unified School District (2011, May 24). *Sponsorship Guidelines*. Los Angeles, CA: Author. Retrieved January 15, 2013, from http://notebook.lausd.net/portal/page?_pageid=33,501466&_dad=ptl&_schema=PTL_EP./.

69. Education Funding Partners (2012, September). Cause marketing: The case for corporate marketing investments in public education to grow minds and mindshare. Golden, CO: Author. Retrieved January 23, 2011, from http://edufundingpartners.com/cause-marketing-and-education-white-paper/.

70. In the 1920s, the National Education Association established its Committee on Propaganda in the Schools to determine the nature of propaganda that was being received by American schools and the policies or other mechanisms in place to deal with it. The committee's report raised the following concerns: (1) The decentralized nature of curriculum development and approval processes in the United States means that each school and school district is forced to depend on its own, often limited, resources for evaluating the accuracy, fairness, and educational value of each sponsored material or program offered to them. (2) The principle of democratic control of curriculum content (generally through an elected school board) is jeopardized by the abundance of unsolicited and unevaluated materials following into the schools from well-funded outside interests. (3) Sponsored materials and programs pose a distraction from the already crowded course of study required to meet state or local standards; Broome, E. (1929,

July). Report of the Committee on Propaganda in the Schools. Presented at the meeting of the National Education Association, Atlanta, GA. According to Sheila Harty, by 1953, the terminology in use had changed to "free materials." Harty, S. (1979). Hucksters in the classroom: A review of industry propaganda in schools. Washington, DC: Center for Study of Responsive Law.

71. Healthy Weight Commitment Foundation (n.d.). Fighting obesity by balancing calories in with calories out. Author. Retrieved December 15, 2014, from http://www.healthyweightcommit.org/about/overview/.

72. Healthy Weight Commitment Foundation (n.d.). Fighting obesity by balancing calories in with calories out. Author. Retrieved December 15, 2014, from http://www.healthyweightcommit.org/about/overview/.

73. For information about the Healthy Weight Commitment Foundation, Together Counts, and Energy Balance 101, see Healthy Weight Commitment Foundation (n.d.). Fighting obesity by balancing calories in with calories out. Author. Retrieved December 15, 2014, from http://www.healthyweightcommit.org/about/overview/; Healthy Weight Commitment Foundation (2014). Together Counts. Retrieved July 1, 2014, from http://www.togethercounts.com/; see sponsored educational materials at Together Counts (n.d.). What Is Energy Balance? Author. Retrieved December 10, 2014, from http://www.togethercounts.com/sites/togethercounts.com/files/module/documents/3-5_0.0.pdf. For the Consensus Statement of the American Society for Nutrition, see Hall, K. D., Heymsfield, S. B., Kemnitz, J. W., Klein, S., Schoeller, D. A., & Speakman, J. R. (2012). Energy balance and its components: Implications for body weight regulation. *American Journal of Clinical Nutrition, 95*, 989–94. And for a readable commentary, see Freedhoff, Y. (2013, December 12). Who cares if 3,500 calories don't make a real life pound? *Weighty Matters*. Retrieved December 15, 2014, from http://www.weightymatters.ca/2013/12/who-cares-if-3500-calories-dont-make.html.

74. SchoolTube, Inc. (2012). SchoolTube channels for sponsors and partners. SchoolTube.com. Retrieved September 7, 2014, from http://www.schooltube.com/info/channels/.

75. SchoolTube, Inc. (2012). SchoolTube channels for sponsors and partners. SchoolTube.com. Retrieved September 7, 2014, from http://www.schooltube.com/info/channels/.

76. American Meat Institute (2012, October 25). Meat Mythcrushers: Americans eat too much meat and its saturated fat content leads to heart disease. SchoolTube.com. Retrieved September 7, 2014, from http://www.schooltube.com/video/97569329ac0641cc914e/Meat%20Mythcrushers:%20Americans%20Eat%20Too%20Much%20Meat%20And%20Its%20Saturated%20Fat%20Content%20Leads%20To%20Heart%20Disease; American Meat Institute (2012, October 25). Meat Mythcrushers: Grass-

fed beef is safer than beef from cattle finished on corn and grains. School-Tube.com. Retrieved September 7, 2014, from http://www.schooltube.com/video/64eb97e6ba4941d98dd7/Meat%20Mythcrushers:%20Grass-Fed%20Beef%20Is%20Safer%20Than%20Beef%20From%20Cattle%20Finishe d%20On%20Corn%20And%20Grains; American Meat Institute (2012, December 13). Video tour of a beef plant featuring Temple Grandin. SchoolTube.com. Retrieved September 7, 2014, from http://www.schooltube.com/video/c176bf54e35d4b639d53/Video%20Tour%20of%20a%20Beef%20Plant%20Featuring%20Temple%20Grandin.

77. Neff, J. (2012, June 18). The truth about what works in digital marketing. *Advertising Age.* Retrieved January 25, 2013, from http://adage.com/article/news/truth-works-digital-marketing/235427/ [subscription required]; Bernoff, J. (2009, July 20). Advertising will change forever: Digital spending will nearly double in 5 years, but ad budgets won't. *Advertising Age.* Retrieved July 20, 2009, from http://adage.com/digitalnext/article?article_id=138023/ [subscription required].

78. Montgomery, K. C., & Chester, J. (2009). Interactive food and beverage marketing: Targeting adolescents in the digital age. *Journal of Adolescent Health, 45,* S18–S29; Moore, E. S. (2006, July). It's child's play: Advergaming and the online marketing of food to children. Menlo Park, CA: The Henry J. Kaiser Family Foundation. Retrieved August 20, 2009, from http://www.kff.org/entmedia/upload/7536.pdf/.

79. Davis, M. R. (2011, October 17). States, districts move to require virtual classes. Retrieved October 20, 2011, from http://www.edweek.org/dd/articles/2011/10/19/01required.h05.html?intc=DD10.11EM/.

80. Molnar, A., Boninger, F., Wilkinson, G., & Fogarty, J. (2009). *Click: The Twelfth Annual Report on Schoolhouse Commercialism Trends: 2008–2009.* Boulder and Tempe: Education and the Public Interest Center & Commercialism in Education Research Unit. Retrieved January 25, 2013, from http://nepc.colorado.edu/publication/schoolhouse-commercialism-2009.

81. Just as a comparison to Coca-Cola's 10.6 billion total social media brand impressions, second-place Apple generated only 719 million impressions. *Business Wire* (2012, September 5). Top ten consumer brands dominate 10.6 billion social media impressions in first syndicated audience measurement report released by PQ Media and uberVU. Retrieved November 20, 2012, from http://www.marketwatch.com/story/top-ten-consumer-brands-dominate-106-billion-social-media-impressions-in-first-syndicated-audience-measurement-report-released-by-pq-media-and-ubervu-2012-09-05/.

82. Quinton, B. (2008, February 1). Coke's Kruse Control. *Chief!Marketer*. Retrieved January 25, 2013, from http://chiefmarketer.com/interactivemarketing/cokes_kruse_control_coca_cola_interactive_0201/.

83. The Coca-Cola Company (2014). Put your school in play. Retrieved September 7, 2014, from http://www.mycokerewards.com/mcrSchools.do?tab=1&WT.ac=mnuS_PD/.

84. Center for Digital Democracy and Berkeley Media Studies Group (n.d.). Case studies: My Coke. *Interactive Food & Beverage Marketing: Targeting Children and Youth in the Digital Age*. Retrieved January 25, 2013, from http://digitalads.org/documents/digiMarketingFull.pdf/.

85. Fair Isaac Corporation (n.d.). The Case for Customer Centricity. *CXO*. Retrieved January 25, 2013, from http://www.cxo.eu.com/article/The-Case-for-Customer-Centricity/; Fair Isaac Corporation (2009). Boosting sales and site traffic, Coca-Cola breaks ground in customer loyalty. *FICO*. Retrieved January 25, 2013, from http://www.fico.com/en/Products/DMApps/Pages/FICO-Customer-Dialogue-Manager.aspx/.

86. Center for Digital Democracy and Berkeley Media Studies Group (n.d.). Case studies. *Interactive Food & Beverage Marketing: Targeting Children and Youth in the Digital Age*. Retrieved January 25, 2013, from http://case-studies.digitalads.org/; Federal Trade Commission (2012, December). A review of food marketing to children and adolescents: Follow-up report (p. 87). Washington, DC: Author. Retrieved December 1, 2014, from http://www.ftc.gov/opa/2012/12/foodmarketing.shtm/; PQ Media (2010, June). PQ Media Global Branded Entertainment Marketing Forecast 2010–2014. Stamford, CT: Author.

87. Chester, J., & Montgomery, K. (2007, May). *Interactive Food & Beverage Marketing: Targeting Children and Youth in the Digital Age*. Berkeley, CA: Public Health Institute. Retrieved January 25, 2013, from http://digitalads.org/documents/digiMarketingFull.pdf/; Clark, W. (2013, March). Coca-Cola's Wendy Clark defends 'crucial' social media. *Advertising Age*. Retrieved April 5, 2013, from http://adage.com/article/cmo-strategy/social-media-matter-marketing-coca-cola/240444/ [subscription required].

88. Moss, M. (2013). *Salt Fat Sugar: How the Food Giants Hooked Us*. New York: Random House, 117.

5

THREATS TO THE INTEGRITY OF CHILDREN'S EDUCATION

Now that School^{TM} is run by the corporations, it's pretty brag, because it teaches us how the world can be used, like mainly how to use our feeds. Also, it's good because that way we know that the big corps are made up of real human beings, and not just jerks out for money, because taking care of children, they care about America's future. It's an investment in tomorrow. When no one was going to pay for the public schools anymore and they were all like filled with guns and drugs and English teachers who were really pimps and stuff, some of the big media congloms got together and gave all this money and bought the schools so that all of them could have computers and pizza for lunch and stuff, which they gave for free, and now we do stuff in classes about how to work technology and how to find bargains and what's the best way to get a job and how to decorate our bedroom.
—from *Feed*, a novel by M. T. Anderson [1]

The 85,000 students enrolled in MPS are a big market, and I believe that corporations that cater to the youth market, such as Sony, Adidas, and Apple, would be willing to pay for naming rights to schools, especially if that included the rights to assign team colors, names and logos. For example, if McDonald's outbid Wendy's, Arby's, and Domino's for the naming rights to a high school, the school's teams might be known as the Golden Archers, with uniforms designed accordingly. Imagine a big game between Nike High and Reebok High—now, that would be a rivalry!

—from "New Money for MPS," a blog post by Gerald S. Glazer, candidate for school director for the Second District, Milwaukee, Wisconsin, March 8, 2011)[2]

Although Titus, the teenage protagonist in the young adult novel *Feed*, is blissfully unaware of how corporations' involvement in his schooling affects his attitudes, values, and education, readers can discern those influences even in the short paragraph presented above. *Feed* is fiction, but it's not too far from reality.[3]

Many believe that there is no problem with corporations "helping" schools carry out their mission. In his State of the Union address in 2013, President Obama emphasized the importance of education for putting students "on a path to a good job" and lauded IBM for providing funds, sponsoring school programs and educational materials, and helping design curricula at P-TECH, a science, technology, engineering, and math (STEM)–oriented school in Brooklyn, New York.[4] Corporate domination of public space—including schools—now seems obvious and natural to those who grew up in recent years. The corporate capture of public space is neither natural nor necessary, however.[5] And while post-school employment is surely important, giving corporate marketers access to schoolchildren is not the obvious best way of assuring students' job prospects. Schools are one of the only places still available where children can to some extent exist outside of our pervasive consumer culture, and schools can be places where children explore possibilities for their lives, their values, and their selves other than those corporations define for them.

We have identified three types of threats to the integrity of children's education associated with marketing in schools:

1. Corporate materials and/or activities may contradict or undermine the school curriculum. Some of the lessons learned from corporate advertising explicitly contradict or subtly undermine lessons that children learn in classes. The most obvious and prevalent example of a subtle challenge to what students learn in classes is that vending machines in schools encourage children to buy and eat food products that their nutrition and science teachers try hard to teach them to avoid.

2. In an already crowded school day, commercializing activities necessarily displace other educational activities. When ASA Entertainment's action sports tour shows up at the local high school, for
example, classes are suspended so that students can attend a mandatory assembly. When Microsoft sponsored the tour in 2008 and
2009, students played new Xbox games, strolled past banner advertisements for other sponsors, and listened to athletes' antismoking
speeches that were the pretext for the program;[6]

3. Corporate materials can undermine the development of scientific,
creative, and critical thinking. Along with providing basic skills
instruction and content knowledge, we look to schools to teach our
children how to think—scientifically, creatively, and critically.
This is no easy task. Researchers and theorists have spent quite a
bit of energy explicating various skills that contribute to effective
thinking and developing approaches to nurturing it in children.
Critical thinking, in particular, requires skills and habits of mind
inhospitable to the success of commercial enterprises in schools.
Critical thinking skills incline students to question and possibly
reject consumerist messages as they identify and evaluate sponsors' points of view and biases, consider alternative points of view,
and generate and consider alternative solutions.

Our analysis leads us to the conclusion that when there is commercial
activity in schools, critical thinking, and the habits of mind associated
with it, are less likely to be encouraged. Paradoxically, to understand how
marketing may undermine critical thinking in schools we have to consider, as Sherlock Holmes did in the story "Silver Blaze," the "dog that
didn't bark." That is, the threat to critical thinking posed by marketing
will become visible when we move beyond what *does happen* in schools
to what *is not happening* in schools at least in part as a result of corporate
involvement.

Educators' ability to foster critical thinking is restricted not just as a
result of corporate involvement. In the United States, school reform emphasizes a testing regime that rewards teachers and administrators when
students memorize facts and master such skills as are necessary to perform well on standardized tests.[7] In this kind of educational environment,
teachers have little incentive, support, or time to employ approaches that
encourage higher-level thinking among their students.[8]

These negative features of the current educational zeitgeist are amplified by corporate involvement in schools: the same types of low-level thinking that are encouraged by the testing regime also often benefit and are encouraged by corporate materials and activities in schools. Even such corporate materials that may at first blush appear refreshingly "creative" or "critical" rarely, if ever, contain any content that may threaten the sponsoring corporation's bottom line.

CRITICAL THINKING

What Is Critical Thinking?

In order to understand how marketing undermines critical thinking in schools, it is first necessary to consider what critical thinking is and how pedagogy and the school environment can encourage its development. [9]

The term "critical thinking" is used most narrowly to refer to "analytical thinking," generally considered to be thinking that dissects, critiques, evaluates, and judges. [10] Used more broadly, however, it includes any of the characteristics of so-called "higher-order thinking." Higher-order thinking "comprises the mental processes, strategies, and representations people use to solve problems, make decisions, and learn new concepts," [11] as contrasted with lower-order thinking, which is thinking associated with remembering, comprehending, and applying knowledge.

Psychologist Robert Sternberg's review of varied philosophical, psychological, and educational approaches led him to posit that the differences between approaches rest primarily with how broadly or narrowly they view the construct of critical thinking, not what they see as its core. [12] Thus, while the names given to the various skills associated with higher-order or critical thinking vary according to the academic tradition of the theorist, the skills themselves are more or less the same. [13]

Others have also found the elements involved in critical thinking are consistent in several aspects. [14] For example, in 1985, E. Jean Gubbins reviewed taxonomies of critical thinking and developed a comprehensive matrix of the skills involved. This matrix defines six sub-areas of critical thinking (and the specific skills involved in each). The six sub-areas of critical thinking identified by Gubbins are problem solving, decision making, inductive and deductive inference making, divergent thinking, evaluative thinking, and philosophy and reasoning (see appendix A for the full matrix).[15]

A colloquial way of summing this up is that critical thinkers can take different points of view; they can identify, understand, and evaluate the assumptions, point of view, and logic behind a given position or proposed solution to a problem; and they can generate and evaluate alternative solutions.

Critical thinking overlaps with "creative thinking." Elizabeth Fairweather and Bonnie Cramond define creative thinking as "thought that results in an idea that is novel and useful."[16] They point out that creative and critical thinking processes are "recursive, parallel, coincidental, and idiosyncratic to the situation and the person."[17] Effective problem solving is seen as often requiring both critical and creative thinking as an individual generates, evaluates, and refines ideas. The practice of critical thinking necessarily tends to encourage an appreciation of the complexity of the issues under consideration, tolerance for ambiguity, and appreciation of the variety of perspectives from which one can approach an issue.[18]

How Students Can Be Encouraged to Think Critically

There are educational programs that have successfully nurtured both critical thinking ability and the disposition, or habit of mind, to use it.[19] Teachers can, and many have, helped their students develop the skills required for critical thinking while introducing subject-specific content.[20]

In a 1997 *American Psychologist* article on intelligence, David Perkins and Tina Grotzer suggest that if intelligence is defined as intelligent behavior over time, it will be influenced to some extent by biology (that is, innate ability), but also by experience and "informed reflective management of thinking."[21] Teachers can provide students with experiences that encourage them to become informed reflective managers of their thinking.

After reviewing a variety of techniques designed to teach higher-level thinking skills, Perkins and Grotzer conclude that successful techniques make students' thought processes explicit, leading students to "reorganize" their thinking. Students learn thinking strategies and concepts, as well as how to pay attention to their own thinking and how to avoid logical errors or faulty use of heuristics.[22] In other words, students learn not only how to structure problems but also how to monitor and correct their own thinking processes as they engage with them.

The Importance of Asking Questions

In the "real world," problems may be complex and not amenable to black-and-white reasoning. Moreover, the available information may be irrelevant or misleading, or the information sources may be biased.[23] Asking questions enables students to unearth the underlying complexities and to define problems so that they are amenable to further logical inquiry. Students can also learn to formulate hypotheses and ways of testing them as they problem-solve.

Inquiry skills are seen as important in science classes, but they are also relevant to history, politics, literature, social relations, and so on.[24] Students can learn to ask questions such as "What additional information would you want before answering that question?" (asks them to determine whether relevant information might be missing); "Are all assertions in the question credible or valid?" (reminds them to check for misleading claims); and "What are two potential solutions to the problem?" (encourages them to think creatively about the possibility of multiple solutions).[25]

In part, such activities can teach students that thoughtful questioning and informed debate in the classroom are appropriate and that confusion is part of the learning process rather than a problem to be avoided or papered over.[26] Also, the process underscores the importance of examining the underlying assumptions and logic behind claims, evaluating those assumptions and the logic, and generating and considering alternative claims.

The Importance of Thinking about Thinking

The effectiveness of strategies that teach "metacognition" (i.e., how to think about your thinking) as a way of promoting critical thinking is well supported by research.[27] Metacognitive strategies help students understand, review, and revise their thought processes. A 2010 study that examined the thought processes of low- and high-performing critical thinkers (matched on cognitive ability, thinking disposition, and academic achievement) found that skilled critical thinkers displayed better use of metacognitive strategies, especially planning for specific steps in thinking and revising their approach after identifying problems.[28]

In a series of studies, Anat Zohar and her colleagues demonstrated the effectiveness of explicitly teaching students "metastrategic knowledge" to foster critical thinking. They define metastrategic knowledge as general knowledge about higher-order thinking strategies such as planning, classifying, establishing and analyzing causal relationships, constructing good arguments, formulating and testing hypotheses, and drawing valid conclusions.[29] In both laboratory and classroom-based research, they found that explicitly teaching children about higher-order thinking strategies improved the children's use of the strategies and their success in relevant academic tasks. This was the case for both high- and low-achieving students and over time.[30]

Zohar and her colleagues echo Perkins and Grotzer in pointing out that whereas students may use components of the various thinking strategies implicitly or explicitly, the advantage of teaching them in class is that there they can be articulated, discussed, and negotiated.[31]

The Challenge of Transfer of Learning

One of the hardest aspects of teaching thinking (or teaching anything for that matter) is getting the learning to "transfer." That a student learns to think in a certain way about her latest science experiment, for example, does not mean that she will automatically apply that learning to relevant real-world problems with different surface characteristics. This is true not only because there are aspects of thinking about a science project that may not carry over to other domains, but also because students do not necessarily access thinking strategies they associate with science in seemingly unrelated situations.[32] To do so many students need ongoing help, modeling, and practice to develop the habits of mind necessary to transfer thinking skills learned in one domain to another.[33]

The Importance of Classroom and School Environments

In addition to explicitly teaching students to think critically and to transfer skills from one domain to another, schools can create a culture of learning and thinking that encourages critical thinking as an integral part of everyday life in and out of school.[34] Researchers and program developers increasingly recognize that programs to teach thinking cannot just be "implemented," but rather must be "enacted, developed, and sustained within a social context."[35] This means that effective teaching of critical thinking is not limited to specific classroom lessons, but also takes place

spontaneously in the classroom and school as teachers create environments that support critical thinking and also capitalize on situations that
arise outside of planned lessons.

The school experience for students includes far more than just the
curriculum. All kinds of "real-world" situations show up for students in
school—such as when they have to negotiate and make decisions about
joint projects, extracurricular activities, and social events, or navigate
complicated social interactions. Teachers are not aware of every such
situation that arises, of course, but when they are aware, they can encourage their students to apply their thinking skills. They can help students
learn to deconstruct their school environment, to ask questions about the
nature of their curriculum and other features of the school.

By encouraging students to ask questions, teachers help students learn
how the thinking skills they learned in class can be of broad use to them
in their lives in and out of school. In addition, to the extent that teachers
model critical thinking themselves, they show students the varieties of
opportunities the students have to transfer what they have learned.[36]

Michael Weinstock and his colleagues, in a study that examined how
students who attended either democratic or regular schools responded to
moral dilemmas, found that teachers, working within a supportive school
structure, could actively encourage critical thinking that transfers to out-
of-classroom situations.[37]

In the Israeli "democratic schools" that were the focus of this research,
teachers encourage their students to express their opinions regarding important class and school issues, including the content of the curriculum,
methods of learning, and social relations within the class and the school.
In weekly, democratically run school meetings, attended by all school
staff, parents, and students, teachers justify their own positions on issues,
demand the same from students, and model respect for disagreement by
taking students' viewpoints seriously even if they differ from their own.

Students from the democratic schools made more autonomous moral
judgments than did students from the regular schools.[38] Causal modeling
showed that this difference in the students' moral judgments could be
attributed to teachers' practice, in the democratic schools, of actively
encouraging their students to think critically. Alternative explanations,
such as the students were given more choices in general in the democratic
school or that parents of democratic school students encouraged them
more to think critically, were not supported.[39]

It appears that supportive school and classroom cultures can sustain the gains in critical thinking made by the explicit teaching of relevant skills. They also appear to encourage intelligent behavior over time and in a variety of situations.[40] When school environments support engagement and critical thinking in the random day-to-day opportunities that pop up (such as when students are making decisions about a school dance, for example), they can provide the advantage of "ubiquity" ascribed to informal science education settings by the National Science Foundation (NSF).[41] The NSF points out that "almost any environment can support informal science education," and that learners need to be supported to make conscious and strategic bridges between what they learn in one setting and another.[42]

Especially relevant to understanding how school commercialism shapes thinking is that school culture helps shape what children attend to, care about, and focus their energies upon.[43] So not only does the culture of schools and classrooms influence whether a child's inclination to think critically develops at all, but it also influences the focus of children's thinking, or what children think *about*. School and classroom environments, for better or worse, help create a "common-sense culture" in which critical thinking is—or is not—desirable and normative.

How Commercializing Activities in School Discourage Critical Thinking

Promoting critical thinking is the essence of what John Dewey termed an "educative" experience.[44] Educative experiences increase students' ability to have fruitful, creative, and enjoyable experiences in the future. *Miseducative* experiences, according to Dewey, are those that arrest or distort the growth of future experience.[45] They may be fun at the time, or even increase some automatic skill, but they narrow the range and richness of possible future experience and thus limit growth.

When for-profit corporations are involved in schools, irrespective of what the particular surface aspects of a given relationship may be, the heart of the relationship is mis-educative. This is because for-profit corporations must maintain a focus on the bottom line—they must make a profit. The mission of the school, on the other hand, is to provide educative experiences for students. The tension between the educative mission of schools and the corporate imperative to earn profits means that when corporations enter schools, there is going to be pressure to create student experiences and shape student attitudes and dispositions in ways that support, or at least do not undermine, corporate profits. This pressure is inherent in the relationship.

Gary Gutting made a similar point when he discussed the implications of the corporate profit motive more generally in a 2011 *New York Times* op-ed. He pondered what corporations do in the case of conflict between profit and responsible action, and concluded: "Given their raison d'être, when push comes to shove corporations will honor their commitments to shareholders' profit."[46] Moreover, he pointed out, from a profit perspective, the appearance of social responsibility is worth more than actual social responsibility.

Both of Gutting's conclusions are relevant to corporate activity in schools, which is portrayed as socially responsible action but almost always involves an attempt to influence students to purchase corporate products and services either immediately or in their future, and to promote the corporate worldview.

In their attempts to influence public policy regarding advertising to children in schools (through lobbying) and public perceptions (through advertising), corporations promote first and foremost their profits, even when that goal undermines genuinely educative experiences.[47] And although it is true that all curriculum has limits, and that some of the schools' noncorporate curriculum may very well be mis-educative as well, corporate commercializing activity in schools has a core element that is, without exception, inherently mis-educative.

Commercializing activities in school thus foster a common-sense culture that favors both the specific brands that get their advertising into the school and a noncritical mindset that facilitates the effectiveness of such advertising. At their most emotive, corporate commercializing activities discourage thinking of any kind ("Hungry? Grab a Snickers!"). Even when they are apparently rational, they discourage aspects of critical thinking that might lead to disagreement with or discrediting of the sponsor's message—especially critical thinking skills having to do with identifying and evaluating sponsors' points of view and biases, considering alternative points of view, and generating and evaluating alternative solutions. In other words, they insinuate sponsors' points of view or product advertising into the daily life of the school in a way designed to have students accept them uncritically as commonsensical and normal.

Even if teachers explicitly teach critical thinking in their classes, they would be unlikely (indeed they would be discouraged) to demonstrate its applicability to corporate messages that are endorsed by the school or district.[48] At best, teachers might be expected to be neutral with respect to corporate messages. While it is accurate to say that such neutrality may not explicitly inhibit students from thinking critically, neither would it encourage them to do so; thus by default, students would not experience an important opportunity to learn how the critical thinking taught in class can be applied to important, real-world issues.

In effect, sponsorship allows the sponsor to shape when and where critical thinking is applied. Whether or not students are successfully attracted to a particular product is less important than the implicit lesson that there is no need to think critically about corporate messages.

Nike's adoption of the fourth grade at the school where Rachel Cloues taught provides a good example.[49] Over the course of the yearlong program, Nike employees played games with the children and gave them branded gifts. In an article she wrote about her experience with Nike's sponsorship in her school, Cloues described watching ". . . as our students were indoctrinated into a corporate culture, experiencing the lovely Nike Campus without being asked to consider where Nike products are made, who makes them, and under what conditions."[50]

Ms. Cloues, however, was wondering about those questions that Nike was happy to avoid. Back at school, she tried to teach her students to think more critically about their consumer choices.[51] She designed a math lesson to help them think about where their sneakers were made and an advertising unit to help them see how media influences their decisions.

She was concerned, however, that such lessons were not supposed to be happening as Nike support flowed into the school. In the end, she wrote, "I didn't have the tools or the support to take either of these projects to any great depth. I also was not comfortable using Nike as an example for critical study. I worried that people at our school would view it as 'inappropriate.'"[52] Her colleagues did find it inappropriate, worried that it would threaten the school's relationship with the company. And when Nike learned about her article, they called her principal and threatened to cancel the program.[53]

Later, as a school librarian in a San Francisco middle school, Cloues documented her library's Target-funded remodel in a 2014 article.[54] Because her school district has an anti-branding policy, it negotiated hard with Target to prevent the company from putting their brand logo in the library. Even so, there was plenty of branding at the grand opening activities. Each child received "a bright red book bag with a giant bulls-eye on it—full of free books marked with Target stickers" and free groceries for their families, donated by the local food bank, were distributed in red Target shopping bags.[55]

All the hoopla made a strong impression on the children. She overheard children begging their parents to take them to the just-opened local Target store, and noted that students talked and wrote about Target for the rest of the year: "That red and white bulls-eye was a presence in our school for the entire year, even without being painted on the library walls."[56]

When we interviewed her and asked if she thought commercializing activities in school diminish children's critical thinking skills, she responded,

> I'm convinced that it does. They're so taken with the things (the plastic giveaways), and they're shown the happy aspect of it. They're shown that this is a place they can work for. Some of us are trying hard to teach about the environment, about workers' rights . . . a more full and balanced perspective of what's happening on this earth. I'm afraid the kids are being brainwashed—for lack of a better term. They're not being asked if there's a counterpart to this . . . is there anything they can do better? Or differently?[57]

Examples of Commercializing Activities in Schools That Limit Critical Thinking

Overall, as we noted in chapter 2, commercializing activities in schools reflect a wide variety of marketing strategies. Unlike regular school activities, which are—or are supposed to be—determined on the basis of their pedagogical value, commercial activities are adopted by schools opportunistically, based on whoever shows up with an appealing marketing idea that can be, even remotely, linked to an educational purpose.

As was evident in Rachel Cloues's experience when Nike "adopted" her school, corporate sponsors usually don't actively proscribe critical pedagogy. Instead—and unsurprisingly—corporate activities such as sponsored programs and educational materials present a worldview consistent with the corporate perspective, including the development of a common-sense culture that takes the presence of products and brands in school for granted and accepts that corporate "partners" in education are legitimate and valuable sources of educational materials, programs, activities, and funds.

On the surface, some sponsored efforts seem to encourage creativity and critical thought, but when we look deeper, we see that such thinking is channeled in a corporate-friendly direction. Teachers and students are on their own to initiate oppositional questions, often in school and classroom environments unsupportive of such questioning. The following examples illustrate our point:

Scholastic, Inc., has produced educational materials for two competing interests in the energy market that exemplify how cynically material is designed and disseminated to bias children's learning toward sponsors' agendas.[58] First, the materials for Shell's "Energize Your Future" curriculum addressed the importance of developing many energy sources and linked Shell to such endeavors. For example, a classroom poster features multiple alternative energy sources and casts Shell as a leader in alternative technologies.[59] In contrast, the materials for the American Coal Foundation's "The United States of Energy" fourth-grade curriculum emphasized the use and production of coal in many states.[60]

The materials in Scholastic's fourth-grade coal curriculum, discontinued in July 2012 as a result of a campaign by environmental and anticommercialism groups,[61] appear at first to be fair and neutral. Closer examination finds that the materials never address the potential negative effects associated with any aspect of the mining, washing, transport, or burning of coal. They are vocal about coal's advantages, but restrained about other energy sources' advantages and completely silent about coal's disadvantages.[62] Finally, although they present cost and availability as ways to evaluate potential sources of energy (coal is presented as relatively inexpensive and available), they fail to consider environmental or health concerns.

Although the coal industry's attempt to use the Scholastic materials to shape the environmental views of fourth-graders was stymied by bad publicity, the industry continues its "educational activity" in the coal-producing states of Kentucky, Virginia, and North Carolina via a nonprofit organization called Coal Education Development and Resource (CEDAR), which explicitly works to forward the mission of "securing coal's future today by educating the leaders of tomorrow."[63] CEDAR is a not-for-profit corporation, formed in Pikeville, Kentucky, in July 1993 by the North Carolina Coal Institute and Coal Operators and Associates of Pikeville, Kentucky, for the purpose of improving the image of the coal industry.[64] It uses monetary prizes to encourage teachers to develop units about the coal industry and to engage students in producing projects for regional coal fairs.[65]

CEDAR focuses students' learning on the engineering and technology of coal mining and on the industry's importance to the local culture and economy. Students' coal fair projects can be in any academic or creative area, and some of the winning projects featured on CEDAR's website are truly impressive.[66] However, environmental and health-related concerns related to coal mining are largely ignored because, although not explicitly forbidden to do so, a student or teacher gunning for a prize would be unlikely to introduce any of these taboo topics.[67]

While it is reasonable for students in coal-producing states to learn in school about an industry important to their local economy, it is mis-educative if these students are never asked to consider and think about the full range of implications of that industry on their lives. As citizens who will eventually be needed to make judgments about their livelihoods, their local economy, and their environment—among other things—they would be better served if they were taught, instead, how they could thoughtfully consider the full range of advantages and disadvantages of this particularly relevant local concern.

School trips are another form of sponsored activity. Our colleague Joseph Fogarty reports that in his country, Ireland, school trips to Tayto Park are advertised to teachers as providing an assortment of educational benefits. Tayto Park is owned and operated by Tayto, the leading potato chip maker in Ireland. Students learn about a variety of plants and animals featured at the park and can lunch in replica Native American "tipis [*sic*]."[68] They also tour the Tayto potato chip factory, where they learn that 10 percent of the local Irish potato crop is made into potato chips, and they walk away with six free "limited edition" bags of the product.[69] Not surprisingly, the "learning section" of the Tayto Park School Tours brochure does not advertise discussion about the nutritional value of potato chips.[70]

Whereas a trip to a potato chip factory may raise some eyebrows, student participation in Google's virtual science fair, in contrast, appears to most observers as beyond reproach. The virtual science fair, after all, provides students with an outlet for creative and critical thinking in the scientific domain. It also sidesteps any critical thinking around either the value of a virtual fair or the assumption that high tech is best and Google products are the default, normative choice for search and other high-tech applications.

Google's marketing department oversees the science fair, and Tom Oliveri, head of product marketing for Google Apps, told the *New York Times* in 2011 that "part of this program is helping students use the apps to discover new things and develop their hypotheses."[71] As the *Times* points out, this strategy is similar to one Apple used in the 1980s and early 1990s, when it provided school computer labs with its computers, desktop publishing software, and CD-ROM drives.

Currently Google is striving to replace Microsoft in offices, and it makes sense from a corporate point of view that a large number of students be taught with and become accustomed to using Google products. To the extent that children become used to Google products in school, the more likely they will be to feel comfortable with and seek those products in their workplaces.[72] Consistent with this strategy, for the past several years Google has, without charge, supplied schools with the premium version of its Google Apps, for which it typically charges corporations.[73] On the one hand, these Google initiatives are a boon for students, who get computer equipment to use and a high-tech science fair. On the other hand they are being used as agents of Google's business plan. The key question for educators is one that is rarely asked when a company offers something for free: do these products represent the best educational choice for the students?

Google is also active in a currently popular type of fundraising incentive program: a contest in which students are encouraged to participate by their schools, which may or may not win money or products as a result. Unlike "scrip" programs (such as those run by many supermarkets, or by the Target corporation, for instance), in which all participating schools get a percentage back from purchases, contests entice many schools and students to participate but save money by offering a prize to only a few winning contestants or schools.

In Google's Doodle 4 Google program, children worldwide are solicited through their schools to create "their own Google doodle" on a yearly theme and submit it for a prize.[74] In 2010 twenty thousand U.S. schools participated, and Google received over thirty-three thousand entries.[75] In

2011, with the program opened up to selected after-school programs and to parents to enroll their children directly, the company received more than 107,000 doodles.[76] As is the case with other incentive programs, the program's agenda, to put the brand front and center in the role of benefactor, is satisfied.

Other contests have been run by Kohl's, Avery, and many other companies.[77] The extent and nature of students' participation in their schools' efforts to win the various contests vary by school, but in these other cases, as with the Google contest, it is likely that students' thinking about the programs was guided in two directions, neither of which involves critical thinking: toward the common-sense assumption of the corporation as benefactor and toward the goal of getting more votes. The corporation appears philanthropic while it uses students to market to themselves and to others.

As Rachel Cloues noted when she told us about her experiences with Nike and Target in her schools, the seeming goodwill of the companies, accompanied by the need for the money they bring, eclipses questions about the corporations' motives for involvement or criticism about their using their involvement for marketing purposes.[78]

In cooperation with Facebook, Kohl's department stores launched their Kohl's Cares for Schools contest in the summer of 2010.[79] In the autumn, as the contest wound toward its conclusion, schools leading the race for a $500,000 prize engaged in a variety of efforts to garner votes, including setting up booths at local community events, creating YouTube videos, and distributing bumper stickers urging people to vote for the school.[80] The twenty schools with the most votes on Facebook won the contest, and everyone who voted was put on the Kohl's mailing list to receive advertisements and promotions.[81]

Also for collecting votes, the five grand prize–winning schools of the Avery Give Back to Schools Program won $10,000 worth of Avery school supplies, 10,000 Box Tops for Education coupons, and $1,000 worth of gift cards. Twenty-five runner-up schools won 5,000 Box Tops coupons.[82]

These sorts of corporate relationships cannot help but shape school practices. According to one Martin County, Kentucky, biology teacher, for example, her school is so reliant on the funds brought in by its school store that even an academic decision such as when to add time to the school day was influenced by the likelihood of store sales.[83] The store is sponsored by and named for Fast Lane, a local convenience store chain that sponsors other programs in the school (most notably the fundraising Fast Lane Classic basketball tournament), and sells Pepsi products in accordance with the school's exclusive pouring rights contract with a local Pepsi bottling plant.[84]

For students in Martin County, both Fast Lane and Pepsi are the normal, common-sense choices for convenience and soft-drink purchases.[85] In school, they are the only option, and out of school, students learn to prefer them because they are familiar.[86] Exclusive agreements with the school thus limit critical thinking by dissuading students from generating, much less evaluating, alternatives to the norm that might serve them better.[87]

Beyond Critical Thinking Concerns

Although we have focused on how commercializing activities in schools discourage students from thinking critically, other significant threats to children's education result from allowing these activities into schools. As we noted earlier, many displace more valuable educationally valid activities, and others contradict or subtly subvert what students learn in classes. Teachers pushing virtual science fairs have less time to promote hands-on fairs; students visiting the Tayto potato chip factory might be traveling to a museum instead, and students doodling for Google might be doing a more meaningful art project. And foods like Tayto chips and Pepsi are exactly the kinds of foods that students are taught in their nutrition classes to avoid.

These threats to the integrity of students' education are all the more worrisome because school commercializing activities are proliferating so quickly. Agreements that allow corporations to appropriate school space, such as walls, lockers, gymnasiums, scoreboards, and buses, are not new, but in the current political and economic climate these tried-and-true marketing methods are blossoming anew and taking on new dimensions.[88]

School bus marketing is a good example of this evolution. Whereas decisions about whether to allow advertising on buses used to be made at the local level, now those decisions are also being made at the state level, allowing the practice to spread even faster. In March 2011, New Jersey became the seventh state (following Arizona, Colorado, New Mexico,

Tennessee, Texas, and Utah) to allow school bus marketing statewide.[89] Several other states (Kentucky, Ohio, and Rhode Island) have school bus advertising bills under consideration.[90] The nature of school bus marketing is also changing in that middleman companies are signing exclusive agreements with multiple districts to provide the advertising. The ability of these companies to offer potential advertisers many districts allows them to sell advertising to large corporations rather than to small local advertisers.

REMEMBER THE CORPORATE BOTTOM LINE

So often, when policy makers consider allowing some kind of corporate presence in a school, they worry about the type of product that would be advertised to children. They assure themselves that they will allow only pro-social ads, or prohibit ads for alcohol or tobacco, or prohibit ads with sexual, political, religious, criminal, violent, or profane undertones or depictions.[91] As one superintendent said, "You want to be careful of what type of advertising. Once you open your building up, if you don't have any policy in place, where do you stop?"[92]

Although we have expressed particular concerns about certain types of products—particularly "junk foods"—the particular product advertised is only part of the problem. The threat to educational integrity associated with advertising and marketing programs in school is more general in nature, and independent of any particular product category.

It is never in a sponsor's interest for children to learn to identify and evaluate its points of view and biases, to consider alternative points of view, or to generate and consider alternative solutions to problems. In the materials we have seen, instead of promoting this kind of higher-level thinking, sponsors promote their message and encourage activities that appear to forward children's education without risking touching on anything that might lead to thinking inconsistent with that message. This is the natural, unsurprising course of action for a corporation. It does not, however, promote the intellectual development of students or serve the broader interests of society.

It bears repeating and keeping at the forefront of any discussion of corporate involvement in the schools: corporations are self-interested entities in business for one purpose—to make money. Publicly traded corporations are required by law to put the interests of their shareholders first. Educating children is not their mission. Thus, corporate involvement with schools necessarily bends what students learn, how they learn, and the nature of the school and classroom environment in a direction that favors the corporate bottom line and attempts to shape the habits of mind that children internalize and carry with them, to the detriment of us all.

NOTES

1. Anderson, M. T. (2004). *Feed.* Somerville, MA: Candlewick Press, 109–10.

2. Glazer, G. S. (2011, March 8). New money for MPS. OnMilwaukee.com. Retrieved March 25, 2011, http://www.onmilwaukee.com/myOMC/blog/show/4873.

3. See, for example, Massie, K. (2009). Bye-bye sports, buses? Elk Grove schools wrestle with budget cuts. Retrieved November 13, 2009, from http://www.news10.net/news/local/story.aspx?storyid=68414&provider=top; Sanders, R. S. (2011, March 31). District considering advertising in schools to generate revenue. *Swartz Creek View.* Retrieved April 3, 2011, from http://swartzcreekview.mihomepaper.com/news/2011-03-31/Front_Page/District_considering_advertising_in_schools_to_gen.html; *News-Press* (2011, February 23). Editorial: Consider school bus advertising. Retrieved March 10, 2011, from http://www.news-press.com/article/20110224/OPINION/102240355/1015/opinion/Editorial-Consider-school-bus-advertising.

4. City University of New York (2014, February 13). President Obama praises CUNY's P-TECH HS in State of the Union speech. CUNY Newswire. Retrieved August 20, 2014, from http://www1.cuny.edu/mu/forum/2013/02/13/obama-praises-cunys-p-tech-hs-in-state-of-union-speech/.

5. Jhally, S. (2005). Advertising as social communication (online course; part one: Why study advertising?). Retrieved July 22, 2009, from http://www.comm287.com/partone/; McLaren, C., & Torchinsky, J. (2009). *Ad Nauseum.* New York: Faber and Faber, Inc. Retrieved July 31, 2009, from http://www.adnauseum.info.

6. ASA Entertainment Group, LLC (2010). Events: School Tours. Retrieved October 28, 2011, from http://www.asaentertainment.com/events/school_tours.html; ASA Entertainment Group, LLC (2010). ASA high school tour—Fall 2010. Author. Retrieved October 28, 2011, from http://beta.bfd.com/profile/F10HighSchoolTour; BMX.com (2009). Inside the XBox 360 Tour. Video posted on YouTube. Retrieved August 19, 2009, from http://www.youtube.com/

watch?v=JfsdY285_fU; bfd.com (2010). Channel 12 News Phoenix (video). Author. Retrieved October 28, 2011, from http://beta.bfd.com/video/channel-12-news-phoenix.

7. Jones, M. G., Jones, B. D., & Hargrove, T. Y. (2003). *The Unintended Consequences of High-Stakes Testing*. Lanham, MD: Rowman & Littlefield, 4–5; Ritchhart, R., & Perkins, D. N. (2005). Learning to think: The challenges of teaching thinking. In Keith J. Holyoak and Robert G. Morrison (eds.), *The Cambridge Handbook of Thinking and Reasoning*. Cambridge, England: Cambridge University Press, 776.

8. Jones, M. G., Jones, B. D, & Hargrove, T. Y. (2003). *The Unintended Consequences of High-Stakes Testing*. Lanham, MD: Rowman & Littlefield; Law, C., & Kaufhold, J. A. (2009, Spring). An analysis of the use of critical thinking skills in reading and language arts instruction. *Reading Improvement, 46*(1), 29–34; McNeil, L., & Valenzuela, A. (2001). The harmful impact of the TAAS System of testing in Texas. In G. Orfield & M. L. Kornhaber (eds.) (2001), *Raising Standards or Raising Barriers? Inequality and High-Stakes Testing in Public Education*. New York: The Century Foundation Press; Nichols, S. L., & Berliner, D. S. (2005). *The Inevitable Corruption of Indicators and Educators through High-Stakes Testing*. Tempe, AZ: Education Policy Research Unit, Education Policy Studies Laboratory, Arizona State University. Retrieved April 20, 2011, from http://nepc.colorado.edu/publication/the-inevitable-corruption-indicators-and-educators-through-high-stakes-testing; Nickerson, R. S. (2010). How to discourage creativity in the classroom. In R. A. Beghetto & J. C. Kaufman (eds.), *Nurturing Creativity in the Classroom*. Cambridge, England: Cambridge University Press, 1–5; Wenglinsky, H. (2004, November 23). Closing the racial achievement gap: The role of reforming instructional practices. *Education Policy Analysis Archives, 12*(64). Retrieved April 20, 2011, from http://epaa.asu.edu/epaa/v12n64/.

9. For a discussion of related terminology to describe the tendency toward and attitudes relevant to critical thinking, see Ritchhart, R. (2002). *Intellectual Character*. San Francisco, CA: John Wiley and Sons, Inc., xxii.

10. Sternberg, R. J., & Spear-Swerling, L. (1996). *Teaching for Thinking*. Washington, DC: American Psychological Association, 151.

11. Sternberg, R. J. (1986). Critical thinking: Its nature, measurement, and improvement. ERIC Document Reproduction Service No. 272882. Retrieved March 30, 2011, from http://www.eric.ed.gov/PDFS/ED272882; Sternberg, R. J., & Spear-Swerling, L. (1996). *Teaching for Thinking*. Washington, DC: American Psychological Association, 151. For a hierarchy of thinking skills, see Bloom. B. S. (ed.) (1956). *Taxonomy of Educational Objectives: The Classification of Educational Goals. Handbook I: Cognitive Domain*s. New York: David Wiley.

12. Sternberg, R. J. (1986). Critical thinking: Its nature, measurement, and improvement. ERIC Document Reproduction Service No. 272882. Retrieved March 30, 2011, from http://www.eric.ed.gov/PDFS/ED272882.

13. Philip Abrami and his colleagues, for instance, discuss psychological approaches that focus on skills such as interpreting, predicting, analyzing, and evaluating; and philosophical approaches that emphasize the ability and disposition to evaluate beliefs effectively and to identify and assess their underlying assumptions. Diane Halpern refers to skills in verbal reasoning, argument analysis, hypothesis testing, likelihood and uncertainty, decision making, and problem solving. Abrami, P. C., Bernard, R. M., Borokhovski, E., Wade, A., Surkes, M. A., Tamim, R., & Zhang, D. (2008, December). Instructional interventions affecting critical thinking skills and dispositions: A stage 1 meta-analysis. *Review of Educational Research, 78*(4), 1102–34; Halpern, D. F. (1998, April). Teaching critical thinking for transfer across domains: Dispositions, skills, structure training, and metacognitive monitoring. *American Psychologist, 53*(4), 449–55 (452).

14. Fairweather, E., & Cramond, B. (2010). In Beghetto, R. A., & Kaufman, J. C. (eds.), *Nurturing Creativity in the Classroom*. Cambridge, England: Cambridge University Press, 113–41; Paul, R. (2009). A draft statement of principles. the National Council for Excellence in Critical Thinking. Retrieved February 9, 2011, from http://www.criticalthinking.org/about/nationalCouncil.cfm; Sternberg, R. J. (1986). Critical thinking: Its nature, measurement, and improvement. ERIC Document Reproduction Service No. 272882. Retrieved March 30, 2011, from http://www.eric.ed.gov/PDFS/ED272882.

15. Gubbins, E. J. (1985). Matrix of thinking skills. Unpublished document. Hartfort, CT: State Department of Education. Cited in Sternberg, Robert J. (1986). Critical thinking: Its nature, measurement, and improvement. ERIC Document Reproduction Service No. 272882. Retrieved March 30, 2011, from http://www.eric.ed.gov/PDFS/ED272882. See also Ennis, R. H. (1986). A taxonomy of critical thinking dispositions and abilities. In J. B. Baron and R. S. Sternberg (eds.), *Teaching Thinking Skills: Theory and Practice*. New York: Freeman, 9–26; Fairweather, E., & Cramond, B. (2010). In Beghetto, R. A. & Kaufman, J. C. (eds.), *Nurturing Creativity in the Classroom*. Cambridge, England: Cambridge University Press, 113–41; Kennedy, M. L. (2010, June). The art of critical thinking. *Information Outlook, 14*(4), 31–34; Ritchhart, R. (2002). *Intellectual Character*. San Francisco, CA: John H. Wiley & Sons, Inc.; Sternberg, R. J. (1986). Critical thinking: Its nature, measurement, and improvement. ERIC Document Reproduction Service No. 272882. Retrieved March 30, 2011, from http://www.eric.ed.gov/PDFS/ED272882.

16. Fairweather, E., & Cramond, B.(2010). In Beghetto, R. A. & Kaufman, J. C. (eds.), *Nurturing Creativity in the Classroom*. Cambridge, England: Cambridge University Press, 118.

17. Fairweather, E., & Cramond, B. (2010). In Beghetto, R. A. & Kaufman, J. C. (eds.), *Nurturing Creativity in the Classroom*. Cambridge, England: Cambridge University Press, 118.

18. Bransford, J. D., & Stein, B. S. (1984). *The Ideal Problem Solver: A Guide for Improving Thinking, Learning, and Creativity*. San Francisco: Freeman; Sternberg, R. J. (1986). Critical thinking: Its nature, measurement, and improvement. ERIC Document Reproduction Service No. 272882. Retrieved March 30, 2011, from http://www.eric.ed.gov/PDFS/ED272882.

19. Abrami, P. C., Bernard, R. M., Borokhovski, E., Wade, A., Surkes, M. A., Tamim, R., & Zhang, D. (2008, December). Instructional interventions affecting critical thinking skills and dispositions: A stage 1 meta-analysis. *Review of Educational Research, 78*(4), 1102–34; Derry, S., Lewis, J. R., & Schauble, L. (1995). Simulating statistical thinking through situated simulations. *Teaching of Psychology*, 22(1), 51–57; Fairweather, E., & Cramond, B. (2010). In Beghetto, R. A., & Kaufman, J. C. (eds.), *Nurturing Creativity in the Classroom*. Cambridge, England: Cambridge University Press, 113–41; Halpern, D. F. (1998, April). Teaching critical thinking for transfer across domains: Dispositions, skills, structure training, and metacognitive monitoring. *American Psychologist, 53*(4), 449–55 (452); Kuhn, D., & Pearsall, S. (1998). Relations between metastrategic knowledge and strategic performance. *Cognitive Development, 13*, 227–47; Lehman, D. R., & Nisbett, R. E. (1990). A longitudinal study of the effects of undergraduate training on reasoning. *Developmental Psychology, 26*(6), 431–42; Perkins, D. N., & Grotzer, T. A. (1997). Teaching intelligence. *American Psychologist, 52*(10), 1125–33; Salmon, A. K. (2008). Promoting a culture of thinking in the young child. *Early Childhood Education Journal, 35*(5), 457–61; Ritchhart, R., & Perkins, D. N. (2005). Learning to think: The challenges of teaching thinking. In Keith J. Holyoak and Robert G. Morrison (eds.), *The Cambridge Handbook of Thinking and Reasoning*. Cambridge, England: Cambridge University Press; Scardarmalia, M., Bereiter, C., & Lamon, M. (1994). The CSILE Project: Trying to bring the classroom into World 3. In K. McGilly (ed.), *Classroom Lessons: Integrating Cognitive Theory and Classroom Practice*. Cambridge, MA: MIT Press, 201–28; Zohar, A., & Peled, B. (2008). The effects of explicit teaching of metastrategic knowledge on low- and high-achieving students. *Learning and Instruction, 18*, 337–53.

20. Abrami, P. C., Bernard, R. M., Borokhovski, E., Wade, A., Surkes, M. A., Tamim, R., & Zhang, D. (2008, December). Instructional interventions affecting critical thinking skills and dispositions: A stage 1 meta-analysis. *Review of Educational Research, 78*(4), 1102–34; Audet, R., & Jordan, L. K. (eds.), (2005). *Integrating Inquiry across the Curriculum*. Thousand Oaks, CA: Corwin Press; Elder, L. (2011, November 25). Achieving critical mass. *Times Higher Education*. Retrieved July 26, 2011, from http://www.timeshighereducation.co.uk/

story.asp?sectioncode=26&storycode=414351&c=1; Halpern, D. F. (1998, April). Teaching critical thinking for transfer across domains: Dispositions, skills, structure training, and metacognitive monitoring. *American Psychologist, 53*(4), 449–55; Resnick, L. B. (1987). *Education and Learning to Think.* Washington, DC: National Academy Press. Retrieved July 26, 2011, from http://www.nap.edu/openbook.php?record_id=1032&page=R1; Ritchhart, R., & Perkins, D. N. (2005). Learning to think: The challenges of teaching thinking. In K. J. Holyoak and R. G. Morrison (eds.), *The Cambridge Handbook of Thinking and Reasoning.* New York: Cambridge University Press, 775–802; Sternberg, R. J. (1986). Critical thinking: Its nature, measurement, and improvement. ERIC Document Reproduction Service No. 272882. Retrieved March 30, 2011, from http://www.eric.ed.gov/PDFS/ED272882.

21. Perkins, D. N., & Grotzer, T. A. (1997). Teaching intelligence. *American Psychologist, 52*(10), 1125–33.

22. Perkins, D. N., & Grotzer, T. A. (1997). Teaching intelligence. *American Psychologist, 52*(10), 1125–33.

23. Halpern, D. F. (1998, April). Teaching critical thinking for transfer across domains: Dispositions, skills, structure training, and metacognitive monitoring. *American Psychologist, 53*(4), 449–55; Klaczynski, P. A. (2007). Education: Theory, practice, and the road less followed. *Journal of Applied Developmental Psychology, 28,* 80–83.

24. Audet, R., & Jordan, L. K. (eds.), (2005). *Integrating Inquiry across the Curriculum.* Thousand Oaks, CA: Corwin Press; Halpern, D. F. (1998, April). Teaching critical thinking for transfer across domains: Dispositions, skills, structure training, and metacognitive monitoring. *American Psychologist, 53*(4), 449–55; Shaughnessy, M. E. (2004). An interview with Deanna Kuhn. *Educational Psychology Review, 16*(3), 267–82.

25. Halpern, D. F. (1998, April). Teaching critical thinking for transfer across domains: Dispositions, skills, structure training, and metacognitive monitoring. *American Psychologist, 53*(4), 449–55.

26. Halpern, D. F. (1998, April). Teaching critical thinking for transfer across domains: Dispositions, skills, structure training, and metacognitive monitoring. *American Psychologist, 53*(4), 449–55; Klaczynski, P. A. (2007). Education: Theory, practice, and the road less followed. *Journal of Applied Developmental Psychology, 28,* 80–83; Zohar, A., & Aharon-Kravetsky, S. (2005). Exploring the effects of cognitive conflict and direct teaching for students of different academic levels. *Journal of Research in Science Teaching, 42*(7), 829–55.

27. Bransford, J., Sherwood, R., Vye, N., & Rieser, J. (1986). Teaching thinking and problem solving: Research foundations. *American Psychologist 41*(10), 1078–89; Kuhn, D. (2005). *Education for Thinking.* Cambridge, MA: Harvard University Press; Ritchhart, R., & Perkins, David N. (2005). Learning to think:

The challenges of teaching thinking. In K. J. Holyoak and R. G. Morrison (eds.), *The Cambridge Handbook of Thinking and Reasoning.* Cambridge, England: Cambridge University Press; Salmon, A. K. (2008). Promoting a culture of thinking in the young child. *Early Childhood Education Journal, 35*(5), 457–61; Schoenfeld, A. H. (1988). Mathematics, technology, and higher order thinking. In R. S. Nickerson and P. P. Zodhiates (eds.), *Technology in Education: Looking toward 2020.* Mahwah, NJ: Lawrence Erlbaum Associates, Inc., 67–96; Zohar, A., & Ben David, A. (2008). Explicit teaching of metastrategic knowledge in authentic classroom situations. *Metacognition Learning, 3*, 59–82.

28. Ku, K. Y. L., & Ho, I. T. (2010). Metacognitive strategies that enhance critical thinking. *Metacognition and Learning, 5*(3), 251–67. Retrieved July 5, 2011, from http://www.springerlink.com.ezproxy1.lib.asu.edu/content/ h51t66v655167701/fulltext.html [subscription required].

29. Zohar, A., & Aharon-Kravetsky, S. (2005). Exploring the effects of cognitive conflict and direct teaching for students of different academic levels. *Journal of Research in Science Teaching, 42*(7), 829–55; Zohar, A., & Ben David, A. (2008). Explicit teaching of metastrategic knowledge in authentic classroom situations. *Metacognition Learning, 3*, 59–82; Zohar, A., & Peled, B. (2008). The effects of explicit teaching of metastrategic knowledge on low- and high-achieving students. *Learning and Instruction, 18*(4), 337–53.

30. Zohar, A., & Ben David, A. (2008). Explicit teaching of metastrategic knowledge in authentic classroom situations. *Metacognition Learning, 3*, 59–82; Zohar, A., & Peled, B. (2008). The effects of explicit teaching of metastrategic knowledge on low- and high-achieving students. *Learning and Instruction, 18*(4), 337–53.

31. Zohar, A., & Ben David, A. (2008). Explicit teaching of metastrategic knowledge in authentic classroom situations. *Metacognition Learning, 3*, 59–82. See also Abrami, P. C., Bernard, R. M., Borokhovski, E., Wade, A., Surkes, M. A., Tamim, R., & Zhang, D. (2008, December). Instructional interventions affecting critical thinking skills and dispositions: A Stage 1 meta-analysis. *Review of Educational Research, 78*(4), 1102–34; Halpern, D. F. (1998, April). Teaching critical thinking for transfer across domains: Dispositions, skills, structure training, and metacognitive monitoring. *American Psychologist, 53*(4), 449–55; Shaughnessy, M. E. (2004). An interview with Deanna Kuhn. *Educational Psychology Review, 16*(3), 267–82.

32. Diane Halpern (1998) points out (p. 453) that the transfer and use of critical thinking skills to a variety of real-world situations is facilitated by the creation of elaborated cognitive structures associated with those skills. Although she does not focus on the classroom and school environments as a source of developing those elaborated cognitive structures, she emphasizes that any program to teach thinking should draw questions and scenarios from the real-world

contexts of the workplace and "in the exercise of citizenship" (p. 453). To the extent that students get practice extending the thinking skills they learn in class to the "real-life" contexts they face out of class, they may be more likely to recognize when other real-life situations emerge that warrant the application of their skills. Halpern, D. F. (1998, April). Teaching critical thinking for transfer across domains: Dispositions, skills, structure training, and metacognitive monitoring. *American Psychologist, 53*(4), 449–55. See also Rogoff, B., & Lave, J. (eds.), (1984). *Everyday Cognition: Its Development in Social Context.* Cambridge, MA: Harvard University Press; Perkins, D. N., & Grotzer, T. (1997). Teaching intelligence. *American Psychologist, 52*(10), 1125–33.

33. Perkins, D. N., & Grotzer, T. (1997). Teaching intelligence. *American Psychologist, 52*(10), 1125–33; Schoenfeld, A. H. (1988). Mathematics, technology, and higher order thinking. In R. S. Nickerson and P. P. Zodhiates (eds.), *Technology in Education: Looking toward 2020.* Mahwah, NJ: Lawrence Erlbaum Associates, Inc., 67–96.

34. Feurzeig, W. (1988). Apprentice tools: Students as practitioners. In R. S. Nickerson and P. P. Zodhiates (eds.), *Technology in Education: Looking toward 2020.* Mahwah, NJ: Lawrence Erlbaum Associates, Inc., 97–120; Halpern, D. F. (1998, April). Teaching critical thinking for transfer across domains: Dispositions, skills, structure training, and metacognitive monitoring. *American Psychologist, 53*(4), 449–55; Sternberg, R. J. (1986). Critical thinking: Its nature, measurement, and improvement. ERIC Document Reproduction Service No. 272882. Retrieved March 30, 2011, from http://www.eric.ed.gov/PDFS/ED272882.

35. Ritchhart, R., & Perkins, D. N. (2005). Learning to think: The challenges of teaching thinking. In K. J. Holyoak and R. G. Morrison (eds.), *The Cambridge Handbook of Thinking and Reasoning.* Cambridge, England: Cambridge University Press, 792; Scardarmalia, M., Bereiter, C., & Lamon, M. (1994). The CSILE Project: Trying to bring the classroom into World 3. In K. McGilly (ed.), *Classroom Lessons: Integrating Cognitive Theory and Classroom Practice.* Cambridge, MA: MIT Press, 201–28; Schoenfeld, A. H. (1988). Mathematics, technology, and higher order thinking. In R. S. Nickerson and P. P. Zodhiates (eds.), *Technology in education: Looking toward 2020.* Mahwah, NJ: Lawrence Erlbaum Associates, Inc., 67–96.

36. Bandura, A. (1977). *Social Learning Theory.* New York: General Learning Press; Fairweather, E., & Cramond, B. (2010). In Beghetto, R. A., & Kaufman, J. C. (eds.), *Nurturing Creativity in the Classroom.* Cambridge, England: Cambridge University Press, 113–41.

37. Weinstock, M., Assor, A., & Broide, G. (2009). Schools as promoters of moral judgement: The essential role of teachers' encouragement of critical thinking. *Social Psychology in Education, 12*, 137–51.

38. Weinstock, M., Assor, A., & Broide, G. (2009). Schools as promoters of moral judgement: The essential role of teachers' encouragement of critical thinking. *Social Psychology in Education, 12*, 137–51.

39. Weinstock, M., Assor, A., & Broide, G. (2009). Schools as promoters of moral judgement: The essential role of teachers' encouragement of critical thinking. *Social Psychology in Education, 12*, 137–51. See also Scardarmalia, M., Bereiter, C., & Lamon, M. (1994). The CSILE Project: Trying to bring the classroom into World 3. In K. McGilly (ed.), *Classroom Lessons: Integrating Cognitive Theory and Classroom Practice*. Cambridge, MA: MIT Press, 201–28.

40. Halpern, D. F. (1998, April). Teaching critical thinking for transfer across domains: Dispositions, skills, structure training, and metacognitive monitoring. *American Psychologist, 53*(4), 449–55; Ritchhart, R., & Perkins, D. N. (2005). Learning to think: The challenges of teaching thinking. In K. J. Holyoak and R. G. Morrison (eds.), *The Cambridge Handbook of Thinking and Reasoning*. Cambridge, England: Cambridge University Press; Rogoff, B., & Lave, J. (eds.), (1984). *Everyday Cognition: Its Development in Social Context*. Cambridge, MA: Harvard University Press; Schoenfeld, A. H. (1988). Mathematics, technology, and higher order thinking. In R. S. Nickerson and P. P. Zodhiates (eds.), *Technology in Education: Looking toward 2020*. Mahwah, NJ: Lawrence Erlbaum Associates, Inc., 67–96.

41. National Science Foundation, Directorate for Education & Human Resources, Research on Learning in Formal and Informal Settings (2010). *Informal Science Education (ISE): Program Solicitation NSF 10-565*. Author. Retrieved April 13, 2011, from http://www.nsf.gov/pubs/2010/nsf10565/nsf10565.htm#pgm_desc_txt.

42. National Science Foundation, Directorate for Education & Human Resources, Research on Learning in Formal and Informal Settings (2010). *Informal Science Education (ISE): Program Solicitation NSF 10-565*. Author. Retrieved April 13, 2011, from http://www.nsf.gov/pubs/2010/nsf10565/nsf10565.htm#pgm_desc_txt.

43. Ritchhart, R., & Perkins, D. N. (2005). Learning to think: The challenges of teaching thinking. In K. J. Holyoak and R. G. Morrison (eds.), *The Cambridge Handbook of Thinking and Reasoning*. Cambridge, England: Cambridge University Press, 792.

44. Dewey, J. (1938). *Experience and Education*. Indianapolis, IN: Kappa Delta Pi, 16–17.

45. Dewey, J. (1938). *Experience and Education*. Indianapolis, IN: Kappa Delta Pi, 13–14.

46. Gutting, G. (2011, October 12). Corporations, people and truth. *New York Times*. Retrieved August 20, 2014, from http://opinionator.blogs.nytimes.com/2011/10/12/corporations-people-and-truth/?_php=true&_type=blogs&_r=0.

47. Bakan, J. (2011). *Childhood under Siege: How Big Business Targets Children*. New York: Free Press, 11; Norris, T. (2011). *Consuming Schools: Commercialism and the End of Politics*. Toronto: University of Toronto Press, 57; Gutting, G. (2011, October 12). Corporations, people and truth. *New York Times*. Retrieved August 20, 2014, from http://opinionator.blogs.nytimes.com/2011/10/12/corporations-people-and-truth/?_php=true&_type=blogs&_r=0.

48. Consistent with this analysis, nutritionist Rosemary Stanton commented as follows about a proposal to ban advertising in Australian schools by companies that sell "junk food": "If you have spellathons, walkathons, anything that's sponsored by a junk food company, it effectively silences the teachers from being critical of those products." Tovey, J. (2011, March 22). Greens want to curb junk food ads. *Sydney Morning Herald*. Retrieved March 27, 2011, from http://www.smh.com.au/nsw/state-election-2011/greens-want-to-curb-junk-food-ads-20110321-1c3xf.html.

49. Cloues, R. (2011). My year with Nike: A story of corporate sponsorship, branding, and ethics in public schools. In E. Marshall & Ö. Sensoy (eds.), *Rethinking Popular Culture and Media*. Milwaukee, WI: Rethinking Schools.

50. Cloues, R. (2011). My year with Nike: A story of corporate sponsorship, branding, and ethics in public schools. In E. Marshall & Ö. Sensoy (eds.), *Rethinking Popular Culture and Media*. Milwaukee, WI: Rethinking Schools.

51. Cloues, R. (2011). My year with Nike: A story of corporate sponsorship, branding, and ethics in public schools. In E. Marshall & Ö. Sensoy (eds.), *Rethinking Popular Culture and Media*. Milwaukee, WI: Rethinking Schools.

52. Cloues, R. (2011). My year with Nike: A story of corporate sponsorship, branding, and ethics in public schools. In E. Marshall & Ö. Sensoy (eds.), *Rethinking Popular Culture and Media*. Milwaukee, WI: Rethinking Schools.

53. Cloues, R. (2014, July 8). Personal communication (telephone) with Faith Boninger.

54. Cloues, R. (2014, Summer). The library that Target built. *Rethinking Schools, 28*(4). Retrieved August 20, 2014, from http://www.rethinkingschools.org/archive/28_04/28_04_cloues.shtml.

55. Cloues, R. (2014, Summer). The library that Target built. *Rethinking Schools, 28*(4). Retrieved August 20, 2014, from http://www.rethinkingschools.org/archive/28_04/28_04_cloues.shtml.

56. Cloues, R. (2014, Summer). The library that Target built. *Rethinking Schools, 28*(4). Retrieved August 20, 2014, from http://www.rethinkingschools.org/archive/28_04/28_04_cloues.shtml.

57. Cloues, R. (2014, July 8). Personal communication (telephone) with Faith Boninger.

58. Scholastic's InSchool Marketing and Solutions unit developed and distributed branded in-school materials for private companies and nonprofit agen-

cies and organizations, including products geared to "Brand Awareness, Direct to Home Marketing, Retail Tie-In, Consumer Loyalty, Cause-Marketing, QSR Programs, One-to-One Marketing, Public Relations Tie-Ins, and more," according to Scholastic's website. The page of the company website that described these programs was revised in the wake of the campaign against "The United States of Energy" and no longer publicly lists these products. In July, 2011, Scholastic announced a reduction of its InSchool Marketing division by approximately 40 percent, much of which is from its corporate-sponsored materials. Lewin, T. (2011, July 31). Children's publisher backing off its corporate ties. *New York Times*. Retrieved August 2, 2011, from http://www.nytimes.com/2011/08/01/education/01scholastic.html?_r=1; Scholastic, Inc. (2011). Scholastic Marketing Partners. Retrieved May 6, 2011, from http://www.scholastic.com/aboutscholastic/scholasticmarketingpartners.htm [no longer available]; Paty, A. H. (2010, November 30). American Coal Foundation and Scholastic, Inc.: Partnering for energy education. Retrieved May 6, 2011, from http://www.coalblog.org/?p=1590.

59. Shell (2011). Educators. Retrieved October 11, 2011, from http://www.shell.us/home/content/usa/environment_society/education/teacher/. Shell and the American Coal Foundation are not the only energy interests attempting to influence children in schools. Climate Science Watch, a sponsored project of the Government Accountability Project, cites BP, Chevron, ConocoPhillips, Halliburton, and Pacific Gas and Electric as funders of energy education programs in schools; *Climate Science Watch* (2010, December 23). Corporate funding in public education—is anyone watching? Author. Retrieved October 28, 2011, from http://www.climatesciencewatch.org/2010/12/23/corporate-funding-in-public-education-is-anyone-watching/. See also National Energy Education Development Project (n.d.). Sponsors. Retrieved October 28, 2011, from http://www.need.org/Sponsors-Partners.

60. Alma Hale Paty's post presents a coal industry perspective on the partnership between the American Coal Foundation and Scholastic: Paty, A. H. (20110, November 30). American Coal Foundation and Scholastic, Inc.: Partnering for energy education. Retrieved May 6, 2011, from http://www.coalblog.org/?p=1590. Scholastic, Inc. (2011, May 13). Statement from Scholastic on "The United States of Energy." Retrieved May 17, 2011, from http://oomscholasticblog.com/2011/05/statement-from-scholastic-on-the-united-states-of-energy.html.

61. As discussed in chapter 2, when a coalition of environmental and anticommercialism groups protested this curriculum, the resulting bad publicity led Scholastic to reduce (but not cease) its production and promotion of sponsored content; May, C. (2011, May 18). Scholastic Inc. bends to the will of environmental activists. *Daily Caller*. Retrieved October 30, 2014, from http://dailycaller.com/2011/05/18/scholastic-inc-bends-to-the-will-of-environmental-

activists/; Lewin, T. (2011, July 31). Children's publisher backing off its corporate ties. *New York Times*. Retrieved August 2, 2011, from http://www.nytimes.com/2011/08/01/education/01scholastic.html?_r=1; Scholastic, Inc. (2011, May 13). Statement from Scholastic on "The United States of Energy." Retrieved May 17, 2011, from http://oomscholasticblog.com/2011/05/statement-from-scholastic-on-the-united-states-of-energy.html.

62. Bigelow, B. (2011). Scholastic, Inc.·Pushing coal: A fourth-grade curriculum lies through omission. *Rethinking Schools, 25*(4); Campaign for a Commercial-Free Childhood (2011, May 14). Scholastic Severs Ties with the Coal Industry. Author. Retrieved May 17, 2011, from http://www.commercialfreechildhood.org/pressreleases/coalandscholasticwin.html; Lewin, T. (2011, May 11). Coal curriculum called unfit for 4th graders. *New York Times*. Retrieved May 18, 2011, from http://www.nytimes.com/2011/05/12/education/12coal.html.

63. CEDAR. Inc. (2011). CEDAR, Inc.: Coal education development and resource. Retrieved May 5, 2011, from http://www.cedarinc.org/.

64. CEDAR, Inc. (n.d.) Coal education development and resource. Retrieved May 5, 2011, from http://www.cedarinc.org/; NCCI (2011). Welcome to NCCI The Coal Institute. Retrieved October 17, 2011, from http://www.thecoalinstitute.org/; in addition to the original organization, CEDAR, Inc., the following child organizations are also active: CEDAR of West Kentucky, CEDAR of Southern West Virginia, and CEDAR of Virginia; CEDAR, Inc. (2010). CEDAR, Inc.: Coal education development and resource: expansion activities. Retrieved October 17, 2011, from http://www.cedarinc.org/coal_fair.htm.

65. CEDAR, Inc. (2006). CEDAR, Inc.: Coal education development and resource. Retrieved May 5, 2011, from http://www.cedarinc.org/ (see subpages for much of what's copied here); CEDAR, Inc. (2010). CEDAR, Inc.: Coal education development and resource: Regional Coal Fair: 1993–2010. Retrieved May 5, 2011, from http://www.cedarinc.org/coal_fair.htm; CEDAR, Inc. (2010). CEDAR, Inc.: Coal education development and resource: Teacher Coal Study Unit (CSU) Program: 1993–2010. Retrieved May 5, 2011, from http://www.cedarinc.org/teacher_CSU.htm; CEDAR, Inc. (2010). CEDAR, Inc.: Coal education development and resource: Program Statistics 1993–2010. Retrieved May 5, 2011, from http://www.cedarinc.org/statistics.htm; Donour, R. (2011, May 8). Personal communication (e-mail) with Nina McCoy.

66. CEDAR, Inc. (n.d.). Featured projects. Retrieved May 25, 2011, from http://www.cedarinc.org/featured_projects.htm.

67. In an e-mail to another high school teacher, a Letcher County, Kentucky, chemistry teacher described CEDAR's work in local schools: "I am not sure if you know the background of the CEDAR program—it is a state-funded program that offers educational grants to teachers that want to show how the coal industry

is a part of our historical, economical, and environmental background. Now with that said—this is strongly supported by coal operators/companies (I think CEDAR has financial support from them). They really want to spotlight the positive side of the industry (environmental—how it produces areas for animal grazing or industrial sites). I am not saying that they would say no to any type of grant that might address some of the negative issues—but your application would more likely be funded if—in the end it makes the coal industry look positive." McCoy, Nina (2011, May 8). Personal communication (email) with Faith Boninger.

68. Tayto Crisps (2010). Tayto Tours school brochure. Retrieved October 30, 2014, from http://www.taytocrisps.ie/wp-content/themes/tayto/assets/files/TP_School_Brochure.pdf.

69. Tayto Crisps (2010). Tayto Tours school brochure. Retrieved October 30, 2014, from http://www.taytocrisps.ie/wp-content/themes/tayto/assets/files/TP_School_Brochure.pdf.

70. For an interesting and entertaining discussion about how potato chip marketing portrays the chips as healthy, see Jarafsky, D. (2014). *The Language of Food: A Linguist Reads the Menu*. New York: W.W. Norton and Company, 107–16.

71. Miller, C. C. (2011, April 4). Promoting science, and Google, to students. *New York Times*. Retrieved April 18, 2011, from http://mobile.nytimes.com/2011/04/04/technology/04fair.xml.

72. Miller, C. C. (2011, April 4). Promoting science, and Google, to students. *New York Times*. Retrieved April 18, 2011, from http://mobile.nytimes.com/2011/04/04/technology/04fair.xml; Fost, D. (2009, October 28). Google co-founder Sergey Brin wants more computers in schools. *Los Angeles Times*. Retrieved November 5, 2009, from http://latimesblogs.latimes.com/technology/2009/10/sergey-brin-put-computers-in-schools-.html.

73. Fost, D. (2009, October 28). Google co-founder Sergey Brin wants more computers in schools. *Los Angeles Times*. Retrieved November 5, 2009, from http://latimesblogs.latimes.com/technology/2009/10/sergey-brin-put-computers-in-schools-.html; Google (n.d.). Google Apps for Education: Discover a better way of learning. Retrieved October 30, 2014, from https://www.google.com/work/apps/education/.

74. Google (2011). Doodle 4 Google. Author. Retrieved July 14, 2011, from http://www.google.ie/doodle4google/index.html; Google (2011). Doodle 4 Google—"I love soccer." Author. Retrieved July 14, 2011, from http://www.google.com/intl/en_au/lovefootball/doodle4google/index.html; Google (2011). Doodle 4 Google "My China" International Children's Painting Competition on Google. Author. Retrieved July 14, 2011, from http://www.google.com/intl/zh-CN/doodle4google/ [translation athttp://translate.google.com/translate?hl=en&sl=zh-CN&u=http://www.google.com/intl/zh-CN/doodle4google/&ei=

Bx4fTqT3HsTTgQfE4vitAw&sa=X&oi=translate&ct=result&resnum=4&ved=
0CDgQ7gEwAw&prev=/search%3Fq%3Ddoodle%2Bfor%2B
google%2Bchina%26hl%3Den%26prmd%3Divns.]

75. Google (2011). *Doodle 4 Google: FAQ*s. Author. Retrieved October 28, 2011, from http://www.google.com/doodle4google/faqs.html.

76. Google (2011). *Doodle 4 Google: FAQ*s. Author. Retrieved October 28, 2011, from http://www.google.com/doodle4google/faqs.html.

77. Avery Dennison Corporation (2011). Avery gives back to schools. Retrieved September 9, 2011, from http://givebacktoschools.avery.com/schools/index; Briggs, J. (2011, June 30). Personal communication (telephone) with Faith Boninger; Rodriguez, M. (2010, September 2). The 'little school that didn't quit' wants your vote for national prize. *Kansas City Star*. Retrieved September 3, 2010, from http://www.kansascity.com/2010/09/01/2193971/the-little-school-that-didnt-quit.html (no longer available).

78. Cloues, R. (2014, July 8). Personal communication (telephone) with Faith Boninger.

79. The Avery Dennison Corporation ran a similar program in 2011, in conjunction with Box Tops for Education, called "Avery Give Back to Schools," but with a smaller payoff. The top five schools at the end of the promotion won $10,000 worth of Avery school supplies, 10,000 Bonus Box Tops coupons, and $1,000 worth of gift cards. Twenty-five runner-up schools won 5,000 Bonus Box Tops coupons. Avery Dennison Corporation (2011). Avery Gives Back to Schools. Retrieved September 9, 2011, from http://givebacktoschools.avery.com/schools/index.

80. Briggs, J. (2011, June 30). Personal communication (telephone) with Faith Boninger; Rodriguez, M. (2010, September 2). The 'little school that didn't quit' wants your vote for national prize. *Kansas City Star*. Retrieved September 3, 2010, from http://www.kansascity.com/2010/09/01/2193971/the-little-school-that-didnt-quit.html [no longer available].

81. Henk, B. (2010, September 9). The unofficial half million dollar$ Kohl's Cares winners. *Marquette Educator*. Retrieved June 30, 2011, from http://marquetteeducator.wordpress.com/2010/09/09/the-half-million-dollar-kohls-cares-winners/; Rodriguez, M. (2010, September 2). The 'little school that didn't quit' wants your vote for national prize. *Kansas City Star*. Retrieved September 3, 2010, from http://www.kansascity.com/2010/09/01/2193971/the-little-school-that-didnt-quit.html [no longer available].

82. Avery Dennison Corporation (2011). Avery gives back to schools. Retrieved October 11, 2011, from http://givebacktoschools.avery.com/; General Mills (2011). Make a difference for your school! Retrieved October 11, 2011, from http://www.boxtops4education.com/.

83. McCoy, N. (2011, October 8). Personal communication (e-mail) with Faith Boninger.

84. The school has a long history with the bottling company. When, in 2000, students in the environmental club participated in a rally in favor of a "bottle bill," the company bused its own employees to the state capitol to rally against the bill. Although she can't prove it, the advisor to the environmental club suspects that company pressure was behind both her principal's reluctance to provide a bus to the capitol for his own students and their state representative's failure to show up for a scheduled meeting with the students. McCoy, N. (2011, May 8). Personal communication (telephone) with Faith Boninger.

85. Kahneman, D., and Miller, D. T. (1986). Norm theory: Comparing reality to its alternatives. *Psychological Review, 93*(2), 136–53.

86. Bornstein, R. F., Leone, D. R., & Galley, D. J. (1987). The generalizability of subliminal mere exposure effects: Influence of stimuli perceived without awareness on social behavior. *Journal of Personality and Social Psychology, 53*(6), 1070–79; Hansen, J., & Wanke, M. (2009). Liking what's familiar: The importance of unconscious familiarity in the mere-exposure effect. *Social Cognition, 27*(2), 161–82; Smith, E. R., & Mackie, D. M. (2000). *Social Psychology* (2nd Ed.). Philadelphia, PA: Taylor and Francis, 260.

87. Kahneman, D., & Miller, D. T. (1986, April). Norm theory: Comparing reality to its alternatives. *Psychological Review, 93*(2), 136–53.

88. My Central New Jersey.com (2011, May 20). School ads a $ign of the times. Author. Retrieved May 23, 2011, from http://www.mycentraljersey.com/article/20110522/NJOPINION0102/305220004/School-ads-a-ign-of-the-times.

89. Jennings, R. (2011, March 17). School buses give ads a ride. *USA Today*. Retrieved April 18, 2011, from http://www.usatoday.com/news/nation/2011-03-16-schoolbusads16_ST_N.htm; Campaign for a Commercial-Free Childhood (2011). School bus ad action center. Retrieved September 9, 2011, from http://www.commercialfreechildhood.org/actions/schoolbusads.html.

90. Campaign for a Commercial-Free Childhood (2011). School bus ad action center. Retrieved September 9, 2011, from http://www.commercialfreechildhood.org/actions/schoolbusads.html; Jennings, R. (2011, March 17). School buses give ads a ride. *USA Today*. Retrieved April 18, 2011, from http://www.usatoday.com/news/nation/2011-03-16-schoolbusads16_ST_N.htm; Russell, B. Z. (2011). School bus ads bill resurfaces with amendments. *Spokesman-Review*. Retrieved April 18, 2011, from http://www.spokesman.com/blogs/boise/2011/mar/24/school-bus-ads-bill-resurfaces-amendments/.

91. Hatch, K. (2011, May 13). Committee gives preliminary OK to ads in Ashland schools. MetroWest Daily News. Retrieved May 24, 2011, from http://www.metrowestdailynews.com/archive/x1046545928/Committee-gives-preliminary-OK-to-ads-in-Ashland-schools#ixzz1NJUppbuY; Slater, S. (2011,

July 21). Dallas County Schools places ads on sides of buses to raise money. *WFAA.com*. Retrieved July 26, 2011, from http://www.wfaa.com/news/local/ Dallas-County-Schools-places-ads-on-sides-of-buses-to-raise-money- 125993698.html; Tuggle, K. (2011, July 29). Will School Bus Ads Drive Revenue for Cash-Strapped Districts? *Foxbusiness.com*. Retrieved August 1, 2010, from http://www.foxbusiness.com/personal-finance/2011/07/29/school-districts- rolling-in-profit-with-bus-side-advertisements/#ixzz1UTTTAuYP.

92. Aiekens, D. (2011, March 14). Schools explore advertising as idea for extra revenue. *St. Cloud Times*. Retrieved March 23, 2011, from http://www. sctimes.com/article/20110315/NEWS01/103150021/1009 [no longer available].

6

ASSESSING THE INTENSITY OF THE THREATS COMMERCIALISM POSES TO CHILDREN'S WELL-BEING

Parents and students tend to regard the school as an authoritative source of reliable information. And since they do, advertising and marketing in schools carries a legitimacy that it would not have in any other marketing venue. The perceived legitimacy of marketing and advertising in schools amplifies their manipulative power and thus the threat they pose to children's psychological well-being, to their physical health, and to the integrity of the education they receive. Of course, not all school advertising and marketing programs are likely to be equally harmful. The specific features of the sponsor, product or service, point of view, and advertising medium may each affect the intensity of the threat posed by a given marketing activity. For this reason, school board members, parents, and policy makers need real-world guidelines for assessing the negative impacts of specific marketing programs.

UNDERSTANDING THE INTENSITY OF THE THREAT POSED BY MARKETING

Marketing in schools is, in our judgment, a relatively greater threat to children's well-being:

- *When the marketing directly targets children.* Many ads, for example, target children via their placement in areas of school property that children frequent. Thus, ads "wrapped" on student lockers target children, whereas ads in an employee newsletter, or in a parking garage not used by K-12 students, do not.[1]
- *When the advertising is for brands and products children use.* On the Orange County Public Schools website, for example, photos show advertising at football games for Florida's Blood Centers, Channel 47, and Tostitos.[2] Of the three, Tostitos is likely the most compelling to students.[3]
- *When the marketing is present in the classroom.* The classroom is the school location most central to student life. Advertisements in the classroom are more likely to threaten children educationally than advertisements in school locations more physically distant from their learning. In recognition of the power of classroom advertising, the North Penn School District banned advertising in its classrooms in 2012.[4]
- *When the marketing is integrated into sponsored educational materials or programs.* Sometimes marketing in the classroom is more subtle than a straightforward advertisement. When corporations create educational materials that promote their worldview or sponsor school activities that encourage students to view them as benefactors rather than self-interested entities, the stealthy marketing of the brand tends to go unrecognized.
- *When the marketing takes up school time.* When students take a Field Trip Factory–designed class trip to the local Petco store, it takes up their class time. Field Trip Factory also provides a coordinated curriculum that can be used in class in preparation for the trip.[5]
- *When the marketing contradicts curriculum lessons.* "Pouring rights" contracts present a clear example of how advertising can contradict school nutrition policy. In Maine, students are taught to avoid foods of minimal nutritional value. Yet according to a 2012 representative study of high schools in the state, 85 percent of the schools have some form of advertising—usually several instances—for foods of minimal nutritional value.[6]

- *When the marketing is directly harmful to children's health or psychological well-being.* The Los Angeles Unified School District (LAUSD) specifically prohibits "sponsorship by corporations that market, sell or produce products that may be harmful to children including, but not limited to, tobacco, alcohol, firearms, gambling, or high fat and calorie foods and drinks."[7]

By addressing both the sponsor and the product, LAUSD policy acknowledges that the two are connected, particularly if the brand is well known. If, hypothetically, a local McDonald's franchise were to provide salads for an LAUSD event and be recognized with a banner that says, "Thank you, McDonald's, for your support!" as per the district's sponsorship guidelines, Big Macs could not help being subtly promoted also.[8] Popular McTeacher nights, disallowed by LAUSD but embraced by many districts, support every product McDonald's offers.[9]

Clearly, when only parents see an advertisement, or receive information about a corporate sponsorship, the threat is minimized. Quiet donations to school foundations or ads such as those in the Orange County Public Schools employee newsletter similarly pose little threat to children's well-being.[10] More threatening would be ads on a marquee in front of the school that students might see but that actually target passing adult traffic.[11] More threatening still are ads and other promotional materials that directly target students.

HOW THREATS CAN INTERACT

A commercializing activity in school may pose multiple threats simultaneously. Consider, for example, the threat posed to children's health associated with a highly visible educational program sponsored by the fast food company Panda Express. When the company sponsors an elementary school's adoption of FranklinCovey's Leader in Me program,[12] the school becomes a Panda Express School and the children identify as Panda Express Kids. When Lakeview Elementary School in Kirkland, Washington, became a Panda Express School, the company sent free food and a big "Panda" to the presentation night at which the school introduced the program to the parents and students.[13]

The sponsorship and supporting activities "brand" the children and encourage uncritical acceptance of Panda Express menu items, a potential health threat because of the high levels of sodium in most of the menu items and the high sugar content of the numerous soft drinks on offer.

Figure 6.1 displays our conception of how the various threats posed by school commercializing activities may interact in the real world.

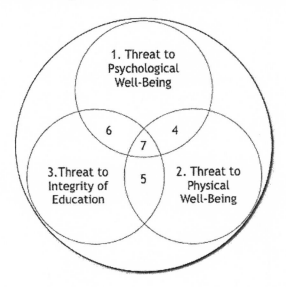

Figure 6.1.   The Interaction of Threats to Children's Psychological Well-Being, Physical Well-Being, and Education

Although the graphic representation in Figure 6.1 may suggest equal and tidy relationships among the types of potential threat posed by commercializing activities in school, in reality the nature and power of the threats will necessarily vary by the particular activity and the context. The examples below illustrate what our analysis looks like when applied to real-life situations:

Example of a Threat Primarily to Children's Psychological Well-Being

Dove's Real Beauty campaign won *Advertising Age*'s recognition as the top campaign of the twenty-first century (so far) and is credited with increasing the brand's soap sales from $2.5 billion to $4 billion.[14] The centerpiece of the ad campaign was a video showing women describing themselves to a portrait artist more critically than did someone else who had just met them; the campaign argued for a broadening of the definition of beauty.

The video "went viral," and the campaign was lauded for challenging the popular conception of beauty. Critics, however, pointed out that Dove's continuing emphasis on physical beauty was neither unusual nor empowering for women.[15] In a 2013 *Salon* article Erin Keane noted, for example:

> The only interesting thing Dove has done since it began this campaign to sell soap in 2004 is overtly shift the emphasis from sexual attraction to peer approval. The real take-away is still that women should care whether a stranger thinks she is beautiful. That's not radical—it's the thesis of every beauty product ad campaign ever.

Consistent with its advertisements, Dove's Self-Esteem Project encourages people to support its "important mission" by engaging in activities that can range from "starting a conversation with a girl in your life to leading self-esteem building workshops in classrooms or to even choosing to buy Dove products."

The company's branded Real Beauty School Program brought the mission to classrooms, with activities and conversation starters designed to raise self-esteem by exposing students to the manipulation of images in the media and engaging them in conversation about how retouched images influence their ideas of beauty and their self-esteem.[16]

Although portrayed as a worthwhile effort to boost girls' self-esteem, the Dove-branded school program is problematic. Even as the materials alert girls to the power of others, especially the media, to influence their own perceptions of beauty and their self-image, their focus is on girls' body image and physical beauty as their primary source of self-esteem.[17]

Included as part of the materials is a list of "companies that benefit from making us think our bodies are imperfect." The list includes "gyms, diet industry, make-up and perfume products, plastic surgeons, [and] pharmaceutical companies." Notably absent from the list are companies that sell body care products. Dove itself markets deodorants and body-firming cream, and its parent company, Unilever, markets wrinkle cream (Pond's Rejuveness) and diet aids (Slim-Fast).

The absence of Dove and Unilever from the list of "companies that make us think our bodies are imperfect" betrays the actual purpose of the ad campaign: to sell more Dove products by attaching the brand to a perceived positive value—a positive value to which Unilever has no particular attachment. Unilever's Axe brand, for example, markets itself to adolescent boys by capitalizing on stereotypical images of girls—brainless beauties who are powerless in their attraction to Axe-scented males.[18]

Example of a Threat Primarily to Children's Physical Well-Being

The New York Jets football team runs several programs in New York and New Jersey public schools. The team partners with the Robert Wood Johnson Foundation and the American Dairy Association and Dairy Council, Inc., in its *Eat Right, Move More* campaign, which encourages schools to provide sixty minutes of exercise for students daily and students to make healthy choices in the cafeteria.[19] The campaign also encourages schools to make their meals healthier and creative via a contest that recognizes schools with the "most creative meal selections" that exceed state and federal guidelines each year. The grand prize–winning school wins $15,000, and is honored both at a Jets home game and a by a school visit from a player.[20] *Eat Right, Move More* is a good example of a relatively nonthreatening cause marketing effort designed to benefit both children and sponsors.

The team's partnership with the Public Schools Athletic League (PSAL) is more problematic. The Jets donated $150,000 to the PSAL in October 2014 as part of its continuing support of the *Heads Up!* program.[21] According to Eric Goldstein, CEO of the office of school sports services at the Department of Education,

> We're really celebrating the contribution the New York Jets make to the New York City Department of Education and the PSAL. Without

the help of the Jets, year on year on year, we wouldn't have 54 football teams, we wouldn't have 50 girls flag football teams, and we wouldn't have several thousand students engaged in the crucial activity of high school football sports.[22]

In prior years the *Heads Up!* program, like *Eat Right, Move More*, may also have been considered a relatively nonthreatening pro-social effort, with the benefit to the team of promoting football as a sport for students to engage in as both players and spectators. Now, however, with evidence mounting about brain injuries that result from playing football, encouraging children to play football can only be considered a health threat—even if part of the donation was used to recondition all the helmets in the PSAL.[23]

Example of a Threat Primarily to Children's Education

In 2012, timed to coordinate with NBC's launch of the new musical drama series *Smash*, NBC and iTheatrics initiated the promotional program *Smash: Make a Musical*. Its ostensible goal was to "create sustainable musical theater programs in underserved schools nationwide."[24] Schools in twenty cities across the United States were encouraged to apply for the program, with ten winning schools selected to have a full Make a Musical program installed in their schools and an additional twenty schools awarded an MTI Broadway Junior Collection "ShowKit" of resources.[25]

Although the idea of initiating sustainable musical theater programs in schools—especially in underserved schools—is laudable, this program did not by any means uniformly help students. In fact, in several ways it did them a disservice. First, it appropriated school time from the approved curriculum for the application process and then, if the school was lucky enough to win, for participation in the program itself.

In the instance of *Smash: Make a Musical*, instructional time spent on musical theater was not "wasted" time, but it was time not designated or approved by the professionals charged with determining school curriculum. Instead, instructional time was diverted to musical theater only because NBC provided incentives. (Many corporations use similar strategies to appropriate instructional time, such as—described elsewhere—

when Panda Express pays for a branded character-education program, or when Nike sponsors a classroom.[26])

In this example, anything students learned or experienced as part of the activity was necessarily bound up with marketing for the TV show. Students were not learning just about musical theater, but rather about musical theater in the context of *Smash: The Musical*.

Finally, irrespective of whether they won or lost the contest, most of the students involved spent a lot of time and effort preparing their application and along the way learning about NBC's program. In many ways the students who lost were more important from a marketing standpoint than the students who won—there were so many more of them.

As it turned out, the series *Smash* was canceled in May 2013, and we have been unable to find any material on the Internet attesting to continuation of *Smash: Make a Musical* after 2013. This illustrates the manner in which this type of marketing program inflects the school's program with no long-term commitment to the school or its students. *Smash: Make a Musical* was created solely because a corporation had a product to push.

Examples of Threats to Children's Psychological Well-Being and Their Education

Entrepreneur Christopher Whittle introduced Channel One News to American classrooms in 1989, offering free television and transmission equipment in a contract that required students to watch a daily twelve-minute news broadcast with two minutes of commercials. In its early years Channel One News was controversial, spurring the National PTA to call for legislation to prohibit businesses from bringing into the school any program that would require students to view advertising in exchange for donations, which some states enacted (e.g., California's Education Code § 35182.5[27]).

Over the years Channel One was bought and sold, and people tended to forget about it—including the National PTA, which archived its resolution condemning commercialism. According to the child advocacy group Campaign for a Commercial-Free Childhood (CCFC), as recently as 2012, 5.5 million students were still forced to watch a daily broadcast that included two minutes of acknowledged commercial time plus unacknowledged product placements (for a total of thirty-two hours per year of displaced instructional time).[28]

Watching Channel One at school has been associated with a variety of psychological threats. In 1993, a study found that children attending schools with Channel One were more materialistic than students attending schools without it.[29]

In the 2011–2012 school year, Channel One began to target elementary in addition to middle and high school students, via its partnership with Promethean, a company that produces whiteboards.[30]

In 2012, CCFC found problematic advertising on websites advertised on the broadcast and its associated website, channelone.com, which is promoted on the broadcast.[31] Ads for websites operated by Channel One's parent company, Alloy Media and Marketing, such as teen.com and gURL.com, contain highly sexualized content, such as racy photos of TV stars and pages on such topics as "How are you when it comes to playing hard to get?" and "Can you leave your house without makeup?"[32] Hypersexualization like this is linked to pressing mental health problems for girls, including eating disorders, low self-esteem, depression, and poor sexual health.[33]

In May 2014, the educational and trade publisher Houghton Mifflin Harcourt purchased Channel One. Although the business model of trading equipment for student eyes mostly remains, Channel One currently offers an advertising-free, subscription-based option.[34]

Examples of Threats to Children's Education and Their Physical Well-Being

Coca-Cola's sponsorship of school playgrounds is accompanied at least in some cases by playground signage.[35] And when the Howe Elementary School of Excellence on Chicago's West Side received a $25,000 recreation grant for a new playground from Coca-Cola's Sprite Spark Parks program, the children wrote thank-you letters to Coke during school hours. For homework, they made healthy resolutions.[36] Nutrition curricula teach children to avoid sweetened soft drinks, and the beverage companies themselves have acknowledged the potential problem with calories associated with such drinks in their voluntary effort to remove them from school sales around the United States.[37]

Both Coca-Cola and its competitor PepsiCo have launched several health and wellness initiatives designed to promote physical activity and movement, in response to concerns that their products may contribute to the obesity problem.[38] Although, as we discussed in chapter 4, these types of initiatives are actually recommended by the Federal Trade Commission,[39] they are problematic in that they shift the onus for obesity from the corporation's responsibility to market healthy food to the consumer's responsibility for making healthy choices.[40]

When that change in conversation takes place in school, as it did with the Howe Elementary children's homework assignment, it shows how corporate involvement can distort what children learn in school. In a situation in which the school just received a $25,000 playground from Coca-Cola, it is only reasonable for the teachers to consider the corporation's view of its products' relationship to obesity, and to present the issue "fairly"—not as an issue of whether sweetened soft drinks are to be avoided, but rather in terms of balance, moderation, and sensible choices. How could they possibly be expected to react otherwise? And how could the children, who just received the playground, think of Coca-Cola as anything but benevolent?

Examples of Threats to Children's Physical and Psychological Well-Being

Axe and Old Spice are brands notorious for marketing masculinity to teen boys.[41] Axe, known for its edgy ads, has probably been banned in more high schools.[42] Old Spice has had some success in staying in schools by connecting its brand with high school football. In the early 2000s it sponsored the SchoolSports Rivalry Tour and the Old Spice Red Zone High School Showcase, and in 2013 it involved high school coaches in nominating their top players to be awarded Old Spice Player of the Year.[43] Psychologist and author Lyn Mikel Brown claims that such products preach an extreme, singular definition of masculinity at a time in their development when boys are grappling uneasily with identity. She argues that these products "cultivate anxiety in boys at younger and younger ages about what it means to man up, to be the kind of boy they're told girls will want and other boys will respect."[44]

In addition, Old Spice products, like many other personal care items marketed to children and teens, contain chemicals that may increase users' risk for certain health problems.[45] The perfumes in these products contain "secret ingredients" that are legalized by a loophole in the Federal Fair Packaging and Labeling Act of 1973. In a laboratory study of seventeen popular perfumes (including products actively marketed to children such as Hannah Montana Secret Celebrity for girls and Old Spice and Axe body sprays for boys), the Environmental Working Group found that the perfumes contained an average of fourteen secret chemicals, ten "sensitizing" chemicals that can lead to allergic reactions, four known hormone disruptors, and twelve chemicals that have not been assessed for safety by the industry or the government.[46] Adolescents, who are going through significant hormonal changes in their transition to adulthood, may be particularly sensitive to exposures to trace levels of hormone-disrupting chemicals.[47]

Examples of Threats to Children's Psychological Well-Being, Physical Well-Being, and Education

The nonprofit organization Junior Achievement (JA) has opened Biz-Town simulation centers for children in more than twenty cities around the United States.[48] The Chick-fil-A Foundation, AT&T, Delta Air Lines, SunTrust, and other sponsors fund the Chick-fil-A Foundation Discovery Center that opened in 2013 in Atlanta, Georgia.[49] Annually, 30,000 middle-schoolers are expected to take school trips to this Discovery Center, which consists of a JA BizTown and JA Financial Park. There, they "work" for one of the sponsor companies and "shop" in the BizTown shop for products provided by other sponsor companies. As one JA appeal to potential sponsor companies put it, BizTown

> introduces students to the free enterprise system through active participation in a simulated town filled with citizens who buy, sell, consume and create products and/or services. Your help in providing select products and services can create a wide variety of positive opportunities for your company, your employers and even your business partners.[50]

As in the case of NBC's *Smash: Make a Musical*, described above, the Atlanta children's time both during the trip and in their four-week preparation for it in school is diverted to a pursuit that benefits the sponsors' interest, which here is indoctrinating them into the consumer system and introducing them to brands that (the companies hope) they will develop fond memories of and want to do business with later. In other words, it contributes to the development of the consumer worldview that emphasizes material rather than nonmaterial pursuits, and to the threats to psychological well-being associated with such a worldview.[51] It also seeks to "brand" students so that they favor particular products and services.

A trip to BizTown is certainly colorful, and Junior Achievement of Georgia works with local school systems to align its curriculum to Georgia Performance Standards and to the Common Core standards, in an effort to support rather than displace the regular curriculum. Even if the curriculum aligns with the Common Core, however, the primary goal of BizTown is to serve the interests of the sponsors. It is designed to teach children the message that the sponsors want to convey, not to think critically about anything related to any of the sponsor companies or about the validity of the economic system that supports those sponsors.

Who exactly the sponsors are at any time in any BizTown determines to what extent health threats are implicated. In Atlanta, Chick-fil-A is the primary sponsor. Some of the thirty thousand children each year work for the simulated Chick-fil-A, and all the children are exposed to it. Although not all of Chick-fil-A's offerings are high in fat, sugar, and/or salt, many are, and are unhealthy when consumed to excess.

Determining the Extent of the Threat Commercializing Activities Pose in Your School

One way of thinking about the extent of the threat posed by a particular commercializing activity is that the greater number of threats implicated, the greater the overall threat to children's well-being. Thus, Atlanta's JA BizTown is especially problematic because it is associated with threats to children's psychological well-being, physical well-being, and education.

As we have already noted, however, not all threats are equal. At times, stakeholders may disagree about whether a particular marketing campaign is harmful or about which marketing campaigns are the most harmful. Some may be more concerned about the health implications of consistent advertising of soft drink brands in school hallways, for example, than by the intensive, but one-time and more culturally normative JA BizTown experience. By considering the relative threat to children's well-being caused by various commercializing activities, and the nature of the threats they pose, stakeholders can better evaluate whether the various "school-business partnerships" offered to them are really worth what they hope to gain from them.

CRAFTING POLICY RESPONSES TO THE THREAT TO CHILDREN'S WELL-BEING POSED BY COMMERCIALIZING ACTIVITIES IN SCHOOL

While it is practical and worthwhile for parents, educators, and policy makers to consider the relative threats posed by various marketing programs, our research has led us to conclude that commercializing activities do not belong in school at all. In our view, the dictum "first, do no harm" should be applied to these activities. Its wisdom underlies the requirement for new pharmaceuticals to be tested and reviewed before being allowed on the market. There are good reasons why drugs are not approved for use until they are proven to cause no harm to potential patients and to provide the benefits claimed.

In contrast, current policy with respect to commercializing activities in schools seems to rest on the assumption that marketing is benign unless proven to be harmful. Our reading of the available evidence, however, suggests that the opposite is the case: marketing to children should be considered harmful unless proven to be benign.

Marketing in schools favors special interests by allowing access to students to any company that buys it by offering money or programming or has a connection to a marketing company that has negotiated a contract with the school. Although school or district policy may claim not to favor its sponsors,[52] in reality, children are likely to perceive products, services, and viewpoints marketed in their school to be approved by the school.[53]

Moreover, social forces in the school setting such as a "reciprocity" effect that calls for conformity to sponsors' wishes in exchange for money spent on advertising or sponsorships[54] can lead to an environment of implicit support for sponsors' products and worldviews.[55]

It is important to note that marketing takes place in an education system that is already inequitable. While advertising schemes such as the placement of marquees to be seen by local traffic are most valuable in higher-income districts,[56] the focus of many harmful marketing activities is on urban schools that serve low-income children.[57] In these situations, the districts are so desperate for money that they are willing to overlook the threats marketing may pose to the children's longer-term well-being.

Finally, as examples such as JA BizTown and NBC's musical theater program illustrate, free-will corporate donations or corporate marketing programs are not reliable or appropriate sources of school funding. Such contributions are dependent on the corporation's business interests, not on an obligation to provide a steady source of funding to schools independent of those interests.

From a business perspective, this is uncontroversial: corporations are legally bound to maximize their stockholders' profit, not to prioritize education or any other outside interest. A corporation's claim to an interest in a particular community because it has customers or employees in that community cannot be considered a valid argument for depending on it as a source of funding or for prioritizing its concerns in the education of the community's children. If the corporation moves its plant to a less expensive location or shutters an unsuccessful store, the corporation's interest in that location ends.[58]

State legislatures may also be capricious, but they are, at least, subject to democratic control and pressure. And because it takes so long to shift state funding formulas in any given direction, they are inherently more stable than corporate largesse.

It can be tempting to school and district administrators to accept or even solicit corporate sponsorships that promise to fill the holes in their budgets. Likewise, it can be tempting to follow the advice to "never look a gift horse in the mouth." Our analysis suggests, however, that in the case of commercializing activities in schools, a critical look is definitely called for.

Commercializing programs in schools bring with them serious threats to children's education and to their psychological and physical well-being. By considering the various threats likely to be presented by various marketing programs, and by considering factors that might amplify or reduce those threats, stakeholders can begin to craft policies that protect children from the harmful effects of school commercialism.

STATE POLICY APPROACHES TO SCHOOL COMMERCIALISM

Given the vulnerability of children to the value system embedded in school commercializing activities, it is important to understand where and how legislators have intervened to offer some measure of protection from what has become the ever-more-pervasive presence of marketing in schools.

Here, we review legislation that permits or forbids specific kinds of marketing activities. We intend this review to provide some sense of legislative possibilities—and of the distance between what policy makers *might* choose to do and what they *are* choosing to do to in terms of protecting children from the threats of unbridled commercialism.

In general, legislators have taken four basic approaches in framing statutory responses to school commercialism. They can (1) permit any or all marketing activities; (2) prohibit and/or restrict outright all or certain types of marketing activity; (3) delegate to some other entity, such as a school board, the authority to determine which marketing activities, if any, will be permitted; and (4) require that school boards engage in specific processes for considering a marketing activity before it can be approved or implemented. [59]

Each approach is discussed below.

Policy That Permits Commercializing Activities in Schools

Despite concerns school bus operators express about its potential safety implications, advertising on school buses has frequently been proposed—and implemented—in response to funding shortfalls. [60] The following states allow advertising on the inside or outside (or both) of school buses: Arizona, California, Colorado, Florida, Indiana, Michigan, Minnesota, New Mexico, Nevada, New Jersey, Pennsylvania, Rhode Island, Tennessee, Texas, Utah, and Wisconsin. [61]

Policy That Prohibits or Restricts Commercializing Activities in Schools

Legislation in New York and California tries to distinguish between "commercial activity" on the one hand and "sponsorship," or indications by districts of "appreciation" for support, on the other. Both limit "commercial activity" in schools while allowing "sponsorship." (Unlike these states, we consider sponsorship to be commercial activity because both promote the values of commercialism and encourage the use of certain brands.)

California's Education Code § 35182.5 allows districts to "sell advertising, products, or services on a nonexclusive basis," and to "post public signs indicating the district's appreciation for the support of a person or business for the district's education program."[62]

New York State Regents Rule § 23.2 prohibits school districts from entering into contracts, agreements, or arrangements that provide for "commercial promotional activity on school premises." However, this rule explicitly allows for commercial "sponsorship" of school activities. Such sponsorship allows a company to sponsor or underwrite an activity on school premises that "does not involve the commercial promotion of a particular product or service."[63]

Some legislation targets particular kinds of products rather than particular types of activity. For example, Maine prohibits brand-specific advertising on school grounds for foods of minimal nutritional value (FMNV).[64] While much advertising for FMNV was likely removed from schools as a result of this legislation, one 2012 study found that most Maine high schools still contained several cases of such advertising.[65] Enforcement is beyond the scope of our current discussion, but we'll note here that the impact of legislation where it does exist is likely to be weakened if provision isn't made for enforcement.

There is some evidence that state-level restrictions have an impact. For example, a 2009 article compared New York, which has imposed the restrictions described above, with Pennsylvania, which is completely silent on school commercialism.[66] Using a definition of commercialism that, like ours, considers sponsorship a form of commercial activity, researchers Brian Brent and Stephen Lunden surveyed 307 New York districts and 197 Pennsylvania districts. They found that compared to the 97 percent of Pennsylvania districts that engaged in one or more commercial activity, only 75 percent of New York districts did so.[67] This is a substantive difference—and yet three out of four New York schools still were found to engage in some form of school commercialism. It is evident that even in a state with restrictions, if those restrictions are relatively weak, school commercialism may remain rampant.

Policy That Delegates Authority to School Boards or Other Entities

Florida, North Carolina, and Wisconsin have comprehensive legislation that delegates authority for developing advertising policies to local school boards, including policies related to the distribution and posting of promotional materials and literature.[68] Such an approach aligns with the desire of local communities to manage their own schools.

However, an implication of letting school boards develop advertising policy is that it may make the boards vulnerable to costly lawsuits when they turn away a litigation-minded advertiser.[69] In a potentially precedent-setting case, when the Massachusetts Bay Transportation Authority's advertising policy was challenged in 1993, a federal court ruled that the policy was unconstitutional. The judge in that case explained that a transit service "cannot open its transit car door to public service advertising and hang only its favorite posters."[70]

A case from Palm Beach County, Florida, brings this point back to school districts. The owner of a local business, Happy/Fun Tutoring, was reaping about twelve clients per month from the signs he had hung at three high schools until the district made him remove the signs, claiming that his employment history—as an actor in and producer of pornography—violated its advertising policy. He sued the school board in May 2013, for violating his civil rights and preventing him from earning a living.[71]

Sabrina Adler, of ChangeLab Solutions, points out that schools' unique educational mission provides districts with more leeway than transportation authorities have with respect to potential First Amendment challenges to their rules limiting certain types of advertising. Importantly, however, and perhaps at issue in the Happy/Fun case, districts must apply their rules consistently and fairly, and be "content neutral."[72]

Policy That Requires a Process for Considering a Commercializing Activity

California's education code, discussed above, specifies strict rules for districts interested in entering into contracts that would provide for the sale or advertising of "carbonated beverages or non-nutritious beverages" or "non-nutritious food" within the district, or that would provide for the provision of electronic services or products, such as Channel One, that require the dissemination of advertising to students.[73] Districts are required to hold public hearings before they can enter into such food- or electronic-related contracts. Additionally, with respect to electronic advertising, the district must provide notice to parents of the impending advertising, allow parents to opt their children out of the program or service, and demonstrate both that the product or service in question is integral to students' education and that the district cannot afford to provide it without the contract that provides for advertising.[74]

CURRENT SCHOOL COMMERCIALISM POLICY LANDSCAPE

A 2004 Government Accountability Office report offers a baseline for state legislative interest in school commercialism.[75] The GAO found that thirty-two states had adopted some form of legislation relating to school commercialism and that then-existing legislation did little to restrict marketing in schools generally. Instead, bills were piecemeal rather than comprehensive, addressing only a narrow aspect of school commercialism, such as product sales (see appendix B).

In the ten years since the GAO report was published, any legal restrictions on school commercialism in state law appear to have done little to prevent advertising in schools from proliferating. Although there is a large body of nonsystematic evidence from press reports and other sources that school districts continue to adopt advertising programs and/ or establish advertising policies, we wanted to develop a sharper and more accurate picture by reviewing school commercialism-related legislative activity for the three-year period 2011–2014.[76]

Current State Legislative and Policy Landscape

We assessed state legislative activity in several ways. First, we searched state and national legislative databases to identify bills that addressed school commercialism. In addition, we searched websites and reviewed newsletters from organizations concerned with commercialism and children or with marketing to children. Finally, we reviewed academic research on and analysis of the impact of marketing to children; conducted regular web searches for keywords associated with school commercialism issues; and conducted interviews with policy experts at education- and commercialism-focused organizations.[77]

From these various sources, we sought information on innovations in marketing, on how school policy makers described school marketing arrangements, and on the positions of various education and noneducation policy organizations toward school commercialism. Together with findings of our legislative search, these sources helped us pull together a picture of the current legislative landscape with respect to school commercialism.

We conducted searches for state legislation using the Open States database (openstates.org) and for federal legislation using the Congress.gov database of legislation of the U.S. Congress (https://beta.congress.gov/legislation).[78]

Our review of 2011–2014 legislative activity found very little legislation related to school commercialism (see appendix C).[79] New Jersey and Tennessee were the only two states to pass legislation directly related to marketing or advertising in schools. In 2011, New Jersey began permitting advertising on school buses.[80] Tennessee has allowed school bus advertising in some form since 1997. In 2012, the state slightly loosened its policy on school bus advertising by removing a limitation on the specifics related to the advertisements' lettering.[81]

In California, the state's school nutrition requirements allow districts and schools to set policy within certain specific limitations. In 2013, the state legislature enacted a variety of changes to the state's school food requirements, among them a few minor adjustments to restrictions on the sale of food and drink items that do not meet the regular state nutrition requirements for what may be sold to students during the school day.[82] The most significant of these with respect to commercialism is removal of the requirement that only students be allowed to sell food at elementary school fundraisers.

Finally, as part of its abortion policy, Kansas law now prohibits districts or schools from accepting any "course materials or instruction relating to human sexuality or sexually transmitted diseases" from an abortion services provider or any of its employees or volunteers.[83]

Current Federal Legislative and Policy Landscape

Compared to state legislation, federal legislation generally has relatively less direct impact on local school policies; and our legislative search found no bills relevant to school commercialism either introduced or passed in 2011–2014. Still, federal interest in agriculture and school lunch programs has generated some policy with implications for schools, as has federal interest in student privacy, which is addressed in the Protection of Pupil Rights Amendment (PPRA) and in the Family Educational Rights and Privacy Act (FERPA).[84] Advances in data collection and analysis have turned children's privacy rights into a "hot-button" issue that we will address in the next chapter.

Federal policy specifically addresses the promotion of local agriculture and governs the sale of food in schools, either as the school lunch or as so-called "competitive foods" sold outside the school lunch program in school cafeterias or other venues, including vending machines, school stores, and snack bars.[85]

As we discussed in chapter 4, the U.S. Department of Agriculture finalized updated rules for school meals in 2012 and for competitive food in schools in 2013.[86] Together, these rules limit the calories, salt, and sugar content of foods available to children in schools. Opponents, including the School Nutrition Association, are contesting the rules' implementation.[87]

As it now stands, schools are free to accept marketing for foods that the new rules prohibit them from selling. In chapter 4, we noted that both food marketing activists and the USDA were aware of this problem. And in February 2014 the USDA proposed a rule designed to strengthen school wellness policies by addressing food marketing. Unfortunately, the rule as proposed has serious loopholes.[88]

Although the proposed rule specifically prohibits a broad array of marketing approaches, it also fails to prohibit quite a few. Branding on "durable equipment" may continue, as may the use of sponsored educational materials, school visits by brand mascots (e.g., Ronald McDonald, who visited fourteen schools in Central Kentucky alone in April 2014), or school-sponsored off-site events, such as McTeacher Nights. The proposed rule also allows schools to continue to advertise food products of little nutritional value after school hours, and to continue to advertise products that meet the nutrition standards, such as diet sodas, all day.[89]

If the USDA's rules are fully implemented, they may improve the nutritional value of the specific food and beverage products sold in schools while at the same time reinforcing commercialism by allowing marketing for brands whose products outside of school are not at all "healthier" as a normal element in the school environment. Thus, by permitting marketing of approved products, the rules open the door to increased marketing more generally.[90]

Finally, in 2014, bills introduced by Rosa DeLauro in the House and by Richard Blumenthal in the Senate would have denied a tax deduction "for marketing directed at children to promote the consumption of food of poor nutritional quality."[91] Although neither of these bills became law, the explicit inclusion of in-school marketing in their definition of marketing was a significant recognition of this practice by the federal government.

Interviews and Media Searches

Our legislative search found only two state laws specifically intended to address school commercialism, and those statutes expanded rather than restricted it. To get a better understanding of legislators' behavior, we interviewed policy experts from a variety of organizations concerned with education policy or marketing in schools to explore the organizations' positions on commercializing activities in schools, what the respondents knew about legislation regarding such activities, and where we might look further to find relevant legislation.

In addition, we conducted a search of newspaper references to commercializing activities in schools. Having systematically searched the popular press for references to commercialism from 1990 to 2006,[92] we updated our data by searching the ten highest-circulation newspapers in the United States for school commercialism-related articles published between January 2011 and June 2014, using the search terms from our prior research.

Finally, we conducted Internet searches using the Google (www.google.com), Bing (www.bing.com), and Mention (www.mention.net) search engines, and regularly reviewed relevant websites, to keep tabs on mentions of commercializing activities in the news (see appendix D).

MISSING IN ACTION: LEGISLATION AND REGULATION THAT RESTRICTS OR BANS SCHOOL COMMERCIALISM

There appear to be several reasons why there has been so little legislative or regulatory activity aimed at banning or sharply restricting commercializing activities in schools.

Industry Opposition Is Fierce

The advertising and food and beverage industries vigorously oppose policy that would limit their behavior and have reacted strongly toward any perceived regulatory threat. Food and beverage industry groups spent over $175 million lobbying between January 2009 and May 2012, much of it fighting the voluntary guidelines for food marketing to children that Congress had requested from the Interagency Working Group.[93] In 2006–2008, when there was no specific threat to their industry on the horizon, these groups spent $83 million.[94] In addition, the industry (mostly the American Beverage Association) spent $3.9 million in the fall of 2012 to defeat two "soda tax" initiatives on local ballots in Richmond and El Monte, California. Proponents of the bills (mostly California Center for Public Health Advocacy) spent $66,546.[95]

Even as it opposed government regulatory efforts, the industry expanded certain self-regulatory activities. Beverage companies have focused their efforts on reducing the calorie count of the beverages sold in schools, in conjunction with the American Beverage Association and Alliance for a Healthier Generation.[96] Both in schools and outside them, the Children's Food and Beverage Advertising Initiative (CFBAI) self-regulates advertising to children.

As discussed in chapter 4, the CFBAI has grown to seventeen member corporations, and on December 31, 2013, it implemented the category-specific, uniform nutrition criteria that it issued in July 2011.[97] By establishing advertising standards for whole categories of products, these criteria improve on prior criteria that varied from company to company.[98] Such moves seem intended to and appear to have been effective at heading off external regulation.

The CFBAI reported "excellent" compliance on the part of member companies that pledged not to advertise branded foods and beverages in elementary schools.[99] However, the CFBAI makes no commitment regarding middle or high schools, and its restrictions in elementary schools do not include such activities as fundraising programs, provision of sponsored educational materials, sponsorship of incentive programs and other programs and activities, sponsored public service announcements, and sponsored gifts to adults on school campuses that children may see. Further, any sponsored items or programs may acknowledge the sponsor.[100]

In a September 2013 speech, Michelle Obama both praised and challenged the food and media industries, asking representatives "to do even more and move even faster to market responsibly to our kids."[101]

Educators Are Largely Unconcerned about School Commercialism

Our media search and interviews with leaders of organizations concerned with education policy indicate that schoolhouse commercialism is not a priority issue for many individuals and organizations.[102] Some organizations, such as StudentsFirst and the National School Boards Association, have never had any policy regarding commercialism.[103] Other organizations had been interested in commercialism at one time, but abandoned their positions as other issues have taken priority and as fundraising has become more of a concern. As mentioned above, the National PTA, for example, had adopted in 1990 a strongly worded resolution that explicitly called for federal regulation or legislation to eliminate certain types of commercial programs—particularly electronic marketing programs.[104] However, that resolution has since been archived.[105]

Similarly, the American Association of School Superintendents (AASA) adopted an anti-commercialism position in the early 1990s, but let it lapse. According to Bruce Hunter, who spoke regularly to superintendents around the country in his position as associate executive director for advocacy, policy, and communication at AASA, commercialism stopped arising among his constituents as an issue. He said, "Although there's talk about field houses and stadiums and scoreboards from commercial interests . . . it's never on the agenda that they want to discuss. It's not controversial at all. Or if it is, if people don't like it, they're not talking about it."[106] Finally the Education Commission of the States (ECS) had commercialism "on its radar" in the 1990s, but also shifted its attention.[107]

Passing Legislation Is Difficult and Expensive

Legislation or policy to eliminate or restrict commercializing activities in schools is difficult to pass: it requires extended effort, ample funds, and the ability to convince legislators and other stakeholders that the issue is even worth addressing. It also requires the ability to conduct the difficult political work necessary to get a law passed. [108]

Maine, with its 2007 legislation banning advertising of foods of minimal value in schools, provides an interesting example. [109] A public health activist who was involved in promoting that state's legislation noted that although that particular bill was relatively easy to pass because it focused on nonnutritious foods at a time when obesity was on the rise, it was still considerably weaker when it finally passed than it was when it was originally proposed. [110]

Josh Golin, associate director of the Campaign for a Commercial-Free Childhood (CCFC), has organized grass-roots opposition to legislative proposals for school bus advertising. He noted that with respect to legislation, "It's easier to play defense than offense." [111] Not only does "offense" require sustained effort, but it also requires a lot of money to compete with the big-money interests opposed to anticommercialism efforts. [112]

It Is Assumed That Marketing Benefits Schools Financially

Schools need money, and many people seem to assume that schools can make money from marketing—or at least that they can avoid spending money on items that corporations are willing to donate. [113] Stakeholders at all levels continue to present participation in commercializing programs in school as an innovative way to raise money for struggling districts, casting business in the role of valuable education partner that can "give back" funds to local communities, contribute to training the next generation of workers, and help schools and teachers function more effectively. [114]

In an interview, Eric Lerum, vice president of national policy at the education reform organization StudentsFirst, noted that policy makers are reluctant to adopt anything that cuts into potential revenue streams. And although research indicates that marketing arrangements bring little, if any, money into schools, the perception that they do, and the subsequent reluctance to interfere with commercial opportunities, persist. [115]

Brian Brent and Stephen Lunden's findings, cited earlier, support Lerum's observation.[116] They reported that although the school district administrators they interviewed reported only modest income from exclusive agreements in their schools (less than $10 per student per year, consistent with other similar research[117]), they also reported that they would still use exclusive agreements if they had more money at their disposal.[118] Brent and Lunden suggested that part of the reason for administrators' stance may be that "districts use exclusive agreements to signal their 'dogged' pursuit of nontax revenues, generating goodwill that can be accessed at budget time."[119]

A GATHERING STORM: DATA COLLECTION AND STUDENT PRIVACY

One area not addressed in our initial legislative search was student privacy. The collection of data from students has increased exponentially in the last several years. Although we didn't set out to study the relationship between gathering data on students and commercialism, as we saw privacy concerns cropping up in our media searches we realized that a whole new area of commercial threat had opened up. In the next chapter we explore the ways in which data collection in school presents a threat not only to students' privacy but also opens them up to marketing and advertising in and out of school. We also review legislative efforts to address this emerging threat to children's well-being.

NOTES

1. Draper, N. (2010, October 18). Schools open lockers to advertising. StarTribune.com. Retrieved November 11, 2014, from http://www.startribune.com/local/north/105226404.html; Orange County Public Schools (n.d.). Garage Advertising, Downtown Orlando. Author. Retrieved January 15, 2013, from https://www.ocps.net/es/cr/Advertisements/billboards,%20445%20W%20Amelia%20Parking%20Garage.pdf/ [no longer available]; Orange County Public Schools (n.d.). Advertising program. Author. Retrieved January 15, 2013, from https://www.ocps.net/es/cr/Pages/AdvertisingProgram.aspx/; Siatowski, B. (2012, June 14). Personal communication (telephone) with Faith Boninger.

2. Orange County Public Schools (n.d.). Sideline down marker bullseye caps. Author. Retrieved November 11, 2014, from https://www.ocps.net/es/cr/Advertisements/OCPS%20HS%20Football%20Bullseye%20Caps%202014.pdf; Orange County Public Schools (n.d.). Pro Crew Vests, 19 high school football crews. Author. Retrieved November 11, 2014, from https://www.ocps.net/es/cr/Advertisements/OCPS%20HS%20Football%20Pro%20Crew%20Vests%202014.pdf.

3. Muncy, J. A., & Hunt, S. D. (1984). Consumer involvement: Definitional issues and research directions. *Advances in Consumer Research, 11*, 193–96. Retrieved November 11, 2014, from http://www.acrwebsite.org/search/view-conference-proceedings.aspx?Id=6241.

4. North Penn School District (2012). North Penn School District School Board Policy: 2603(a): Administration: Advertising. Author. Retrieved January 16, 2013, from http://www.npenn.org/cms/lib/PA09000087/Centricity/Domain/26/Board_Policies/2000_Administration/2603%20-%20Advertising.pdf/.

5. Field Trip Factory (2012). Furs, Feathers and Fins. Retrieved September 7, 2014, from http://fieldtripfactory.com/programs/petco.

6. Polacsek, M., O'Roarke, K., O'Brien, L., Blum, J. W., & Donahue, S. (2012, March–April). Examining compliance with a statewide law banning junk food and beverage marketing in Maine schools. *Public Health Reports, 127*, 216–23. Retrieved January 28, 2013, from http://www.une.edu/news/2012/upload/PHRarticle-Marketing-Polacsek.pdf/.

7. Los Angeles Unified School District (2011, May 24). *Sponsorship Guidelines*. Los Angeles, CA: Author. Retrieved January 15, 2013, from http://notebook.lausd.net/portal/page?_pageid=33,501466&_dad=ptl&_schema=PTL_EP/.

8. Kanner, A. D. (2008, November). Now, class, a word from our sponsor. *Designer/Builder*. Retrieved December 9, 2014, from http://www.commercialfreechildhood.org/sites/default/files/kanner_nowclassaword.pdf.

9. David, C. V. (2013, January 9). SAES teachers, principal flip burgers for school cause. *Saipan Tribune*. Retrieved January 15, 2013, from http://www.saipantribune.com/newsstory.aspx?cat=1&newsID=124461/; Picchi, A. (2014, December 11). Why McDonald's says it wants "to be in the school." *CBS News*. Retrieved December 13, 2014, from http://www.cbsnews.com/news/why-mcdonalds-says-it-wants-to-be-in-the-schools/.

10. Orange County Public Schools (n.d.). Garage Advertising, Downtown Orlando. Author. Retrieved January 15, 2013, from https://www.ocps.net/es/cr/Advertisements/billboards,%20445%20W%20Amelia%20Parking%20Garage.pdf/. In Rock Hill, South Carolina, schools have found a different way to direct advertising away from children, by putting advertisements on utility vehicles: Cetrone, S. (2011, October 30). Rock Hill schools find moneymakers. Heraldon-

line.com. Retrieved October 30, 2011, from http://www.heraldonline.com/2011/10/30/3484708/rock-hill-schools-find-moneymakers.html/.

11. Retrieved December 5, 2012 from http://www.Impactlocal.com/(n.d.).

12. FranklinCovey Education (2014). Sponsors. Retrieved September 15, 2014, from http://www.theleaderinme.org/sponsors/; Lakeview Elementary receives Panda Express grant for the 'Leader in Me' program, parent night Thursday (2012, November 1). *Kirkland Reporter.* Retrieved March 8, 2013, from http://www.kirklandreporter.com/community/176796571.html/.

13. Purcell, Y. (2012, December 3). Personal communication (e-mail) with Faith Boninger.

14. *Advertising Age* (n.d.). Top ad campaigns of the 21st century. Author. Retrieved January 15, 2015, from http://adage.com/lp/top15/#tapproject.

15. *Advertising Age* (n.d.). Top ad campaigns of the 21st century. Author. Retrieved January 15, 2015, from http://adage.com/lp/top15/#tapproject; Friedman, A. (2013, April 18). Beauty above all else: The problem with Dove's new viral ad. *New York Magazine.* Retrieved January 22, 2015, from http://nymag.com/thecut/2013/04/beauty-above-all-else-doves-viral-ad-problem.html; Keane, E. (2013, April 18). Stop posting that Dove ad: "Real beauty" campaign is not feminist. *Salon.* Retrieved January 22, 2015, from http://www.salon.com/2013/04/18/stop_posting_that_dove_ad_real_beauty_campaign_is_not_feminist/.

16. Although the program could theoretically be used with boys also, girls are its target audience. Dove (n.d.). Real Beauty School Program. Retrieved January 15, 2015, from http://www.dove.ca/en/docs/pdf/real_beauty_school_program_en.pdf.

17. See also Friedman, A. (2013, April 18). Beauty above all else: The problem with Dove's new viral ad. *New York Magazine.* Retrieved January 22, 2015, from http://nymag.com/thecut/2013/04/beauty-above-all-else-doves-viral-ad-problem.html.

18. Zeilinger, J. (2013, August 1). Axe commercial suggests that women's increasing hotness is a danger to men. *Huffington Post.* Retrieved January 19, 2015, from http://www.huffingtonpost.com/2013/08/01/axe-commercial-suggests-that-women-ruin-everything_n_3689409.html. See, for example, Axe (2012, August 20). Hot Putt. Retrieved February 5, 2015, from https://www.youtube.com/watch?v=RpTGaENQNNg.

19. New York Jets (2014). Community: Eat Right, Move More. Retrieved September 16, 2014, from http://www.newyorkjets.com/community/be-lean-and-green/eat-right-move-more.html/; Linden High School wins nutrition contest by N.Y. Jets and N.J. Department of Agriculture (2012, May 11). *Suburban News.* Retrieved May 14, 2012, from http://www.nj.com/suburbannews/index.ssf/2012/05/linden_high_school_wins_nutrit.html/.

20. New York Jets (2014). Community: Eat Right, Move More. Retrieved September 16, 2014, from http://www.newyorkjets.com/community/be-lean-and-green/eat-right-move-more.html.

21. Brennan, T. J. (2014, October 2). Jets make $150,000 donation to PSAL *New York Jets*. Retrieved September 16, 2014 from http://www.newyorkjets.com/news/article-5/Jets-Make-150000-Donation-to-PSAL/47d96fb1-0f11-41cb-9ea0-9d82d19c3327.

22. Brennan, T. J. (2014, October 2). Jets make $150,000 donation to PSAL *New York Jets*. Retrieved September 16, 2014, from http://www.newyorkjets.com/news/article-5/Jets-Make-150000-Donation-to-PSAL/47d96fb1-0f11-41cb-9ea0-9d82d19c3327.

23. Solotaroff, P. (2013, January 31). This is your brain on football. *Rolling Stone, 1157,* 56–61 and 71. Retrieved February 5, 2013, from http://archive.rollingstone.com/Desktop#/20130131/C1 [subscription required]; Wilking, C., Golin, J., & Feick, C. (2015, January). Out of bounds: The NFL's intensive campaign to target children. Campaign for a Commercial-Free Childhood. Retrieved January 28, 2015, from http://commercialfreechildhood.org/sites/default/files/outofbounds.pdf.

24. BWW News Desk (2012, January 6). SMASH launches 'Make a Musical' initiative. Retrieved January 17, 2012, from http://tv.broadwayworld.com/article/SMASH-Launches-Make-a-Musical-Initiative-20120106_page1/ [no longer available].

25. BWW News Desk (2012, January 6). SMASH launches 'Make a Musical' initiative. Retrieved January 17, 2012, from http://tv.broadwayworld.com/article/SMASH-Launches-Make-a-Musical-Initiative-20120106_page1/ [no longer available].

26. CFA Properties, Inc. (2012). In your community. Retrieved February 14, 2013, from http://www.chick-fil-a.com/Kids/Local/; FranklinCovey Education (2013). Sponsors. Retrieved February 14, 2013, from http://www.theleaderinme.org/sponsors/; Cloues, R. (2011). My year with Nike: A story of corporate sponsorship, branding, and ethics in public schools. In E. Marshall & Ö. Sensoy (eds.), *Rethinking Popular Culture and Media*. Milwaukee, WI: Rethinking Schools; Cloues, R. (2014, July 8). Personal communication (telephone) with Faith Boninger.

27. Cal Ed Code § 35182.5 (2015); National PTA (1990). Sample resolution against commercialism in schools. Retrieved November 20, 2014, from http://www.ibiblio.org/commercialfree/action/resolution.html.

28. Campaign for a Commercial-Free Childhood (2012, July 30). Letter to Thomas R. Bice. Author. Retrieved November 13, 2014, from http://commercialfreechildhood.org/sites/default/files/channelone letter.pdf.

29. Greenberg, B. S., & Brand, J. E. (1993). Television news and advertising in schools: The "Channel One" controversy. *Journal of Communication, 43*(1), 143–51; see also Kurtz, C. J. (2013, January). Channel One may not be in best interests of students. *Mercury.* Retrieved January 16, 2013, from http://www.pottsmerc.com/article/20121115/OPINION02/121119657/channel-one-may-not-be-in-best-interests-of-students/.

30. Campaign for a Commercial-Free Childhood (2012, July 30). Letter to Thomas R. Bice. Author. Retrieved November 13, 2014, from http://commercialfreechildhood.org/sites/default/files/channeloneletter.pdf.

31. Campaign for a Commercial-Free Childhood (2012, July 30). Letter to Thomas R. Bice. Author. Retrieved November 13, 2014, from http://commercialfreechildhood.org/sites/default/files/channeloneletter.pdf.

32. Retrieved January 17, 2013 from http://www.gurl.com/.

33. The website does not contain commercials and links to hypersexualized content have been removed. Campaign for a Commercial-Free Childhood (2012, July 30). Letter to Thomas R. Bice. Author. Retrieved January 17, 2013, from http://commercialfreechildhood.org/sites/default/files/channeloneletter.pdf/; Wykes, M., & Gunter, B. (2005). *The Media and Body Image: If Looks Could Kill.* London: Sage.

34. Channel One News (n.d.). Daily Transcript. Author. Retrieved November 20, 2014, from http://www.channelone.com/transcript.

35. Deardorff, J. (2012, February 5). Beverage-makers build playgrounds, draw criticism. *Chicago Tribune.* Retrieved on May 1, 2012, from http://articles.chicagotribune.com/2012-02-05/news/ct-met-exercise-coke-pepsi-20120205_1_coke-new-playground-fitness-challenge/; Deardorff, J. (2012, March 5). Does Coke market to kids? You decide. *Chicago Tribune.* Retrieved on May 1, 2012, from http://articles.chicagotribune.com/2012-03-05/features/chi-does-coke-market-to-kids-you-decide-20120304_1_coca-cola-coke-beverage-brands/.

36. Deardorff, J. (2012, February 5). Beverage-makers build playgrounds, draw criticism. *Chicago Tribune.* Retrieved on May 1, 2012, from http://articles.chicagotribune.com/2012-02-05/news/ct-met-exercise-coke-pepsi-20120205_1_coke-new-playground-fitness-challenge/.

37. American Beverage Association (2010, March 8). Alliance school beverage guidelines: Final report. Author. Retrieved January 21, 2015, from http://www.ameribev.org/files/240_School%20Beverage%20Guidelines%20Final%20Progress%20Report.pdf; Wescott, R. F., Fitzpatrick, B. M., & Phillips, E. (2012, October). Industry self-regulation to improve student health: Quantifying changes in beverage shipments to schools. *American Journal of Public Health, 102*(10), 1928–35.

38. Deardorff, J. (2012, February 5). Beverage-makers build playgrounds, draw criticism. *Chicago Tribune.* Retrieved on May 1, 2012, from http://articles.

chicagotribune.com/2012-02-05/news/ct-met-exercise-coke-pepsi-20120205_1_
coke-new-playground-fitness-challenge/; Deardorff, J. (2012, February 5). Critics pounce on Coke, Pepsi health initiatives. *Chicago Tribune*. Retrieved January
17, 2013, from http://articles.chicagotribune.com/2012-02-05/news/ct-met-coke-
pepsi-health-20120205_1_coca-cola-north-america-health-groups-healthy-
lifestyle-choices/.

39. Federal Trade Commission (2012, December). A review of food marketing to children and adolescents: Follow-up report. Washington, DC: Author.
Retrieved December 21, 2012, from http://www.ftc.gov/os/2012/12/
121221foodmarketingreport.pdf/.

40. For an interesting discussion of the shift of onus to students, see Powell,
D., & Gard, M. (2014, April 14). The governmentality of childhood obesity:
Coca-Cola, public health and primary schools. *Discourse: Studies in the Cultural
Politics of Education*. Retrieved May 5, 2014, from http://dx.doi.org/10.1080/
01596306.2014.905045.

41. Young, A. (2010, March 31). Axe vs. Old Spice: Whose media plan came
up smelling best? *Advertising Age*. Retrieved February 5, 2013, from http://
adage.com/article/media/axe-spice-media-plan-worked/143066/.

42. Lindstrom, M. (2011, October 24). Can a commercial be too sexy for its
own good? Ask Axe. *Atlantic*. Retrieved March 20, 2013, from http://www.
theatlantic.com/business/archive/2011/10/can-a-commercial-be-too-sexy-for-its-
own-good-ask-axe/246863/. See also: Caulfield, P. (2013, March 20). Ax the
Axe! Pa. high school tells students to stop using Axe Body Spray after one
suffers 'life-threatening' allergic reaction. *New York Daily News*. Retrieved
March 20, 2013, from http://www.nydailynews.com/news/national/pa-high-
school-tells-students-stop-axe-body-spray-article-1.1293847#ixzz2O6ZaBUGi/.

43. Mnfb.com (2011, February 18). Whiteside nominated as Old Spice player
of the year. Retrieved February 5, 2013, from http://www.marplenewtownfoot-
ball.com/wp/2011/02/18/whiteside-nominated-as-old-spice-player-of-the-year/;
Promo (2005, September 14). Old Spice sponsors high school football rivalries.
Chief Marketer! Retrieved February 5, 2013, from http://chiefmarketer.com/
news/old-spice-sponsors-high-school-football-rivalries/.

44. Brown, L. M., cited in Hoffman, J. (2010, January 29). Masculinity in a
spray can. *New York Times*. Retrieved February 5, 2013, from http://www.
nytimes.com/2010/01/31/fashion/31smell.html/. For commentary on hypersexuality in boys, see also Jhally, S. (2005). Advertising as social communication
(online course; part three: Advertising and Social Issues). Retrieved July 22,
2009, from http://www.comm287.com/partthree/.

45. Environmental Working Group & the Campaign for Safe Cosmetics
(2010, May). Not so sexy: Hidden chemicals in perfume and cologne. Washing-

ton, DC: Author. Retrieved March 11, 2013, from http://www.ewg.org/research/not-so-sexy/.

46. Environmental Working Group & the Campaign for Safe Cosmetics (2010, May). Not so sexy: Hidden chemicals in perfume and cologne. Washington, DC: Author. Retrieved March 11, 2013, from http://www.ewg.org/research/not-so-sexy/. See also Caulfield, P. (2013, March 20). Ax the Axe! Pa. high school tells students to stop using Axe Body Spray after one suffers 'life-threatening' allergic reaction. *New York Daily News*. Retrieved March 20, 2013, from http://www.nydailynews.com/news/national/pa-high-school-tells-students-stop-axe-body-spray-article-1.1293847#ixzz2O6ZaBUGi/.

47. Environmental Working Group (2008, September 24). Teen girls' body burden of hormone-altering cosmetics chemicals: adolescent exposures to cosmetic chemicals of concern. Washington, DC: Author. Retrieved March 11, 2013, from http://www.ewg.org/research/teen-girls-body-burden-hormone-altering-cosmetics-chemicals/; Houlihan, J. (2008, June 19). Comments for public meeting on "International Cooperation on Cosmetics Regulations (ICCR) Preparations." Washington, DC: Environmental Working Group. Retrieved June 29, 2010, from http://www.ewg.org/node/26733/.

48. Saporta, M. (2012, April 20). JA and Chick-fil-A plan finance park, BizTown. *Atlanta Business Chronicle*. Retrieved January 17, 2013, from http://www.bizjournals.com/atlanta/print-edition/2012/04/20/ja-and-chick-fil-a-plan-finance-park.html/; Young, C. (2013, January 10). Junior Achievement, Chick-fil-A launch discovery center. *NeighborNewspapers.com*. Retrieved January 17, 2013, from http://neighbornewspapers.com/view/full_story/21371700/article-Junior-Achievement--Chick-fil-A-launch-discovery-center/.

49. Junior Achievement of Georgia (n.d.). Junior Achievement's Chick-fil-A Foundation Discovery Center. Retrieved September 12, 2014, from https://www.juniorachievement.org/web/ja-georgia/ja-discovery-center; Saporta, M. (2012, April 20). JA and Chick-fil-A plan Finance Park, BizTown. *Atlanta Business Chronicle*. Retrieved January 17, 2013, from http://www.bizjournals.com/atlanta/print-edition/2012/04/20/ja-and-chick-fil-a-plan-finance-park.html/; Young, C. (2013, January 10). Junior Achievement, Chick-fil-A launch discovery center. NeighborNewspapers.com. Retrieved January 17, 2013, from http://neighbornewspapers.com/view/full_story/21371700/article-Junior-Achievement--Chick-fil-A-launch-discovery-center/.

50. Junior Achievement of Arizona, Inc. (2012). JA Biztown Shop. Author. Retrieved January 15, 2013, from http://www.jaaz.org/support/biztown-shop/.

51. Kasser, T. (2002). *The High Price of Materialism*. Cambridge, MA: MIT Press. See also Jhally, S., & Barr, W. (n.d.). Advertising, cultural criticism, and pedagogy: An interview with Sut Jhally (conducted by William O'Barr). Re-

trieved November 23, 2010, from http://www.sutjhally.com/articles/
advertisingcultura/.

52. For an example of a policy that denies support for advertised brands, see
LAUSD's sponsorship guidelines: Los Angeles Unified School District (2011,
May 24). Sponsorship Guidelines. Retrieved April 27, 2012, from http://
notebook.lausd.net/portal/page?_pageid=33,501466&_dad=ptl&_schema=PTL_
EP/.

53. Articles that support the idea that contextual cues lead students to interpret
the school's support for the advertised brands: Eagly, A. E., & Chaiken, S.
(1983). Process theories of attitude formation and change: The elaboration likelihood model and the heuristic systematic models. In A. E. Eagly and S. Chaiken
(eds.), *The Psychology of Attitudes*. Fort Worth, TX: Harcourt Brace Jovanovich,
305–25; Mallinckrodt, V., & Mizerski, D. (2007). The effects of playing an
advergame on young children's perceptions, preferences and request. *Journal of
Advertising, 36*, 87–100; Nairn, A., & Fine, C. (2008). Who's messing with my
mind? The implications of dual-process models for the ethics of advertising to
children. *International Journal of Advertising*, 27(3), 447–70; Petty, R. E., &
Cacioppo, J. T. (1986). *Communication and Persuasion: Central and Peripheral
Routes to Attitude Change*. New York: Springer; Tellis, G. J. (2004). *Effective
Advertising: Understanding When, How, and Why Advertising Works*. Thousand
Oaks, CA: Sage.

54. Burger, J. M., Sanchez, J., Imberi, J. E., & Grande, L. R. (2009). The
norm of reciprocity as an internalized social norm: Returning favors even when
no one finds out. *Social Influence, 4*(1), 11–17. Retrieved November 25, 2014,
from http://www.scu.edu/cas/psychology/faculty/upload/Burger-et-al-SI-2009.
pdf.

55. Molnar, A., Boninger, F., & Fogarty, J. (2011). *The Educational Cost of
Schoolhouse Commercialism—The Fourteenth Annual Report on Schoolhouse
Commercializing Trends: 2010–2011*. Boulder, CO: National Education Policy
Center. Retrieved December 5, 2012, from http://nepc.colorado.edu/publication/
schoolhouse-commercialism-2011/; Cloues, R. (2011). My year with Nike: A
story of corporate sponsorship, branding, and ethics in public schools. In E.
Marshall & Ö. Sensoy (eds.), *Rethinking Popular Culture and Media*. Milwaukee, WI: Rethinking Schools; Cloues, R. (2014, July 8). Personal communication
(telephone) with Faith Boninger.

56. For example, see http://www.Impactlocal.com (n.d.). Retrieved November 21, 2014.

57. Sacramento Bee (2003, July 27). Addicted schools: Dependence on soda
money is a shame. *Sacramento Bee*. Retrieved November 21, 2014, from http://
epsl.asu.edu/ceru/CERU_2003_Articles_Of_Interest.htm.

58. Two different, but related, examples shed light on this phenomenon: The first is that unlike school districts, private entities that run charter schools can decide to "go out of business" without warning, leaving children to find new schools, as happened with several Florida charter schools in 2014. See Yi, K., & Shipley, A. (2014, June 18). Florida's charter schools unsupervised: Taxpayers, students lose when school operators exploit weak laws. *SunSentinel*. Retrieved November 21, 2014, from http://interactive.sun-sentinel.com/charter-schools-unsupervised/investigation.html. The second is more distant from a school setting: when American Airlines and US Airways merged, the new American Airlines decided it no longer benefited from sponsoring what until now had been US Airways Arena in Phoenix. It did not renew its naming rights contract, leaving the Phoenix Suns to scramble for a new sponsor. See Gilbertson, D. (2014, September 4). Suns shopping for new US Airways Center sponsor. *Arizona Republic*. Retrieved November 21, 2014, from http://www.azcentral.com/story/travel/2014/09/04/suns-shopping-new-us-airways-center-sponsor/15072067/.

59. Molnar, A., Koski, W. S., & Boninger, F. (2010, January 13). Policy and statutory responses to advertising and marketing in schools. Boulder and Tempe: Education and the Public Interest Center and Commercialism in Education Research Unit. Retrieved October 11, 2013, from http://nepc.colorado.edu/publication/policy-and-statutory.

60. Boehm, J. (2013, January 3). EV school districts have different views on bus advertising. *East Valley Tribune*. Retrieved January 6, 2014, from http://www.eastvalleytribune.com/local/chandler/article_2ca7bfac-6f4d-11e3-b937-001a4bcf887a.html; Blankinship, D. G. (2010, March 20). Could school bus ads save school budgets? *USA Today*. Retrieved August 16, 2013, from http://usatoday30.usatoday.com/news/education/2010-03-20-school-bus-ads_N.htm; National Association of State Directors of Pupil Transportation Devices (2011, March 4). Position paper: Advertising on school buses. Author. Retrieved October 23, 2013, from http://www.nasdpts.org/Documents/Paper-AdvertisingOnSB-3-11.pdf.

61. Campaign for a Commercial Free Childhood (n.d.). 2012 School Bus Ad Action Center. Author. Retrieved March 7, 2014, from http://www.commercialfreechildhood.org/action/2012-school-bus-ad-action-center; Campaign for a Commercial Free Childhood (n.d.). 2012 School Bus Ad Action Center. Author. Retrieved March 7, 2014, from http://www.commercialfreechildhood.org/action/2013schoolbusads.

62. Cal Ed Code § 35182.5 (2015).

63. 8 NYCRR §23.1 (2002).

64. An Act to Protect Children's Health on School Grounds, 20-A M.R.S. § 6662 (2014); Polacsek, M., O'Roarke, K., O'Brien, L., Blum, J. W., & Donahue, S. (2012, March–April). Examining compliance with a statewide law banning

junk food and beverage marketing in Maine schools. *Public Health Reports, 127,* 216–23. Retrieved January 28, 2013, from http://www.une.edu/news/2012/ upload/PHRarticle-Marketing-Polacsek.pdf.

65. Polacsek, M., O'Roarke, K., O'Brien, L., Blum, J. W., & Donahue, S. (2012, March–April). Examining compliance with a statewide law banning junk food and beverage marketing in Maine schools. *Public Health Reports, 127,* 216–23. Retrieved January 28, 2013, from http://www.une.edu/news/2012/ upload/PHRarticle-Marketing-Polacsek.pdf.

66. Brent, B. O., & Lunden, S. (2009). Much ado about very little: The benefits and costs of school-based commercial activities. *Leadership and Policy in Schools, 8,* 307–36; Roller, B. (2013, August 22). Personal communication (telephone) with Faith Boninger.

67. Brent, B. O., & Lunden, S. (2009). Much ado about very little: The benefits and costs of school-based commercial activities. *Leadership and Policy in Schools, 8,* 307–36.

68. Fla. Stat. § 1001.43 (2014); N.C. Gen. Stat. § 115C-98 (2014); Wis. Stat. § 118.12 (2014).

69. Blankinship, D. G. (2010, March 20). Could school bus ads save school budgets? *USA Today.* Retrieved August 16, 2013, from http://usatoday30. usatoday.com/news/education/2010-03-20-school-bus-ads_N.htm; National Association of State Directors of Pupil Transportation Devices (2011, March 4). Position paper: Advertising on school buses. Author. Retrieved October 23, 2013, from http://www.nasdpts.org/Documents/Paper-AdvertisingOnSB-3-11. pdf; Leibowitz, B. (2013, May 9). Math tutor—and porn producer—suing Palm Beach schools for prohibiting his tutoring ads. *CBS News.* Retrieved May 25, 2013, from http://www.cbsnews.com/8301-504083_162-57583791-504083/ math-tutor-and-porn-producer-suing-palm-beach-schools-for-prohibiting-his-tutoring-ads/.

70. National Association of State Directors of Pupil Transportation Devices (2011, March 4). Position paper: Advertising on school buses. Author. Retrieved October 23, 2013, from http://www.nasdpts.org/Documents/Paper-AdvertisingOnSB-3-11.pdf.

71. Leibowitz, B. (2013, May 9). Math tutor— and porn producer—suing Palm Beach schools for prohibiting his tutoring ads. *CBS News.* Retrieved May 25, 2013, from http://www.cbsnews.com/8301-504083_162-57583791-504083/ math-tutor-and-porn-producer-suing-palm-beach-schools-for-prohibiting-his-tutoring-ads/. The case was dismissed October 27, 2014. Bonner-Williams, B. (2015, January 22, 2015). Personal communication (telephone) with Faith Boninger.

72. Adler, S. (2013, October 30). Personal communication (e-mail) with Faith Boninger. ChangeLab Solutions offers model code for districts and states to limit

advertising for food and beverages at school in fair and content-neutral ways. See ChangeLab Solutions (n.d.). District policy restricting food and beverage advertising on school grounds. Author. Retrieved January 28, 2014, from http://changelabsolutions.org/publications/district-policy-school-food-ads; ChangeLab Solutions (2013, November). Model statute limiting food marketing at schools. Author. Retrieved January 28, 2014, from http://changelabsolutions.org/publications/food-marketing-schools.

73. Cal Ed Code § 35182.5 (2015).

74. Cal Ed Code § 35182.5 (2015).

75. Government Accountability Office (GAO). Commercial activities in schools: Use of student data is limited and additional dissemination of guidance could help districts develop policies (GAO-04-810). Retrieved January 14, 2014, from http://www.gao.gov/assets/250/243777.pdf.

76. See also our previous work leading up to the current research: Molnar, A., Koski, W. S., & Boninger, F. (2010, January 13). *Policy and Statutory Responses to Advertising and Marketing in Schools*. Boulder, CO: National Education Policy Center. Retrieved November 21, 2014, from http://nepc.colorado.edu/publication/policy-and-statutory; Molnar, A., Boninger, F., Libby, K., & Fogarty, J. (2014, March 11). *Schoolhouse Commercialism Leaves Policymakers Behind*. Boulder, CO: National Education Policy Center. Retrieved November 21, 2014, from http://nepc.colorado.edu/publication/schoolhouse-commercialism-2013.

77. Media Searches for Recent Developments, conducted 2012–2013. We conducted Internet searches using the Google (www.google.com), Bing (www.bing.com), and Mention (www.mention.net) search engines; and reviewed academic research on, and analysis of, the impact of marketing to children. E-mail news alerts from the following key organizations were used to help identify commercialism-related issues for follow-up Internet and/or academic research: Advertising Age (adage.com), Canadian Centre for Policy Alternatives (http://www.policyalternatives.ca/), Consortium for Media Literacy (http://www.consortiumformedialiteracy.org/), Kidscreen (http://kidscreen.com/), Federal Communications Commission (FCC) (http://www.fcc.gov/), and MedPage Today (http://www.medpagetoday.com/). Interviews, conducted 2013: We conducted telephone interviews with policy experts at the following organizations: American Association of School Superintendents (AASA), American Legislative Exchange Council (ALEC), Campaign for a Commercial-Free Childhood (CCFC), Center for Science in the Public Interest (CSPI), ChangeLab Solutions (National Policy & Legal Analysis Network to Prevent Childhood Obesity [NPLAN]), Education Commission of the States (ECS), National School Boards Association (NSBA), and StudentsFirst. Interviews explored the organizations' positions on commercializing activities in schools, what the respondents knew

about legislation regarding such activities, and where we might look further to find relevant legislation.

78. We reviewed three online state legislative databases to determine which provided comprehensive and accessible information and would allow others to easily replicate our research. The review criteria were that the database provide complete legislative language, be accessible online, be free or inexpensive, be updated regularly, and be searchable using search terms relevant to school commercialism. The National Conference of State Legislatures (NCSL) database (http://www.ncsl.org/) uses preselected categories that did not allow us to search specifically for commercialism-related legislation, making it unsearchable for what we were looking for. The Legiscan (www.legiscan.org) database allowed us to create search terms relevant to our research and to search for all bills introduced, but not to limit our search to bills that were eventually signed into law. This became important as we saw that searches for all bills introduced included bills that died in committee, bills that did not pass, and bills that contained our search words but were not actually relevant to school commercialism—sometimes so many (thousands) that we could only reasonably examine a small subset of them. These "fatal flaws" led us to eliminate these two databases.

It may be possible to systematically search for relevant legislation using supplemental programming techniques that comb through and sort bills after combining data from multiple databases and legislation. However, this would not be the online, inexpensive, easily replicable search we sought.

Although the Open States database allowed us to limit our search to bills that were signed into law, it did have a few drawbacks that complicated the search and therefore the results obtained. First, because we were searching for key words, sometimes it returned bills that contained the specified words but did not address school commercialism in any form.

Second, Open States' output is uneven by state: its search goes back different lengths of time for different states. For example, it scans Illinois bills as far back as 2003, but Missouri bills only to 2012.

The simple fix for this problem, to limit the search for all states to bills introduced beginning in 2012, was not supported by the program. Because of the large numbers of bills introduced (for example, containing the words "sponsor" and "school" but in ways other than what we were looking for in terms of corporate-sponsored school programs, activities, or educational materials) compared to the smaller numbers of bills signed into law, these limitations especially inflate the number bills introduced. For this reason, we focus here on the bills that were signed into law, which we were able to examine more closely because they came back in fewer numbers.

Third, we were dismayed to find that the same searches done on different days yielded different numbers of bills. To examine the implications of that potentially distressing phenomenon, we searched for all our search terms for five days to see what kind of variation we would get. The variation turned out to be immaterial, as it happened typically in cases of very large numbers of bills introduced and did not occur for the culled set of most relevant search terms we eventually settled on. The site https://beta.congress.gov/legislation is the successor to Thomas.

79. We initially had to limit our search for legislation in calendar years 2012–2013; these results are published in our annual report referenced below. Subsequently, in order to broaden our exploration to the last two legislative sessions, we expanded the search to include bills introduced between January 1, 2011, and December 31, 2014, and on bills signed into law in that time period. We did not explore all the bills introduced for their relevance to school commercialism. Because many of them are likely to be irrelevant, these numbers provide a general indication of interest in the issue. Findings of our initial 2012–2013 search are reported in Molnar, A., Boninger, F., Libby, K. M., & Fogarty, J. (2014). *Schoolhouse Commercialism Leaves Policymakers Behind—The Sixteenth Annual Report on Schoolhouse Commercializing Trends: 2012–2013.* Boulder, CO: National Education Policy Center. Retrieved September 15, 2014, from http://nepc.colorado.edu/publication/schoolhouse-commercialism-2013.

80. An act concerning advertisements on school buses and supplementing chapter 7F and chapter 39 of Title 18A of the New Jersey Statutes, N.J. Stat. § 18A:39-31 (2014).

81. An Act to Amend Tennessee Code Annotated, Section 49-6-2109, relative to advertising on school buses, Tenn. Code Ann. § 49-6-2109 (2014).

82. An act to amend Sections 8423, 8482.3, 8483.3, 35182.5, 38091, 38100, 49430, 49431, 49431.2, 49431.5, 49431.7, and 49432 of, to repeal Sections 38085, 49433, 49433.5, 49433.7, 49433.9, 49435, and 49436 of, and to repeal and add Section 49434 of, the Education Code, relating to school nutrition. Cal Ed Code § 8423 (2015), Cal Ed Code § 8482.3 (2015), Cal Ed Code § 8483.3 (2015), Cal Ed Code § 3182.5 (2015), Cal Ed Code § 38091 (2015), Cal Ed Code § 38100 (2015), Cal Ed Code § 49430 (2015), Cal Ed Code § 49431 (2015), Cal Ed Code § 49431.2 (2015), Cal Ed Code § 49431.5 (2015), Cal Ed Code § 49431.7 (2015), Cal Ed Code § 49434 (2015).

83. AN ACT concerning abortion; relating to the funding of abortion services; relating to restrictions on late-term abortions; relating to the woman's right-to-know act; amending K.S.A. 2012 Supp. 40-2246, 65-6701, 65-6703, 65-6709, 65-6710, 76-3308, 79-32,117, 79-32,138, 79-32,182b, 79-32,195, 79-32,261 and 79-3606 and repealing the existing sections. Kan. Stat. Ann. § 65-6734 (2013).

84. Protection of Pupil Rights (PPRA), 20 USC 1232h (2015).

85. National School Lunch Program, 7 CFR Part 210 (2015).

86. Shah, N. (2012, January 31). USDA rules give school meals a healthy makeover. *Education Week.* Retrieved January 28, 2014, from http://www. edweek.org/ew/articles/2012/02/01/19lunch.h31.html; Shah, N. (2013, June 27). Rules for school vending machines, snacks unveiled. *Education Week.* Retrieved June 27, 2013, from http://blogs.edweek.org/edweek/rulesforengagement/2013/ 06/rules_for_school_vending_machines_snacks_unveiled.html?cmp=ENL-EU-NEWS2.

87. Confessore, N. (2014, October 7). How school lunch became the latest political battleground. *New York Times.* Retrieved November 21, 2014, from http://www.nytimes.com/2014/10/12/magazine/how-school-lunch-became-the-latest-political-battleground.html?_r=0; Obama, M. (2014, May 28). The campaign for junk food. *New York Times.* Retrieved September 15, 2014, from http:// www.nytimes.com/2014/05/29/opinion/michelle-obama-on-attempts-to-roll-back-healthy-reforms.html?_r=0.

88. U.S. Department of Agriculture, Food and Nutrition Service (2014, February 26). Local school wellness policy implementation under the Healthy, Hunger-Free Kids Act of 2010, 7 CFR Parts 210 and 220, RIN 0584-AE25: Proposed Rule. *Federal Register, 79*(38), 10693–706. Retrieved January 19, 2015, from http://www.fns.usda.gov/sites/default/files/2014-04100.pdf; Golin, J., & Simon, M. (2014, April 25). USDA's proposal on food marketing in schools could harm children. Campaign for a Commercial-Free Childhood. Retrieved September 15, 2014, from http://www.commercialfreechildhood.org/blog/usda%E2%80%99s-proposal-food-marketing-schools-could-harm-children; Harrington, E. (2014, February 25). Michelle Obama pushing ban on junk food advertising in schools. *Washington Free Beacon.* Retrieved February 26, 2014, from http://freebeacon. com/michelle-obama-pushing-ban-on-junk-food-advertising-in-schools/.

89. Golin, J., & Simon, M. (2014, April 25). USDA's proposal on food marketing in schools could harm children. Campaign for a Commercial-Free Childhood. Retrieved September 15, 2014, from http://www. commercialfreechildhood.org/blog/usda's-proposal-food-marketing-schools-could-harm-children; School wellness policy implementation under the Healthy, Hunger-Free Kids Act of 2010, 7 CFR Parts 210 and 220, RIN 0584-AE25 (pp. 24-25). Retrieved February 26, 2014, from https://s3.amazonaws.com/public-inspection.federalregister.gov/2014-04100.pdf.

90. Golin, J., & Simon, M. (2014, April 25). USDA's proposal on food marketing in schools could harm children. Campaign for a Commercial-Free Childhood. Retrieved September 15, 2014, from http://www. commercialfreechildhood.org/blog/usda%E2%80%99s-proposal-food-marketing-schools-could-harm-children.

91. To amend the Internal Revenue Code of 1986 to deny any deduction for marketing directed at children to promote the consumption of food of poor nutri-

tional quality, H.R. 2831 (2013), 113th Congress (2013–2014). Retrieved January 20, 2015, from http://thomas.loc.gov/cgi-bin/bdquery/z?d113:HR02831:|/home/LegislativeData.php|S.%202342; Stop subsidizing Childhood Obesity Act., S. 2342 113th Congress (2013–2014). Retrieved January 20, 2015, from http://thomas.loc.gov/cgi-bin/bdquery/z?d113:SN02342:|/home/LegislativeData.php|.

92. For the most direct comparison, see Molnar, A. (2003). *No Student Left Unsold: The Sixth Annual Report on Commercializing Activities in Schools.* Tempe, AZ: Education Policy Studies Laboratory. Retrieved September 15, 2014, from http://nepc.colorado.edu/publication/no-student-left-unsold.

93. The Interagency Working Group (IWG) was established by Congress in 2009. The agencies involved were the Federal Trade Commission (FTC), Centers for Disease Control (CDC), Department of Agriculture (USDA) and Food and Drug Administration (FDA); the IWG's mandate was to draft voluntary nutrition standards for children's food marketing.

This number does not include broader lobbying efforts by the Chamber of Commerce, the National Association of Manufacturers, and media and advertising interests that opposed the federal plan but that also lobby on other issues. Lobbying disclosure reports do not specify how much they spent targeting the food marketing proposal. The Reuters analysis was based on records from the Federal Election Commission, the Secretary of the Senate, and the Center for Responsive Politics, a nonpartisan group that tracks money in politics; Wilson, D., & Roberts, J. (2012, April 27). Special Report: How Washington went soft on childhood obesity. *Reuters.* Retrieved January 29, 2013, from http://www.reuters.com/article/2012/04/27/us-usa-foodlobby-idUSBRE83Q0ED20120427/.

94. Wilson, D., & Roberts, J. (2012, April 27). Special Report: How Washington went soft on childhood obesity. *Reuters.* Retrieved January 29, 2013, from http://www.reuters.com/article/2012/04/27/us-usa-foodlobby-idUSBRE83Q0ED20120427/.

95. Goldstein, H. (2013, August 19 and 20). Personal communication (telephone) with Faith Boninger.

96. American Beverage Association (2010, March 8). Alliance school beverage guidelines: Final report. Retrieved January 21, 2015, from http://www.ameribev.org/files/240_School%20Beverage%20Guidelines%20Final%20Progress%20Report.pdf; Wescott, R. F., Fitzpatrick, B. M., & Phillips, E. (2012, October). Industry self-regulation to improve student health: Quantifying changes in beverage shipments to schools. *American Journal of Public Health, 102*(10), 1928–35.

97. Council of Better Business Bureaus, Inc. (2011, July). Children's Food and Beverage Advertising Initiative, Council of Better Business Bureaus, Inc., Category-Specific Uniform Nutrition Criteria. Author. Retrieved January 22,

2015, from http://www.bbb.org/us/storage/16/documents/cfbai/CFBAI-Category-Specific-Uniform-Nutrition-Criteria.pdf.

98. Council of Better Business Bureaus (2013). About the Initiative. Author. Retrieved September 13, 2013, from http://www.bbb.org/us/about-the-initiative/; Council of Better Business Bureaus 9 (2013, June). CFBAI's category-specific uniform nutrition criteria. Author. Retrieved January 15, 2015, from http://www.bbb.org/us/storage/16/documents/cfbai/CFBAI-Category-Specific-Uniform-Nutrition-Criteria.pdf; Klimscak, K. (2013, August 14). Personal communication (telephone) with Faith Boninger.

99. Council of Better Business Bureaus, Inc. (2009). *The Children's Food & Beverage Advertising Initiative: A Report on Compliance and Progress during 2011.* Arlington, VA: Author (p. 15). Retrieved November 18, 2013, from http://www.bbb.org/us/storage/16/documents/cfbai/CFBAI%20Report%20on%20Compliance%20and%20Progress%20During%202011.pdf.

100. Council of Better Business Bureaus, Inc. (2009). *BBB's Children's Food & Beverage Advertising Initiative: Fact Sheet on the Elementary School Advertising Principles.* Arlington, VA: Author. Retrieved November 18, 2013, from http://www.bbb.org/us/storage/0/Shared%20Documents/ESFactSheetFinal Word.pdf; Council of Better Business Bureaus, Inc. (2009). *CSPI Response 12.14.09.* Arlington, VA: Author (p. 6). Retrieved November 18, 2013, from http://www.bbb.org/us/storage/0/Shared%20Documents/CSPI%20response%2012-14-09.pdf.

101. Obama, M. (2013, September 18). Remarks by the First Lady during White House convening on food marketing to children. The White House: Office of the First Lady. Retrieved October 28, 2013, from http://www.whitehouse.gov/the-press-office/2013/09/18/remarks-first-lady-during-white-house-convening-food-marketing-children.

102. For example, see Bahramy, S. (2013, March 12). Personal communication (e-mail) with Faith Boninger.

103. Barth, P. (2013, April 23). Personal communication (telephone) with Faith Boninger; Lerum, E. (2013, April 26). Personal communication (telephone) with Faith Boninger.

104. National PTA (1990). Commercial exploitation of students in school (resolution). This document is not currently found on the National PTA website. It is included in the archive of the Center for Commercial Free Public Education, housed at the online library Ibiblio.org. Retrieved July 31, 2013, from http://www.ibiblio.org/commercialfree/action/resolution.html/. The National PTA states on its website that its current Position Statement on Education Emphasis "was written to update and combine resolutions and position statements concerning 'Education Emphasis.'" "Commercial Exploitation of Students in School" is included in a list of "original resolutions and position statements" to be "archived

in the Historical Records as reference on this issue." See National PTA (n.d.). *Position Statement—Education Emphasis.* Washington, DC: Author. Retrieved August 1, 2013, from http://www.pta.org/about/content.cfm?ItemNumber=3443.

105. Bahramy, S. (2013, March 12). Personal communication (e-mail) with Faith Boninger. Ironically, given the earlier position, among the National PTA's sponsors is the interactive education company Promethean, which partners with Channel One. In June 2012, Channel One, Promethean, and the National PTA announced a collaboration to create the "Parent Connection" program, which delivers daily Channel One News broadcasts shown in the classroom directly to parents' mobile phones. The stated goal of the program is to encourage at-home discussion of the broadcast. National PTA (n.d.). Sponsors and Partners. Retrieved August 1, 2013, from http://pta.org/about/content.cfm?ItemNumber=3019&navItemNumber=555; Promethean (2012, June 26). Promethean and Channel One News Announce The Parent Connection. Author. Retrieved August 1, 2013, from http://www1.prometheanworld.com/dutch/server.php?show=ConWebDoc.18432.

106. Hunter, B. (2013, May 15). Personal communication (telephone) with Faith Boninger.

107. Zinth, J. D., & Christie, K. (2013, May 1). Personal communication (telephone) with Ken Libby.

108. Golin, J. (2013, May 9). Personal communication (telephone) with Faith Boninger; Kramer, A. (2013, November 19). Efforts to reduce unhealthy food marketing to kids: Understanding the past to foster success in the present. Presentation to Food Marketing Workgroup.

109. 20-A M.R.S. § 6662 (2014).

110. O'Roarke, K. (2013, April 26). Personal communication (telephone) with Faith Boninger.

111. Golin, J. (2013, May 9). Personal communication (telephone) with Faith Boninger.

112. Goldstein, H. (2013, August 19). Personal communication (e-mail) with Faith Boninger; Wilson, D., & Roberts, J. (2012, April 27). Special Report: How Washington went soft on childhood obesity. *Reuters.* Retrieved January 29, 2013, from http://www.reuters.com/article/2012/04/27/us-usa-foodlobby-idUSBRE83Q0ED20120427/.

113. Barth, P. (2013, April 23). Personal communication (telephone) with Faith Boninger; Burns, C. (2012, December 5). Personal communication (telephone) with Faith Boninger; Hunter, B. (2013, May 15). Personal communication (telephone) with Faith Boninger; Lerum, E. (2013, April 26). Personal communication (telephone) with Faith Boninger; Rundquist, J. (2013, March 17). More N.J. schools turning to advertising to make ends meet. Nj.com. Retrieved

August 15, 2013, from http://www.nj.com/news/index.ssf/2013/03/schools_
look_at_advertising_to.html.

114. See, for example, inBloom, Inc., and Affiliates (2013). FAQ. Author.
Retrieved August 29, 2013, from https://www.inbloom.org/faq; Obama, B. H.
(2013, February 12). *Remarks by the President in the State of the Union Address*.
The White House, Office of the Press Secretary. Retrieved January 7, 2014, from
http://www.whitehouse.gov/the-press-office/2013/02/12/remarks-president-
state-union-address; Target Brands, Inc. (2014). Give with Target: back to school
with something extra. Author. Retrieved January 8, 2014, from https://corporate.
target.com/discover/article/Give-with-Target-back-to-school-with-something-e;
Verizon (2013). *Education in 2012*. Author. Retrieved on May 26, 2013, from
http://responsibility.verizon.com/education/2012#vils.

115. Batada, A., & Wootan, M. G. (2008). *Food and Beverage Marketing
Survey: Montgomery County Public Schools*. Center for Science in the Public
Interest. Retrieved April 30, 2012, from http://cspinet.org/nutritionpolicy/
MCPS_foodmarketing_report2008.pdf; Ben Ishai, E. (2012, February). School
commercialism: High cost, low revenues. *Public Citizen*. Retrieved April 27,
2012, from http://www.commercialalert.org/PDFs/SchoolCommercialism
Report_PC.pdf; Brent, B. O. & Lunden, S. (2009). Much ado about very little:
The benefits and costs of school-based commercial activities. *Leadership and
Policy in Schools, 8*(3), 307–36; Craypo, L., Francisco, S. S., Boyle, M., &
Samuels, S. (2006). Food and beverage marketing on California high school
campuses survey: Findings and recommendations. California Project Lean. Re-
trieved April 30, 2012, from http://www.californiaprojectlean.org/docuserfiles//
SchoolMarketingReport2006.pdf; Molnar, A., Garcia, D. R., Boninger, F., &
Merrill, B. (2006, January 1). A national survey of the types and extent of the
marketing of foods of minimal nutritional value in schools. Commercialism in
Education Research Unit, Arizona State University. Retrieved April 27, 2012,
from http://nepc.colorado.edu/publication/national-survey-types-and-extent-
marketing-foods-minimal-nutritional-value-schools.

116. Brent, B. O., & Lunden, S. (2009). Much ado about very little: The benefits and costs of school-based commercial activities. *Leadership and Policy in
Schools, 8*, 307–36 (330).

117. Molnar, A., Garcia, D. R., Boninger, F., & Merrill, B. (2006, January). A
national survey of the types and extent of the marketing of foods of minimal
nutritional value in schools. Commercialism in Education Research Unit, Arizona State University. Retrieved April 27, 2012, from http://nepc.colorado.edu/
publication/national-survey-types-and-extent-marketing-foods-minimal-
nutritional-value-schools; Nestle, M. (2000). Soft drink "pouring rights": Marketing empty calories. *Public Health Reports, 115*, 308–19. Retrieved October

25, 2013, from http://www.asu.edu/educ/epsl/CERU/Documents/cace-00-03. htm.

118. Brent, B. O., & Lunden, S. (2009). Much ado about very little: The benefits and costs of school-based commercial activities. *Leadership and Policy in Schools, 8*, 307–36 (330).

119. Brent, B. O., & Lunden, S. (2009). Much ado about very little: The benefits and costs of school-based commercial activities. *Leadership and Policy in Schools, 8*, 307–36 (324).

7

DIGITAL MARKETING AND THREATS TO CHILDREN'S PRIVACY

Any parent will tell you that today's children are fully and continuously connected. As Internet safety advocate Larry Magid commented in 2009, "They don't go online, they ARE online."[1] This means children are also continuously exposed to digital marketing through their use of the Internet and applications on telephones, tablets, and computers.

The interactive nature of the Internet offers marketers many ways to reach children. Marketers create brand presence for children to interact with in the virtual worlds, social networks, and instant messaging environments in which they live. As early as 2001, *Business Week* reported that 98 percent of children's websites permitted advertising, and that more than two-thirds of websites designed for children relied on advertising as their primary revenue source.[2] In 2009, the digital measurement company comScore, Inc., reported that U.S. Internet users of all ages viewed a total of 4.5 trillion display ads during 2008, with the average person viewing more than 2,000 ads per month.[3]

Marketers attract children to branded entertainment sites, to watch and pass on "viral" commercial videos made for viewer dissemination, and to become brand advocates by engaging in buzz marketing and by creating their own advertisements for products.[4]

SCHOOLS AS DIGITAL MARKETING VENUES

Children encounter digital marketing when they use technology on their own during "private" time, but they also increasingly encounter it as part of their schooling. To some extent students themselves drive this development; for example, it only makes sense for high school sports teams to communicate via social media, where teens communicate anyway. Teachers and schools, however, don't just go where the students already are; they also encourage students to spend more time immersed in virtual environments. It is, therefore, important to consider whether the schools' efforts to promote student use of the Internet are being done in a responsible way and for age-appropriate, educationally valid reasons.

Schools now routinely incorporate digital technology in the form of educational software, educational websites, and "1:1" programs that provide laptops or tablets to each student, allowing and encouraging teachers to incorporate technology into their lessons.[5]

In 2009, a survey conducted by the Consumer Electronics Association found that 65 percent of teens reported the use of technology in their classes, with 41 percent reporting spending time in a computer class or lab. At that time, 71 percent of private school students reported needing access to a computer outside of school for their studies, as did 47 percent of public school students. Of teens reporting electronics usage at school, 82 percent reported using a cell phone most often, and 46 percent said they use a laptop at school.[6]

Those numbers have increased since 2009. A 2014 study released by the Sesame Workshop reported that 74 percent of K-8 teachers use digital games for instructional purposes, with 55 percent of teachers reporting that their students play games digitally for school assignments at least weekly.[7] Whereas 80 percent of teachers reported that their students primarily play games specifically created for an educational audience, 13 percent reported that their students play commercial games or commercial games that have been adapted for educational use.[8]

In initial interviews for a study of digital marketing, elementary school teachers in Portland, Maine, told researcher Michele Polacsek that their elementary school students spend, on average, three hours per day in school on some kind of digital device.[9]

In addition, via webinars for educational professionals and articles addressed to both professionals and parents, professional organizations such as edWeb.net, nonprofits such as Common Sense Media, and professional publications such as *Education Week* all pound the drum for increasing computer use in school.[10]

SCHOOLS AS A PORTAL TO THE INTERNET

As children move around the Internet, using educational sites and jumping off from them to surf other sites, their activity is constantly tracked and recorded for future use.[11] A 2014 *Politico* article pointed out that students are tracked by education technology companies as they play online games, watch videos, read books, take quizzes, and work on assignments from home.[12]

The data recorded may include information about their locations, homework schedules, Internet browsing habits, and academic progress.[13] Students also create marketable profiles when they take surveys in school and when they take standardized tests.[14] Because these data are not part of the "educational record" protected under the Family Educational Rights and Privacy Act of 1974 (FERPA), they may be used to target marketing to children and their families, or to build profiles on them that would be of interest to such potential purchasers as colleges, universities, and businesses that seek to market products to students, potential employers, or military recruiters.[15]

A December 2013 report released by the Center on Law and Information Policy at Fordham Law School, examining district contracts with third-party data-cloud-providing services, found that 95 percent of districts now rely on cloud-services providers for such purposes as data mining for student performance, support for classroom activities, student guidance, data hosting, and so on. However, fewer than 25 percent of the agreements specify the permitted purposes for disclosures of student information, fewer than 7 percent of the contracts restrict the sale or marketing of student information by vendors, and many agreements allow vendors to unilaterally change the terms. Many also allow vendors to retain student data in perpetuity.[16]

Joel Reidenberg, the lead author of the Fordham report, warned that districts do not have the expertise to ensure that the contracts they sign with vendors adequately protect student privacy. Moreover, in the absence of formal policy, conditions (such as whether to include a field for

Social Security number, for instance) are dictated by the technological choices made by private companies whose interests are first and foremost to promote profits and avoid liability, not to protect student privacy. [17]

OPPORTUNITY FOR A "CALIFORNIA EFFECT"

In September 2014, California enacted three laws that address some of the concerns raised by the Fordham report and also regulate data that is not typically categorized as part of the educational record.

California Education Code § 49073.6 regulates contracts for services that gather and maintain information about students from social media. [18] It explicitly forbids companies that provide a social media service from sharing the information collected, from selling the information, and from using the information for any purpose other than the contracted purpose, which may be school or student safety only. It requires educational agencies to inform parents and provide for public comment before contracting for service. Finally, it requires the service provider to offer students and their parents means to see, correct, or delete the information gathered about them, to delete individual student data when students turn eighteen or dis-enroll, and to delete all student data completely upon completion of the contract.

California Education Code § 49073.1 addresses the ownership of "pupil-generated content" (such as "essays, research reports, portfolios, creative writing, music or other audio files, photographs, and account information"). [19] It requires that when an educational agency contracts with a provider to store or manage pupil-generated content, the contract must specify how students may retain ownership and control of the content, and must prohibit the service provider from using this content in any way other than specifically contracted for—including using personally identifiable information from the records to target advertising.

This law also requires contracts to include statements that specify that the educational agency—not the service provider—owns and controls its students' records, to describe the precautions the service provider will take to ensure the security and confidentiality of student records, and to describe how the agency and the service provider will jointly ensure compliance with the federal Family Educational Rights and Privacy Act (FERPA).

California Business and Professions Code §§ 22584-22585 regulates Internet sites, online services, online applications, and mobile applications designed and marketed for K–12 school purposes.[20] It prohibits operators of such services from engaging in targeted advertising, from collecting information to create profiles of K–12 students (except as needed to conduct the educational purposes for which it was contracted), and from selling or disclosing students' information. This legislative enactment was described by the *San Jose Mercury News* as the "stiffest U.S. bill to protect K–12 students' online data."[21]

A week after California's governor signed these three laws, a group of fourteen education technology companies took a voluntary pledge to protect student privacy, beginning January 2015.[22]

The companies promised to refrain from collecting, maintaining, using, or sharing student personal information beyond that immediately needed for the contracted educational purposes, from selling student information, from using or disclosing student information for the purpose of developing behavioral targeting for advertisements to students, from knowingly retaining student personal information beyond the time period necessary to complete their contract, and from changing without notice their privacy policies or other policies regarding the use of student personal information.[23]

The companies also promised to limit data collection to that needed for their contracted purpose, to disclose clearly in an easy-to-understand manner the nature of data collected about students and why it may be shared with third parties, to support parent access to and correction of student personally identifiable information, to protect the security of the data collected, and to make sure, in the event of an acquisition of the company, that its successor commits to the same safeguards.[24]

The industry's voluntary pledge and the new California student privacy laws are steps forward; however, key privacy issues remain unresolved. Microsoft and other "big players" in education technology immediately signed on to the pledge, no doubt in the hope of reassuring parents and educators that they can entrust their children's data to them. Google and Apple have since signed on, but education publishing and assessment giant Pearson has not.[25] Nevertheless, as Jules Polonetsky, executive director of the Future Privacy Forum, told the *New York Times*, "We hope this is a useful way for companies that want to be trusted partners in schools to make it clear they are on the side of responsible data use."[26]

In February 2015, President Obama announced a bipartisan effort to create a "Student Digital Privacy Act," presumably modeled on California's "Student Online Personal Information Protection Act."[27] Although the text of this federal bill has not yet been made public, its stated intention is to limit use of data collected about students to "educational and legitimate research purposes."[28]

These moves on the part of legislators and private companies align with public opinion. A January 2014 survey found that 86 percent of adult respondents agreed that "oversight is necessary to ensure [children's] private information is not exploited for commercial purposes and stays out of the hands of the wrong people."[29]

THE NATURE OF THE INTERNET AS A MARKETING ENVIRONMENT

When schools direct children to the Internet, even for educational purposes, they put them in an environment full of marketing. Children are likely to wander from education sites to other sites to play (and be marketed to), but even if they don't wander and do stay focused on their work, many sites that claim to be educational or that children use for educational purposes (such as search engines, educational game sites, or research help sites) serve them ads while they work.[30] Some of these ads are for things that look like fun for children, and many children will, not surprisingly, click through to have a look.

For example, we spent a little time playing on www.funbrain.com, a site that offers games to help making learning to standards more fun for children.[31] When we played math baseball (at a level that an elementary school student might play), among the ads we were served were some for products related to www.Poptropica.com, Funbrain's parent site. The ad for "the ultimate Poptropica sticker collection" led to an opportunity to buy the stickers along with an assortment of games and books. The ad for Poptropica music led to an opportunity to purchase it from Amazon or iTunes.

The ability to track visitors makes the Internet a different kind of advertising environment from, for example, a baseball stadium filled with ads directed at baseball lovers, or even from a school littered with advertising directed specifically toward children. When marketers track a child's activity on her computer, they can then specifically direct ads to that child based on her activity. For the purpose of serving ads to this child, her name and other identifying information do not really matter; the behavior that indicates her likes and dislikes is much more important.[32]

Behavioral tracking is part of what child privacy activists Jeff Chester and Kathryn Montgomery call a "360-degree" marketing strategy.[33] It's a marketing strategy that targets children wherever they may be and engages with them in as many environments as possible (i.e., on television, offline, and online). Whereas marketers cannot monitor children's television viewing and other offline activities, they can and do monitor children's online behavior and record the data for the purpose of subsequently targeting marketing to them.[34]

Websites' privacy policies are often long, complex documents, and few people read them before clicking "accept." Nevertheless, the policies can be revealing to anyone who takes the time to consider to what they are being asked to agree to. Funbrain's privacy policy, for example, explains that it collects "personal information" and "anonymized information." Family Education Network (FEN, Funbrain's parent company, is a subsidiary of Pearson Education, Inc.) "collects IP addresses for system administration, to report aggregate information to our advertisers, sponsors, and partners, and to audit the use of our site."[35]

FEN does not "knowingly collect, use, or distribute personal information from children under the age of 13 without prior verifiable consent from a parent or guardian." When we played math baseball, though, we were not asked to report our ages. FEN does not take responsibility for the activity of other sites to which users may connect via its site—for example, Amazon or iTunes, where we could have purchased stickers, books, or music, and other sites we could have explored from there.[36]

It is worth noting that privacy policies need not be complex. For example, the policy could be as simple as "We will not knowingly share any information with anyone for any purpose and we will not market to you." In other words, complex policies appear designed to obscure and protect advertising and other potential revenue-generating opportunities.

When children enter the Internet environment, even if they enter from a responsible site with a transparent privacy policy, they are quickly exposed to other commercial sites that may be less concerned about their privacy. For parents and educators the hard truth is this: when schools send children into the open online environment, they are in reality often offering up their students to be tracked for the purpose of serving them ads for products that algorithms predict they will want to buy.

Tracking software also records adult behavior on the Internet, of course, although many adults may be unaware of it. Since educators are, however, responsible for the children entrusted to their care, they cannot afford to be uninformed about potential threats to student privacy. Educators are obliged to not only to learn how student data may be gathered and exploited but also to develop privacy policies that protect their students from such exploitation.

CONCERNS ABOUT THE COLLECTION AND TRACKING OF STUDENT DATA

Parents, privacy advocates, and legislators have expressed a number of concerns about the tracking of student data. Trends in parent activism and legislative activity suggest that primarily, they worry that companies will collect, sell, and use for advertising purposes information that personally identifies children, such as their names, Social Security numbers, addresses, and telephone numbers.[37]

They also worry that companies will hold and sell students' data, allowing colleges, employers, medical insurance providers, and other future decision-makers to make consequential decisions about them.[38] Privacy policies, contracts, or laws that prohibit collection of personally identifiable data address this concern.

And they worry about the possibility of data security breaches.[39] For good reason: when tech-savvy parents examined the security provided by software used in their children's classes, they found weaknesses that could have allowed unauthorized users to access children's private information.[40] One of these parents, Tony Porterfield, continued his investigation to examine nearly twenty products used by schools and districts, including school district-wide social networks, classroom assessment programs, and learning applications. He told the *New York Times* that he found several potential security risks, only some of which were addressed when he alerted the companies responsible.[41]

Parents and legislators seem to worry much less about companies collecting behavioral tracking data that does not personally identify children than they do about the collection of unique personal information.

Although these data are "anonymized" (the marketer doesn't really care who they are in this instance), they can be used to target children with ads matched to their particular interests. And, even without a child's name or Social Security number, a company with enough other details about that child can trace her back and identify her.[42] Privacy policies, contracts, or laws that prohibit collection of personally identifiable data do not address this issue.

The Rise and Fall of inBloom

School accountability standards, and a business, political, and cultural zeitgeist that favors technological approaches to improving educational outcomes, encourage districts to collect and report increasingly more data about their students. Districts working with many different vendors using different computer software systems find that those systems are often incompatible with one another.

To help streamline the use of data collected about students, the Bill & Melinda Gates Foundation and the Carnegie Corporation of New York funded a non-profit organization, called inBloom, to provide a "vendor-neutral data service." The idea of the service was, purportedly, to serve as a repository for all the information collected about students, "to make it easier for teachers, parents and students to get a coherent picture of student progress, give them more options to be involved and informed, and make learning more engaging for students."[43]

Several states and districts, including Colorado, Delaware, Georgia, Illinois, Kentucky, North Carolina, Massachusetts, Louisiana, and New York, initially signed up to participate in inBloom's data collection effort, and in March 2013, the *Atlanta Business Chronicle* reported that twenty-one education technology companies had already announced plans to develop applications to work with inBloom.[44] By the end of the 2013–2014 school year, however, the tide had turned: every one of the participating states and districts had pulled out. What happened?

Advocacy groups such as Campaign for a Commercial-Free Childhood, Class Size Matters, NYC Public School Parents, and a band of progressive education bloggers (including Carol Burris, Jason France, Susan Ohanian, and Diane Ravitch) opposed the mass adoption of inBloom[45] and they helped rally opposition to the program.

Critics questioned inBloom's commitment to and ability to protect student privacy. In particular, they challenged the motives of its funders and partners (particularly Rupert Murdoch's News Corp, whose subsidiary, Wireless Generation, built part of the inBloom software infrastructure). They also questioned the security of the system, and the potential violations of privacy associated with the massive collection and maintenance over time of personally identifiable student data. [46]

inBloom's responses to these concerns did not reassure its critics. It claimed that neither funders nor partners would have access to student data and that vendors would be allowed to access student records through inBloom only if the relevant state or district allowed it. [47] With respect to data storage and disclosure, it asserted that its Data Store provided "the privacy and security functionality required by" FERPA[48]; that each state and district was responsible for the security of its own students' data; and that according to FERPA, districts may disclose personally identifiable student information if they want to. [49]

Also, inBloom did not provide an option to "opt out." Parents who wanted to opt out were referred back to their school district. [50] Significantly, decisions about whether to sign on with inBloom, along with the policy that would encourage districts to use its services, were made at the state level. Once a state opted in, it became extremely difficult for school districts to opt out. [51]

The development and initial adoption of inBloom illustrates the intersection of corporate-friendly education reform and commercializing activities in schools. [52] Districts need the technology offered by additional vendors to comply with the testing requirements of the Common Core state standards and of legislation that requires them to offer online learning and testing. Such legislation is being encouraged across the United States by organizations such as the American Legislative Exchange Council (ALEC), the Business Roundtable, the Chamber of Commerce, and a variety of corporate-oriented foundations. [53]

School districts also need the technology to inform their own decision making. But to the extent that private vendors are used to collect and/or store student information, it creates the possibility that the information can be exploited commercially for purposes other than those for which it was collected. Indeed, as things now stand, unless specifically prohibited from doing so contractually or by law, a private vendor who is contracted to collect or store data for purposes of legitimate district decision making may also use those data for its own commercial purposes or share it with third parties who do.[54]

Therefore, inBloom may have been abandoned, but the need to protect student data remains a significant issue for parents and policy makers.[55] The trend of collecting and using student data shows no sign of slowing. The threats posed by districts contracting with a variety of vendors remain.[56] Without expertise or legal protection to help them navigate the contracts presented to them, districts may sign off on contract language that does not adequately protect student privacy.[57]

Student Privacy Bill of Rights

In a March 2014 *Washington Post* article, Khaliah Barnes, director of the Student Privacy Project and administrative law counsel for the non-profit Electronic Privacy Information Center (EPIC), explained the significant features of effective regulation of student privacy in her organization's *Student Privacy Bill of Rights*.[58] EPIC calls for the following:

1. Access and Amendment: Students have the right to access and amend their erroneous, misleading, or otherwise inappropriate records, regardless of who collects or maintains the information.

   - There are gaps in current laws and proposed frameworks concerning students' access and amendment to their data. Schools, companies, government agencies, and other entities that collect any student information should provide students access to this information. This includes access to any automated decision-making rule-based systems (i.e, personalized learning algorithms) and behavioral information.

2. Focused Collection: Students have the right to reasonably limit student data that companies and schools collect and retain.

   - EdTech companies should collect only as much student data as they need to complete specified purposes. "Educational purposes" and "educational quality" are frequent examples of broad and fluid purposes that grant EdTech carte blanche to collect troves of student data. A more focused collection would, for example, specify that the collection is necessary to "improve fifth-grade reading skills" or "enhance college-level physics courses." In focusing student data collection for specific purposes, schools and companies should consider the sensitivity of the data and the associated privacy risks.

3. Respect for Context: Students have the right to expect that companies and schools will collect, use, and disclose student information solely in ways that are compatible with the context in which students provide data.

   • Schools and companies should never repurpose student data without express written student consent. This includes using student data to serve generalized or targeted advertisements. The Education Department's guidance states that federal student privacy laws do not prohibit schools or districts "from allowing a provider acting as a school official from serving ads to all students in email or other online services." This allows service providers to repurpose the information. Schools provide private companies access to student data to help enhance education quality. When companies use this access for general marketing purposes, they have repurposed the student data and turned the classroom into a marketplace.

4. Security: Students have the right to secure and responsible data practices.

   • Amid recent, large-scale student data breaches, schools and companies must increase their data safeguards to ward against "unauthorized access, use, destruction, or modification; and improper disclosure" as described in the CPBR.[59] Companies should immediately notify schools, students, and appropriate law enforcement of any breach. And schools should immediately notify students when there is a breach. Schools should refrain from collecting information if they cannot adequately protect it. Securing student information also entails deleting and de-identifying information after it has been used for its initial and primary purposes (no secondary uses allowed!).

5. Transparency: Students have the right to clear and accessible information privacy and security practices.

   • Schools and companies should publish the types of information they collect, the purposes for which the information will be used, and the security practices in place. Schools and companies should also publish algorithms behind their decision-making.

6. Accountability: Students should have the right to hold schools and private companies handling student data accountable for adhering to the Student Privacy Bill of Rights.

   • Schools and companies should be accountable to enforcement authorities and students for violating these practices.[60]

The discussion that follows below reveals how current federal and state privacy laws fall short on one or more of these measures.

USE AND ABUSE OF STUDENT DATA: THE LEGISLATIVE LANDSCAPE

Federal Law Regarding Student Privacy

Federal law protects student privacy via Section 1232h of the Education Code and the Family Educational Rights and Privacy Act of 1974 (FERPA).[61]

Protection of Pupil Rights (20 U.S. Code § 1232h)

20 U.S. Code § 1232h addresses the collection, disclosure, or use of personal information collected from students for marketing purposes or for sale of the information. Local education agencies (LEAs) must notify parents of any activities involving collection, disclosure, or use of personal information obtained from students for marketing purposes and allow parents both the opportunity to inspect any data collection instruments and to opt their children out of any survey of protected information.[62] That is: districts and schools are still allowed to engage in gathering

student information for marketing purposes; but they have to tell parents they are doing it and allow parents who are aware of privacy concerns to remove their children's information from the school's reach.

Family Educational Rights and Privacy Act (FERPA)

When inBloom's management was questioned about the security and disclosure of the data they planned to store, they answered by saying that all their policies were compliant with FERPA.[63] Critics were concerned because FERPA actually provides a fairly weak set of regulations.[64] This continues to be the case.

FERPA applies to any public or private elementary, secondary, or post-secondary school and any state or LEA that receives federal funds, which in effect includes almost all public and private schools. It works by denying funding to any agency or institution that violates its regulations. FERPA's scope is limited to "educational records" (i.e., it excludes such items as data collected by education technology websites and applications and the "pupil-generated content" now protected by California law, except where Personally Identifying Information from education records is implicated).[65]

FERPA gives parents the right to obtain a copy of their institution's policy concerning access to educational records, to halt the release of personally identifiable information, and to review their children's education records and request corrections, if necessary.[66] It also originally prohibited educational institutions from disclosing "personally identifiable information in education records" without parental consent.[67] However, it has been weakened in recent years to allow schools to provide data to private companies without parental consent.[68]

Moreover, several exceptions allow for disclosure of student records to certain parties or under certain conditions without parental consent. For the purposes of our discussion, the most significant among these parties and conditions are that records may be released without consent to *school officials* with a legitimate educational interest and to organizations conducting studies for or on behalf of a school, and also to *authorized representatives* of the U.S. comptroller general, U.S. education secretary, or state educational authorities.[69]

Changes to FERPA in 2008 and 2011 expanded the definitions of both school officials and authorized representatives. The Department of Education now considers "school officials" to include "contractors, consultants, volunteers, and other parties to whom an educational agency or institution has outsourced institutional services or functions it would otherwise use employees to perform." The department also considers "authorized representatives" to be any individuals or entities that local or state educational authorities, the U.S. secretary of education, or the U.S. comptroller general select as an authorized representative.[70]

FERPA also allows schools to release "directory information," which includes students' names and addresses, to the public. FERPA permits parents to opt out of having their child's directory information disclosed.

The Department of Education's guidelines of "best practices" for schools and districts recommends case-by-case evaluation of any online educational services to determine whether FERPA-protected information is implicated; if so, of course, the school or district must ensure that FERPA requirements are met.[71]

The guidelines also recommend that schools and districts maintain written contracts for any use of online educational services, and that these contracts contain provisions for which data will be collected; with whom they may be shared; how they will be stored; how they will be secured; how they may be accessed by students, parents, and the school; when they will be destroyed; and whether the school or district may be indemnified for a vendor's failure to comply with relevant laws.[72] These guidelines, which do not hold the force of law, may help the schools and districts held responsible under FERPA to define their contract terms.

An Unsuccessful Attempt to Strengthen FERPA: The Protecting Student Privacy Act of 2014

In the summer of 2014, Senators Edward J. Markey and Orrin Hatch introduced the Protecting Student Privacy Act of 2014 to strengthen parent and student rights under FERPA. This bill would have prohibited agencies from entering into contracts with vendors ("outside parties") that do not secure sensitive student data or who use students' personally identifiable information to advertise or market to them. It would have required agencies to minimize the data provided to outside parties when possible, maintain records of which outside parties have been given access to information, and require those outside parties both to maintain lists of whom they have provided access to and to destroy records when their specified reason for accessing them is completed. Finally, it would have provided parents the rights to know which outside parties have access to their child's information and to review and amend the personal information about their children held by outside parties. [73]

Had it passed, the Markey/Hatch bill would have increased protections to student privacy; however, it also fell short in important ways. The bill applied only to the official "education record" and left out data collected about students as they use education technology. And instead of putting an affirmative burden of compliance on outside parties with access to student data, it placed oversight and enforcement with agencies that lack the resources and expertise to do so successfully.

State Laws Passed in 2011–2014

We used the Open States and National Conference of State Legislatures databases to gather information about state legislative activity related to K–12 student privacy. [74] We found thirty-four bills related to student privacy that were signed into law between 2011 and 2014 (see appendix E for a list of these bills along with our analysis of their major provisions and gaps in protection, exclusions, and omissions). [75] The number of privacy-related bills passed increased over time: three laws were enacted in 2011, two in 2012, eight in 2013, and twenty-one in 2014.

Assessment of the State Legislative Landscape Regarding Student Data Privacy

We examined the thirty-four state bills to assess which data the laws address, the methods by which they protect those data, and—our primary interest—whether they insulate students from having information collected about them that may be used to market to them.

Our questions fall into four general categories. First, we wanted to know to which data each law applies. Does the law address data that is part of the educational record, data that is collected by education technology companies as part of their contracted work with a school or district, data that is collected by Internet websites and applications used by students for educational purposes, or something else? Although protecting information in the educational record is a good start, as we have discussed, much data can be and is collected from students' use of educational technology and also from their use of computers in school.

Second, we wanted to assess children's and their parents' rights regarding the data that is collected. Do parents (and children when they turn eighteen) have the right to see the information collected, to challenge it, or opt out of its collection, storage, or use?[76] As things now stand, incorrect information can in many instances be spread about students without them or their parents having the right to see and correct that information.

Third, we wanted to know whether and how state legislatures protect students from unwarranted secondary use of their information. Do state laws prohibit companies from using the data they collect or store for advertising and marketing purposes? And are they required to delete the data when they are no longer using it for the purpose for which it was collected?

If data collection has a specific, declared educational purpose and those data are deleted when that purpose is completed, students and parents can be more secure that their information will not subsequently be used for other, unapproved purposes.

Finally, we wanted to know how the laws address the security of the information collected. Do they require data security procedures? Whom do they hold responsible for compliance: the school or district ("local education agency" [LEA]), vendors, and/or a state agency? To the extent that any of these parties is held responsible for breaches of the security or appropriate use of the data collected, they have a stake in ensuring that breaches do not occur.

To Which Data Do State Laws Apply?

Twenty-nine of the thirty-four student privacy-related laws passed by state legislatures in 2011–2014 address data collected and saved as part of students' individual educational records. Some state laws addressed narrowly defined educational data issues. Montana's 20-1-213 MCA, for example, addresses only basic school attendance data that is transferred from schools to the Montana Youth Challenge Program.[77] Other states, such as Oklahoma, enacted comprehensive legislation.[78]

Oklahoma's Student Data Accessibility, Transparency, and Accountability Act of 2013 covers: state and national assessment results; course taking and completion, credits earned, and other transcript information, including course grades and GPA; date of birth, grade level, and expected graduation date/graduation cohort; degree, diploma, credential attainment, and other school exit information such as general educational development and drop-out data; attendance and mobility; data required to calculate the federal four-year adjusted cohort graduation rate, including exit and drop-out information; discipline reports limited to objective information needed to produce the federal Title IV Annual Incident Report; remediation; special education data; and demographic data and program participation information.[79]

Oklahoma also restricts the information that can be included as part of a student's educational record. The now defunct inBloom data system illustrates the concern. It had room for over four hundred optional data fields.[80] Even though inBloom did not require districts to provide all those pieces of information, the existence of the fields invited them to do so, and parents worried about what information was in fact collected, who would have access to it, and how it could be used in the future. Oklahoma specifically excludes the following from a student's educational record: juvenile delinquency records, criminal records, medical and health records, student Social Security numbers, and student biometric information.[81]

New Hampshire's 2014 act to regulate the collection and disclosure of student data goes even further, excluding the following from being maintained in its statewide longitudinal data system:

a. Name of the student's parents or other family members.
b. Address of the student or student's family.
c. Student email or other electronic address.
d. Student or family telephone number.
e. Student or parent credit card account number, insurance account number, or financial services account number.
f. Juvenile delinquency records.
g. Criminal records.
h. Medical and dental insurance information.
i. Student birth information, other than birth date and town of birth.
j. Student Social Security number.
k. Student biometric information.
l. Student postsecondary workforce information including the employer's name, and the name of a college attended outside of New Hampshire.
m. Height and weight.
n. Body mass index (BMI).

o. Political affiliations or beliefs of student or parents.

p. Family income, excluding free and reduced lunch program eligibility as determined by Food Nutrition Services of the United States Department of Agriculture.

q. Mother's maiden name.

r. Parent's Social Security number.

s. Mental and psychological problems of the student or the student's family.

t. Sex behavior or attitudes.

u. Indication of a student pregnancy.

v. Religious or ethical practices, affiliations, or beliefs of the student or the student's parents.[82]

The Oklahoma and New Hampshire statutes are similar to those in Florida, Louisiana, Kansas, New York, North Carolina, and Ohio that explicitly forbid or limit the collection and use of "biometric" information.[83] The definition of "biometric" in the New Hampshire statute is typical: "a record of one or more measurable biological or behavioral characteristics that can be used for automated recognition of an individual. Examples include fingerprints, retina and iris patterns, voiceprints, DNA sequence, facial characteristics, and handwriting."[84]

Few states have addressed forms of data other than students' educational records. As we discussed earlier, California regulates "pupil-generated content," social media services, and Internet sites, online services, online applications, and mobile applications designed and marketed for K–12 school purposes.[85] Colorado addresses online education services, including websites and applications.[86] Rhode Island covers pupil-generated content and any data processed by cloud providers.[87]

In addition, Louisiana and New Hampshire prohibit schools from demanding students' personal electronic account information; New Hampshire forbids electronic surveillance of students (to identify them, transmit information about them, or monitor or track them), without a public hearing leading to school board approval and parental consent.[88]

What Are Students' and Parents' Rights?

FERPA gives parents the right to see their children's data and, if they object to some aspect of the data stored, to submit a claim to the Education Department's Family Policy Compliance Office (FPCO) to "investigate, process, and review complaints and violations under [FERPA]."[89]

As federal law, FERPA is valid in all states. Although many of the state bills require schools and districts (LEAs) to annually alert parents of their rights under FERPA, only California and New York explicitly provide parents the right to correct their children's data.

California's Education Code § 49073.1 requires contracts with vendors to include a description of the procedures by which a parent, legal guardian, or eligible student may review personally identifiable information in the student's records and correct erroneous information.[90]

New York's Education Law § 2-d calls for the creation of a parents' bill of rights that, according to the New York State Education Department, does the same thing: that is, requires all contracts to contain information about how parents can challenge the accuracy of any data that is collected (although it explicitly denies "private right of action," by which parents can directly sue the Education Department or an educational agency).[91]

Some states allow parents to opt in or out of data collection and/or sharing. Requiring parents to "opt in" is the stronger protection. New York requires parental opt-in for a company to release information[92]; Idaho requires it for secondary uses of the data[93]; Louisiana and Montana require it for release of personally identifying data[94]; and Kansas and Oklahoma require it for biometric data.[95] Oklahoma law allows parents to opt out for data other than what it considers to be necessary items of the educational record.[96]

How Is Student Data Protected?

State laws may require that security measures be taken without specifying the nature of those measures. Alternatively, they may require such specific security measures as de-identification (via aggregation, encryption, or the assignment of unidentifiable codes), or the destruction of the data. Fourteen states require some kind of security measure. Only California, Kansas, New York, Rhode Island, and Oklahoma laws hold private companies responsible for security breaches; Texas holds researchers who obtain data responsible.[97]

Eight states require specification of how data will be used, or at least imply that requirement in their language (California, Colorado, Kansas, Idaho, New York, North Carolina, Oklahoma, and Wyoming).[98] Eight states require destruction of the data collected (California, Colorado, Kansas, Idaho, New York, Louisiana, North Carolina, and Wyoming).[99] The destruction of student data when it is no longer needed for the purpose(s) for which it was collected not only prevents security breaches but also precludes the information being used for purposes that were not intended when it was first collected.

Of the thirty-four laws we examined, only eight (in California, Colorado, Idaho, Montana, New York, Rhode Island, and Wyoming) explicitly prohibit the use for commercial purposes of the student information they address.[100]

THE LEGISLATIVE AGENDA: MUCH REMAINS UNDONE

Although a number of bills exist to address student data privacy issues, legislatures have rarely addressed student data that are not part of official educational records. California and Colorado are the only states whose laws we examined that cover data that may be collected by companies that provide education technology or websites and applications.

Schools continue to send children to the Internet to conduct research and to work and play on education-related websites and mobile applications. By doing so, they in effect send them off unsupervised to sail the digital marketing seas—where, as we discussed in chapters 3 and 4, they are susceptible to and targeted for marketing.

A significant improvement in children's privacy protections occurred in December 2012, when the Federal Trade Commission updated rules under the Children's Online Privacy Protection Act (COPPA). COPPA applies to children under the age of thirteen.[101]

Among the rule changes are several expanded definitions that close loopholes that previously allowed third parties to collect personal information from children via "plug-ins." Also significant is an expanded definition of "personal information," which now includes location (such as street address and city) available from mobile devices, photos, videos, audio recordings, screen or user names, and persistent identifiers (such as "cookies" and other hidden software).

Although these changes to COPPA are significant, they apply only to children under the age of thirteen. Especially at risk are teens, whom COPPA does not protect, who are online more than young children both in and out of school, and who, as we discussed in chapters 3 and 4, are especially susceptible to the marketing for which they are targeted.

Although it may be impossible to impose a parental approval require-ment for the online activity of teens, teenagers' personal information needs to be safeguarded. Jennifer Harris and her colleagues at the Univer-sity of Connecticut's Rudd Center for Food Policy and Obesity have argued, for example, that children need policy protections from unhealthy food marketing until the age of fourteen.[102]

HOW TO BETTER PROTECT CHILDREN'S PRIVACY

As we have argued throughout, commercializing activities in schools threaten children's psychological well-being, their physical health, and the integrity of their education. The use of digital technologies in educa-tion is pervasive and growing. While these technologies show great promise, they also hold the potential to harm students profoundly if not properly managed to ensure that they serve the best interests of students. It is unrealistic to expect schools to reverse the trend toward the use of educational software, Internet websites, and mobile applications; the challenge now is to protect children from the potential harms to which these developments expose them.

To the extent that schools continue to direct high school students to online resources, and because teens are so susceptible to digital marketing strategies, they should be protected from digital marketing in the same way younger children are. We recommend that the Federal Trade Com-mission extend the Children's Online Privacy Protection Act (COPPA) protections to age fourteen, and strengthen the protections offered to ado-lescents ages fifteen to eighteen.

Further, our review of national and state legislation on student data privacy suggests that although some states have addressed important con-cerns, overall there are still many significant gaps in the privacy protec-tions for students.

Particularly limited are opportunities for parents to correct errors in the data collected about their children, or to opt out of data collection entirely. Although the Family Educational Rights and Privacy Act (FER-PA) gives parents the right to lodge a complaint with the Education Department, it does not give them "private right of action"—i.e., the power to sue on their own behalf. [103] Further, the only "opt out" right that FERPA offers parents is to opt out of the release of "directory" information. States that require local education agencies (LEAs) to inform parents of their federal rights, therefore, do not offer parents all that much.

Another significant gap is the failure to require LEAs and private vendors to specify in advance the purpose for which any given piece of information is collected, to limit the use of that information to its original intended purpose, and to destroy the information when the purpose is completed. Such requirements would prevent the collection of more data than necessary and would also prevent LEAs and vendors from engaging in secondary use of the data, particularly for commercial purposes. Laws that require LEAs to provide public documentation of which data are being collected and for what purposes would encourage transparency and promote compliance.

Only a handful of states explicitly prohibit the use for commercial purposes of the student information they address in their legislation, or hold private companies legally responsible for breaches of student privacy and/or data security. Without explicit sanctions against vendors, vendors' motivation for profit may very well overcome their motivation to protect student privacy. Legislation that calls for transparency or that places the onus of compliance on state officials or districts rather than on vendors is not likely to effectively secure children's personal information or adequately protect them from commercial exploitation.

As legislators develop statutory language and district leaders develop their contracting policies, a good resource for them to start with is the set of comprehensive guidelines offered by the Electronic Privacy Information Center's Student Privacy Bill of Rights. [104] These guidelines are stronger and more comprehensive than the 2014 "best practices" offered by the U.S. Department of Education. [105]

We also recommend that policy makers develop policies that encompass not only the privacy of student educational records but also the wide variety of student data (including anonymized data) that may now be collected and shared. These policies should explicitly address the potential commercial use of any data collected.

Finally, we recommend that the burden of protecting student data be placed not only on schools but also on any private vendors with access to student data. This would align the interests of all parties, public and private, in protecting student privacy.

NOTES

1. Magid, L. (2009, June 16). Teen online safety mostly about behavior. Retrieved July 22, 2009, from http://www.safekids.com/2009/06/16/teen-online-safety-mostly-about-behavior.

2. Neuborne, E. (2001, August 13). For kids on the web, it's an ad, ad, ad, ad world: How to help yours see the sales pitches behind online games. *Business Week*. Retrieved August 20, 2009, from http://www.businessweek.com/magazine/content/01_33/b3745121.htm.

3. comScore, Inc. (2009, January 30). *2008 Digital Year in Review*. Reston, VA: Author. Retrieved August 4, 2009, from http://www.comscore.com/Press_Events/Presentations_Whitepapers/2009/2008_Digital_Year_in_Review.

4. MacMullan, J., Wright, H., Linders, H., & de Vera, A. (2009, March). New media, same old tricks: A survey of the marketing of food to children on food company websites. Consumers International. Retrieved August 20, 2009, from http://consint.live.rss-hosting.co.uk/files/98978/FileName/Newmedia,sameoldtricks-ENWebversionFINAL100309.pdf; Chester, J., & Montgomery, K. (2007, May). Interactive food and beverage marketing: Targeting children and youth in the digital age. Berkeley, CA: Public Health Institute. Retrieved August 19, 2009, from http://digitalads.org/documents/digiMarketingFull.pdf.

5. Greenwich Public Schools (2014, December 23). iPads for Elementary Students, Chromebooks for Secondary Students. Author. Retrieved January 2, 2015, from http://www.greenwichschools.org/uploaded/district/pdfs/News_Archives/News_Archives_2014-15/PR_-_DLE_Phase_III_Device_122314.pdf; Waldman, B. (2014, October 14). Technology Is Not the Answer: A Student's Perspective. *Education Week*. Retrieved January 2, 2015, from http://www.edweek.org/ew/articles/2014/10/15/08waldman.h34.html?cmp=ENL-EU-NEWS2.

6. Consumer Electronics Association (2009, August 18). CEA study shows teens want more technology in the classroom: eight in ten teens report using cell phones more than any other device at school. (Press Release). Author. Retrieved August 22, 2009, from http://www.ce.org/Press/CurrentNews/press_release_detail.asp?id=11776.

7. Takeuchi, L. M., &Vaala, S. (2014, October). Level Up Learning: A National Survey on Teaching with Digital Games. The Joan Ganz Cooney Center at Sesame Workshop. Retrieved October 21, 2014, from http://www.joanganzcooneycenter.org/publication/level-up-learning-a-national-survey-on-teaching-with-digital-games/.

8. Takeuchi, L. M., & Vaala, S. (2014, October). Level Up Learning: A National Survey on Teaching with Digital Games. The Joan Ganz Cooney Center

at Sesame Workshop. Retrieved October 21, 2014, from http://www.joanganzcooneycenter.org/publication/level-up-learning-a-national-survey-on-teaching-with-digital-games/.

9. Polacsek, M. (2014). [Digital Food Marketing]. Unpublished raw data.

10. Some examples of webinars promoted to education professionals are: "Amplifying Student Potential with Tablets & Chromebooks," offered by *Education Week* on December 17, 2014, with content provided by Google for Education; "Empowering Students with Project-Based Learning and Google Tablets," offered by *Education Week* on November 24, 2014, with content provided by Google for Education; "How Much Digital Literacy Do Students Need?" offered by *Education Week* on November 24, 2014, with content provided by learning.com and underwritten by Carnegie Corporation of New York; "Building Better Ed-Tech Strategies for the Pre-K-5 Crowd," offered by *Education Week* on October 21, 2014. Education Week webinar listings retrieved January 2, 2014, from http://www.edweek.org/ew/marketplace/webinars/webinars.html#archived;"App Smashing: Combining Apps for Innovative Student Projects," offered by Common Sense Media on November 24, 2014; "Teachers as Designers of Technology, Pedagogy, and Content (TPACK)" offered by Common Sense Media on October 30, 2014; "Khan Academy's Video-based Instruction," offered by Common Sense Media on August 27, 2014. Common Sense Media webinar listings retrieved January 2, 2014, from https://www.graphite.org/appy-hour; "Top 5 Digital Tools of 2014," offered by edWeb.net on December 15, 2014; "Journeys in Blended Learning: Key Landmarks for Your School's Progress," offered by edWeb.net on December 16, 2014; "Encouraging Student Collaboration Using TodaysMeet and Lino," offered by edWeb.net on December 16, 2014. edWeb.net webinar listings retrieved January 2, 2014, from http://home.edweb.net/upcoming-webinars/.

11. Chester, J., & Montgomery, K. (2007, May). Interactive food and beverage marketing: Targeting children and youth in the digital age. Berkeley, CA: Public Health Institute. Retrieved October 7, 2014, from http://digitalads.org/documents/digiMarketingFull.pdf. Montgomery, K. C. & Chester, J. (2009). Interactive food and beverage marketing: Targeting adolescents in the digital age. *Journal of Adolescent Health, 45*, S18–S29; Simon, S. (2014, May 15). Data mining your children. *Politico*. Retrieved October 3, 2014, from http://www.politico.com/story/2014/05/data-mining-your-children-106676.html.

12. Simon, S. (2014, May 15). Data mining your children. *Politico*. Retrieved October 3, 2014, from http://www.politico.com/story/2014/05/data-mining-your-children-106676.html/

13. Simon, S. (2014, May 15). Data mining your children. *Politico*. Retrieved October 3, 2014, from http://www.politico.com/story/2014/05/data-mining-your-children-106676.html.

14. Simon, S. (2014, May 15). For sale: Student 'hopes and dreams.' *Politico.* Retrieved October 7, 2014, from http://www.politico.com/story/2014/05/student-data-privacy-market-106692.html.

15. Simon, S. (2014, May 15). For sale: Student 'hopes and dreams.' *Politico.* Retrieved October 7, 2014, from http://www.politico.com/story/2014/05/student-data-privacy-market-106692.html. For federal privacy law, see: Family Educational Rights and Privacy Act (FERPA). 20 U.S.C. § 1232g (2012).

16. Reidenberg, J. R., Russell, N. C., Kovnot, J., Norton, T. B., Cloutier, R., & Alvarado, D. (2013, December 12). Privacy and Cloud Computing in Public Schools. *Center on Law and Information Policy at Fordham Law School.* Retrieved January 10, 2013, from http://ir.lawnet.fordham.edu/clip/2/.

17. Reidenberg, J. R. (2014, January 13, 2014). Personal communication (telephone) with Faith Boninger.

18. "An act to add Section 49073.6 to the Education Code, relating to pupil records," Cal Ed Code § 49073.6 (2015)

19. "An act to add Section 49073.1 to the Education Code, relating to pupil records," Cal Ed Code § 49073.1 (2015).

20. "Student Online Personal Information Protection Act," Cal Bus & Prof Code, §§ 22584-22585 (2015).

21. Noguchi, S. (2014, August 31). California Legislature Passes Stiffest U.S. Bill to Protect K-12 Students' Online Data. *San Jose Mercury News.* Retrieved January 2, 2015, from http://www.mercurynews.com/education/ci_26444107/online-privacy-california-passes-nations-stiffest-protections-k?source=infinite.

22. Future of Privacy Forum and The Software & Information Industry Association (2014). Student Privacy Pledge. Retrieved October 16, 2014, from http://studentprivacypledge.org/. The number of pledge signers grew to 127 by April 1, 2015.

23. Future of Privacy Forum and The Software & Information Industry Association (2014). Student Privacy Pledge. Retrieved October 16, 2014, from http://studentprivacypledge.org/.

24. Future of Privacy Forum and The Software & Information Industry Association (2014). Student Privacy Pledge. Retrieved October 16, 2014, from http://studentprivacypledge.org/.

25. Future of Privacy Forum and The Software & Information Industry Association (2014). Student Privacy Pledge: Signatories—Currently 127. Retrieved April 1, 2015, from http://studentprivacypledge.org/?page_id=22.

26. Singer, N. (2014, October 7). Microsoft and Other Firms Pledge to Protect Student Data. *New York Times.* Retrieved October 16, 2014, from http://www.nytimes.com/2014/10/07/business/microsoft-and-other-firms-pledge-to-protect-student-data.html.

27. Brown, E. (2014, January 19). Obama to propose new student privacy legislation. *Washington Post*. Retrieved February 9, 2015, from http://www.washingtonpost.com/local/education/obama-to-propose-new-student-privacy-legislation/2015/01/18/2ad6a8ae-9d92-11e4-bcfb-059ec7a93ddc_story.html; Herold, B. (2015, January 29). Draft of President Obama's Student-Data-Privacy Bill Raises Questions. *Education Week*. Retrieved March 30, 2015, from http://blogs.edweek.org/edweek/DigitalEducation/2015/01/federal_student-data-privacy_draft_bill.html; "Student Online Personal Information Protection Act," Cal Bus & Prof Code § 22584 (2015).

28. Podesta, J. (2015, February 5). Big Data and Privacy: 1 Year Out. *The White House Blog*. Retrieved February 11, 2015, from http://www.whitehouse.gov/blog/2015/02/05/big-data-and-privacy-1-year-out.

29. Common Sense Media (2014, January). Student Privacy Survey. Author. Retrieved January 26, 2015, from https://www.commonsensemedia.org/sites/default/files/uploads/about_us/student_privacy_survey.pdf.

30. Although Bing for Schools and Google Apps for Education do not serve ads when children use them on school computers, they do when used from home (Bing for Schools) or when children are not logged in to their Google Apps for Education account (Google Apps for Education). In school or at home, they necessarily lead children to sites that they do not control and that often do serve ads and track user behavior for further marketing purposes. Google (n.d.). Google for Education. Retrieved February 16, 2015, from https://www.google.com/edu/trust/; Wallaert, M. (2014, February 28). Personal communication (e-mail) with Faith Boninger.

31. Retrieved October 15, 2014 from www.funbrain.com.

32. A 2010 *Wall Street Journal* investigation of data tracking and sales via Internet sites found that Dictionary.com was a top venue using tracking technology. Angwin, J. (2010, July 30). The Web's New Gold Mine: Your Secrets. *Wall Street Journal*. Retrieved October 29, 2014, from http://online.wsj.com/articles/SB10001424052748703940904575395073512989404.

33. Chester, J., and Montgomery, K. (2007, May). *Interactive food and beverage marketing: Targeting children and youth in the digital age*. Berkeley, CA: Public Health Institute. Retrieved August 19, 2009, from http://digitalads.org/documents/digiMarketingFull.pdf.

34. Chester, J., and Montgomery, K. (2007, May). *Interactive food and beverage marketing: Targeting children and youth in the digital age*. Berkeley, CA: Public Health Institute. Retrieved August 19, 2009, from http://digitalads.org/documents/digiMarketingFull.pdf; Angwin, J. and Tigas, M. (2015, January 14). Zombie Cookie: The Tracking Cookie That You Can't Kill. *ProPublica*. Retrieved January 15, 2015, from http://www.propublica.org/article/zombie-

cookie-the-tracking-cookie-that-you-cant-kill?utm_source=et&utm_medium=
email&utm_campaign=dailynewsletter&utm_content=&utm_name=.

35. Pearson Education, Inc. (2000–2014). Privacy Statement (October 2013).
Retrieved October 15, 2014, from http://fen.com/resources/privacy-policy-
children.html.

36. Pearson Education, Inc. (2000–2014). Privacy Statement (October 2013).
Retrieved October 15, 2014, from http://fen.com/resources/privacy-policy-
children.html.

37. Campaign for Commercial-Free Childhood (n.d.). Protect Illinois Students' Privacy. Retrieved February 9, 2015, from http://www.
commercialfreechildhood.org/illinoisinbloom.

38. Fleisher, L. (2014, March 23). Big Data Enters the Classroom. *Wall Street
Journal*. Retrieved March 25, 2014, from http://online.wsj.com/news/articles/
SB10001424052702304756104579451241225610478.

39. Class Size Matters (n.d.). New York State inBloom one-page flyer. Author. Retrieved February 9, 2015, from http://www.classsizematters.org/wp-
content/uploads/2013/12/Privacy-Fact-Sheet-rev-5.pdf; NYC Public School Parents (2013, July 24). FAQ on inBloom Inc.: what is the state and your school
district doing? Author. Retrieved August 30, 2013, from http://
nycpublicschoolparents.blogspot.com/2013/07/faq-on-inbloom-inc-what-is-
your-school.html.

40. Noguchi, S. (2014, August 31). California Legislature passes stiffest U.S.
bill to protect K-12 students' online data. *Mercurynews.com*. Retrieved January
2, 2015, from http://www.mercurynews.com/education/ci_26444107/online-
privacy-california-passes-nations-stiffest-protections-k; Singer, S. (2015, February 8). Uncovering Security Flaws in Digital Education Products for Schoolchildren. *New York Times*. Retrieved February 6, 2015, from http://www.nytimes.
com/2015/02/09/technology/uncovering-security-flaws-in-digital-education-
products-for-schoolchildren.html?hp&action=click&pgtype=Homepage&
module=mini-moth&region=top-stories-below&WT.nav=top-stories-below&_
r=1 .

41. Singer, S. (2015, February 8). Uncovering Security Flaws in Digital Education Products for Schoolchildren. *New York Times*. Retrieved February 6,
2015, from http://www.nytimes.com/2015/02/09/technology/uncovering-
security-flaws-in-digital-education-products-for-schoolchildren.html?hp&
action=click&pgtype=Homepage&module=mini-moth&region=top-stories-
below&WT.nav=top-stories-below&_r=1.

42. Kaye, K. (2015, March 23). Sophisticated Health Data Industry Needs
Self-Reflection. *Advertising Age*. Retrieved April 1, 2015, from http://adage.
com/article/privacy-and-regulation/sophisticated-health-data-industry-reflection/
297719/; Wheaton, K. (2015, March 23). Hocus Pocus! Your Data Has Been

Anonymized! Now They'll Never Find You! *Advertising Age*. Retrieved March 30, 2015, from http://adage.com/article/ken-wheaton/data-anonymized-find/297713/.

43. Carr, D. F. (2013, March 26). Hope Battles Fear Over Student Data Integration. *Information Week*. Retrieved August 29, 2013, from http://www.informationweek.com/education/instructional-it/hope-battles-fear-over-student-data-inte/240151687?pgno=1;Bing; inBloom, Inc. and Affiliates (2013). FAQ. Author. Retrieved August 29, 2013, from https://www.inbloom.org/faq.

44. Saporta, M., & Sams, D. (2013, March 1). InBloom may spark 'edtech' boom. *Atlanta Business Chronicle*. Retrieved January 7, 2014, from http://www.bizjournals.com/atlanta/print-edition/2013/03/01/inbloom-may-spark-edtech-boom.html.

45. Carol Burris is a frequent guest blogger at the *Washington Post*, The Answer Sheet blog, http://www.washingtonpost.com/blogs/answer-sheet/; Jason France blogs as Crazy Crawfish, https://crazycrawfish.wordpress.com; Susan Ohanian blogs at http://www.susanohanian.org/; Diane Ravitch blogs at http://dianeravitch.net/

46. American Federation of Teachers (2013, May 31). AFT Statement on Privacy and Security Concerns about inBloom and Other Data Collection Efforts. Author. Retrieved August 30, 2013, from http://www.aft.org/newspubs/press/2013/053113.cfm; Crazy Crawfish (2013, March 28). Your Children for Sale . . . Sold! *Crazy Crawfish's Blog*. Retrieved August 30, 2013, from https://crazycrawfish.wordpress.com/2013/03/28/your-children-for-sale-sold/; NYC Public School Parents (2013, July 24). FAQ on inBloom Inc.: What is the state and your school district doing? Author. Retrieved August 30, 2013, from http://nycpublicschoolparents.blogspot.com/2013/07/faq-on-inbloom-inc-what-is-your-school.html; Ohanian, S. (2013, July 18). NC Lieutenant Governor Has 67 Questions about Common Core. *Susanohanian.org*. Retrieved August 30, 2013, from http://www.susanohanian.org/core.php?id=530; Ravitch, D. (2013, April 8). Why is the US Department of Education Weakening FERPA? *Diane Ravitch's Blog*, Retrieved August 30, 2013, from http://dianeravitch.net/2013/04/08/why-is-the-us-department-of-education-weakening-ferpa/; Simon, S. (3013, March 3). K-12 student database jazzes tech startups, spooks parents. *Reuters*. Retrieved August 30, 2013, from http://www.reuters.com/article/2013/03/03/us-education-database-idUSBRE92204W20130303.

47. inBloom, Inc., and Affiliates (2013). FAQ. Author. Retrieved August 29, 2013, from https://www.inbloom.org/faq; inBloom, Inc., and Affiliates (2013). Privacy Commitment. Author. Retrieved August 29, 2013, from https://www.inbloom.org/privacy-commitment.

48. Family Educational Rights and Privacy Act (FERPA). 20 U.S.C. § 1232g (2012).

49. inBloom, Inc., and Affiliates (2013). FAQ. Author. Retrieved August 29, 2013, from https://www.inbloom.org/faq; inBloom, Inc., and Affiliates (2013). Privacy Commitment. Author. Retrieved August 29, 2013, from https://www.inbloom.org/privacy-commitment; Ravitch, D. (2013, April 8). Why Is the US Department of Education Weakening FERPA? *Diane Ravitch's Blog.* Retrieved August 30, 2013, from http://dianeravitch.net/2013/04/08/why-is-the-us-department-of-education-weakening-ferpa/.

50. inBloom, Inc. and Affiliates (2013). FAQ. Author. Retrieved August 29, 2013, from https://www.inbloom.org/faq.

51. Stern, G. (2013, October 28). Several area districts to forfeit funding over state plans for student data collection. *Lohud.com.* Retrieved November 18, 2013, from http://www.lohud.com/article/20131027/NEWS/310270027?gcheck=1&nclick_check=1; Kamisar, B. (2013, November 13). New York Parents Sue to Block inBloom Program. *Education Week.* Retrieved January 7, 2014, from http://blogs.edweek.org/edweek/marketplacek12/2013/11/lawsuit_filed_in_new_york_to_halt_inbloom_program.html?qs=new+york+inbloom.

52. Ravitch, D. (2013, May 31). How Will inBloom Help Students and Schools? *Diane Ravitch's Blog.* Retrieved August 29, 2013, from http://dianeravitch.net/2013/05/31/how-will-inbloom-help-students-and-schools/.

53. American Legislative Exchange Council (2014). Statewide Online Education Act. Author. Retrieved January 7, 2014, from http://www.alec.org/model-legislation/statewide-online-education-act/; Ravitch, D. (2013, May 31). How Will inBloom Help Students and Schools? *Diane Ravitch's Blog.* Retrieved August 29, 2013, from http://dianeravitch.net/2013/05/31/how-will-inbloom-help-students-and-schools/.

54. Simon, S. (2015, February 9). Pearson's philanthropy entwined with business interests. *Politico.* Retrieved February 12, 2015, from http://www.politico.com/story/2015/02/pearsons-philanthropy-entwined-with-business-interests-115034.html

55. Resmovits, J. (2013, January 22). Immense Unease over Advertisers Nabbing Student Data: Poll. *Huffington Post.* Retrieved January 29, 2014, from http://www.huffingtonpost.com/2014/01/22/student-data-privacy-poll_n_4640688.html?utm_hp_ref=politics&ir=Politics; Singer, N. (2014, February 25). Regulators weigh in on online educational services. *New York Times.* Retrieved February 26, 2014, from http://bits.blogs.nytimes.com/2014/02/25/regulators-weigh-in-on-online-educational-services/?_php=true&_type=blogs&_r=0; U.S. Department of Education, Privacy Technical Assistance Center (2014, February 25). *Protecting Student Privacy While Using Online Educational Services: Requirements and Best Practices.* Author. Retrieved February 26, 2014, from http://ptac.ed.gov/sites/default/files/Student%20Privacy%20and%20Online%20Educational%20Services%20%28February%202014%29.pdf.

56. Fitzgerald, B. (2014, April 3). New York Pulls Out of inBloom. Ho Hum. Funny Monkey. Retrieved January 15, 2015, from http://funnymonkey.com/blog/new-york-pulls-out-inbloom-ho-hum.

57. Reidenberg, J. R. (2014, January 13). Personal communication (telephone) with Faith Boninger.

58. Barnes, K. (2014, March 6). Why a 'Student Privacy Bill of Rights' is desperately needed. *Washington Post*. Retrieved January 7, 2014, from http://www.washingtonpost.com/blogs/answer-sheet/wp/2014/03/06/why-a-student-privacy-bill-of-rights-is-desperately-needed/.

59. President Obama's Consumer Privacy Bill of Rights, released February 23, 2012. Retrieved February 16, 2015, from http://www.whitehouse.gov/sites/default/files/privacy-final.pdf.

60. Electronic Privacy Information Center (n.d.). Student Privacy Bill of Rights. Author. Retrieved January 7, 2014, from https://epic.org/privacy/student/bill-of-rights.html.

61. 20 U.S.C. § 1232h; Family Educational Rights and Privacy Act (FERPA) 20 U.S.C. § 1232g (2012).

62. 20 U.S. Code § 1232h; The Protection of Pupil Rights Amendment (PPRA, 20 U.S.C. § 1232h; 34 CFR Part 98) is only one piece of the section on protection of pupil rights. This 1978 amendment, also known as the Hatch Amendment, specifically addressed the collection of personal data for "survey, analysis, or evaluation" purposes. The collection and use of information for marketing purposes is addressed later in the section.

63. inBloom, Inc., and Affiliates (2013). FAQ. Author. Retrieved August 29, 2013, from https://www.inbloom.org/faq; inBloom, Inc., and Affiliates (2013). Privacy Commitment. Author. Retrieved August 29, 2013, from https://www.inbloom.org/privacy-commitment; Ravitch, D. (2013, April 8). Why Is the US Department of Education Weakening FERPA? *Diane Ravitch's Blog.* Retrieved August 30, 2013, from http://dianeravitch.net/2013/04/08/why-is-the-us-department-of-education-weakening-ferpa/.

64. Electronic Privacy Information Center (EPIC) (n.d.). Family Educational Rights and Privacy Act (FERPA). Author. Retrieved October 21, 2014, from http://epic.org/privacy/student/ferpa/default.html; Electronic Privacy Information Center (EPIC) (n.d.). EPIC v. The U.S. Department of Education. Author. Retrieved October 21, 2014, from http://epic.org/apa/ferpa/; Family Educational Rights and Privacy Act (FERPA) 20 U.S.C. § 1232g (2012); Ravitch, D. (2013, April 8). Why Is the US Department of Education Weakening FERPA? *Diane Ravitch's Blog.* Retrieved August 30, 2013, from http://dianeravitch.net/2013/04/08/why-is-the-us-department-of-education-weakening-ferpa/.

65. Privacy Technical Assistance Center (2014, February). *Protecting Student Privacy While Using Online Educational Services: Requirements and Best Prac-*

tices. U.S. Department of Education. Retrieved February 16, 2015, from http://
tech.ed.gov/wp-content/uploads/2014/09/Student-Privacy-and-Online-
Educational-Services-February-2014.pdf.

66. However, the law does not provide parents private right of action to insti-
tute a lawsuit. Parents can submit a complaint to the Family Policy Compliance
Office, which is designated to review complaints and violations under FERPA.
Barnes, K. (2014, October 31). Personal communication (telephone) with Faith
Boninger.

67. Electronic Privacy Information Center (n.d.). Family Educational Rights
and Privacy Act (FERPA). Author. Retrieved January 5, 2015, from https://epic.
org/privacy/student/ferpa/default.html; Family Educational Rights and Privacy
Act (FERPA) 20 U.S.C. § 1232g (2012).

68. For greater detail, see: Electronic Privacy Information Center (EPIC)
(n.d.). EPIC v. The U.S. Department of Education. Author. Retrieved January 5,
2015, from https://epic.org/apa/ferpa/default.html; Family Educational Rights
and Privacy Act (FERPA) 20 U.S.C. § 1232g (2012); Rotenberg, M. & Barnes,
K. (2013, January 28). Amassing Student Data and Dissipating Privacy Rights.
Educause Review Online. Retrieved January 5, 2015, from http://www.educause.
edu/ero/article/amassing-student-data-and-dissipating-privacy-rights.

69. 34 CFR § 99.31(a)(3); 34 CFR § 99.35(a)(1); Electronic Privacy Information Center (EPIC) (n.d.). EPIC v. The U.S. Department of Education. Author.
Retrieved October 21, 2014, from http://epic.org/apa/ferpa/; Ravitch, D. (2013,
April 8). Why Is the US Department of Education Weakening FERPA? *Diane
Ravitch's Blog.* Retrieved August 30, 2013, from http://dianeravitch.net/2013/04/
08/why-is-the-us-department-of-education-weakening-ferpa/; United States Department of Education (2012). Family Educational Rights and Privacy Act Regulations. Author. Retrieved October 21, 2014, from http://www2.ed.gov/policy/
gen/guid/fpco/pdf/2012-final-regs.pdf.

70. Family Educational Rights and Privacy Act (FERPA) 20 U.S.C. § 1232g
(2012); Rotenberg, M. & Barnes, K (2013, January 28). Amassing Student Data
and Dissipating Privacy Rights. *Educause Review Online.* Retrieved January 5,
2015, from http://www.educause.edu/ero/article/amassing-student-data-and-
dissipating-privacy-rights.

71. Privacy Technical Assistance Center (2014, February). *Protecting Student
Privacy While Using Online Educational Services: Requirements and Best Practices.* U.S. Department of Education. Retrieved February 16, 2015, from http://
tech.ed.gov/wp-content/uploads/2014/09/Student-Privacy-and-Online-
Educational-Services-February-2014.pdf.

72. Privacy Technical Assistance Center (2014, February). *Protecting Student
Privacy While Using Online Educational Services: Requirements and Best Practices.* U.S. Department of Education. Retrieved February 16, 2015, from http://

tech.ed.gov/wp-content/uploads/2014/09/Student-Privacy-and-Online-Educational-Services-February-2014.pdf.

73. Retrieved October 21, 2014, from http://www.markey.senate.gov/imo/media/doc/2014-07-14_StudentPriv_BillText.pdf.

74. We conducted a combination of legislative searches to find bills passed in the last two legislative sessions. We modeled our first search on our prior work, described in chapter 6. Using the Open States database, we searched for the following two terms:

1. privacy AND ("student information" OR "student data")
2. sale AND ("student information" OR "student data")

This search allowed us to choose our own syntax and to examine specifically the possibility that legislatures would address the commercial sale of student information. It also allowed us to find both enacted legislation and bills that were introduced but not enacted. The latter data point is a gross measure because we did not examine each of the introduced bills, but it does give some indication of how much state legislatures considered student privacy issues.

We complemented the Open States search by searching the National Council of State Legislatures (NCSL) database using the keyword "privacy" for state education bills signed into law. Limited to bills that had been classified as education-related, this second search unearthed several relevant enacted bills that slipped through our Open States search. The Open States database can be accessed at http://openstates.org/. The NCSL database can be accessed at http://www.ncsl.org/research/education/education-bill-tracking-database.aspx. Although threats to student privacy are certainly a problem at the post-secondary level as well, we limit our inquiry here to K–12.

75. Our search of the Open States database using the search term *privacy AND ("student information" OR "student data")* yielded 251 bills introduced that contained those words. Of those, fifty-nine were signed into law. We followed the same process for the search term *privacy AND ("student information" OR "student data")*: 145 introduced bills contained those words, with forty-three of them signed into law. We reviewed these laws for relevance (many bills contain these words in irrelevant contexts) and overlap, leaving twenty-six relevant bills that became law.

76. Important, but outside the scope of our inquiry here, are the issues faced by families historically marginalized by schools and for whom the stakes are particularly high (e.g., undocumented students, students and families whose native language is not English, or homeless children). These children and their families may be frightened of data collection for any purpose. 20-1-213 MCA (2013).

77. 20-1-213 MCA (2013).

78. "Student Data Accessibility, Transparency, and Accountability Act of 2013," 70 Okl. St. § 3-168 (2014); "Parents' Bill of Rights," 25 Okl. St. § 2001 (2014); 25 Okl. St. § 2002 (2014); 25 Okl. St. § 2003 (2014).

79. "Student Data Accessibility, Transparency, and Accountability Act of 2013," 70 Okl. St. § 3-168 (2014).

80. Bogle, A. (n.d.). What the Failure of inBloom Means for the Student-Data Industry. *Slate.com*. Retrieved April 29, 2014, from http://www.slate.com/blogs/future_tense/2014/04/24/what_the_failure_of_inbloom_means_for_the_student_data_industry.html.

81. "Student Data Accessibility, Transparency, and Accountability Act of 2013," 70 Okl. St. § 3-168 (2014); 25 Okl. St. § 2002 (2014).

82. "An act relative to the collection and disclosure of student data," N.H. Rev. Stat. Ann. §§ 189:65-189: 68 (LexisNexis 2014).

83. "An act relative to the collection and disclosure of student data," N.H. Rev. Stat. Ann. §§ 189:65-189: 68 (LexisNexis 2014); "Student Data Accessibility, Transparency, and Accountability Act of 2013." 70 Okl. St. § 3-168 (2014); Fla. Stat. § 1002.22 (2014); Fla. Stat. § 1002.221 (2014); Fla. Stat. § 1008.386 (2014); Fla. Stat. § 1011.622 (2014); "Kansas Student Data Privacy Act," K.S.A. § 72-6214 (2013); La. R.S. § 17:3913 (2015); NY CLS Educ § 2-c (2014); NY CLS Educ § 2-d (2014); "An Act to Ensure the Privacy and Security of Student Educational Records, as Recommended by the Joint Legislative Oversight Committee on Information Technology," N.C. Gen. Stat. § 115C-402.5 (2014) and N.C. Gen. Stat. § 115C-402.15 (2014); Ohio Rev. Code Ann. § 3301.0714 (LexisNexis 2014).

84. "An act relative to the collection and disclosure of student data," N.H. Rev. Stat. Ann. §§ 189:65-189: 68 (LexisNexis 2014).

85. "An act to add Section 49073.1 to the Education Code, relating to pupil records," Cal Ed Code § 49073.1 (2015); "An act to add Section 49073.6 to the Education Code, relating to pupil records," Cal Ed Code § 49073.6 (2015); "Student Online Personal Information Protection Act," Cal Bus & Prof Code § 22584 (2015).

86. "Student Data Protection, Accessibility, Transparency, and Accountability Act of 2014," C.R.S. 22-2-309 (2014).

87. R.I. Gen. Laws §§ 16-103-3 - 16-103-4 (2014).

88. "Personal Online Account Privacy Protection Act," La. R.S. §§ 51:1951-1955 (2014); "AN ACT relative to the collection and disclosure of student data," N.H. Rev. Stat. Ann. §§ 189:65-189: 68 (2014). In addition, Maine enacted legislation in 2014 to require a study of social media privacy in school (20-A M.R.S. § 19351 [2014]).

89. Electronic Privacy Information Center (n.d.). EPIC Student Privacy Freedom of Information Act Request: Department of Education's FERPA Enforcement. Author. Retrieved January 7, 2015, from https://www.epic.org/foia/ed/ferpa/default.html.

90. Cal Ed Code § 49073.6 (2015).

91. NY CLS Educ § 2-d (2014). New York State Education Department (2014, July 29). Parents' Bill of Rights for Data Privacy and Security. Author. Retrieved January 8, 2015, from http://www.p12.nysed.gov/docs/parents-bill-of-rights.pdf.

92. NY CLS Educ § 2-c (2014); NY CLS Educ § 2-d (2014).

93. "Student Data Accessibility, Transparency and Accountability Act of 2014," Idaho Code § 33-133 (2014).

94. "An act to enact R.S. 17:3913 and 3996(B)(34), relative to student information; to limit the type of information to be collected on students; to prohibit the collection of certain information; to prohibit the sharing of student information; to provide exceptions; to provide for access by parents and specified others to certain student information stored in public school computer systems; to provide for student identification numbers; to provide definitions; to provide criminal penalties; and to provide for related matters," La. R.S. § 17:3913 (2014), La. R.S. § 3996(B) (2014); 20-7-104, MCA (2013).

95. "Kansas Student Data Privacy Act," K.S.A. § 72-6214 (2013); "Parents' Bill of Rights," 25 Okl. St. § 2001 (2014); 25 Okl. St. § 2002 (2014); 25 Okl. St. § 2003 (2014).

96. "Parents' Bill of Rights," 25 Okl. St. § 2001 (2014); 25 Okl. St. § 2002 (2014); 25 Okl. St. § 2003 (2014). Although Ohio law excludes personally identifying information from the data that can be held by the state historical society, it does allow parents to opt in to allow the historical society to hold that information. Ohio Rev. Code Ann. § 149.381 (LexisNexis 2014).

97. "An act to add Section 49073.1 to the Education Code, relating to pupil records," Cal Ed Code § 49073.1 (2015); "Kansas Student Data Privacy Act," K.S.A. § 72-6214 (2013); NY CLS Educ § 2-c (2014), NY CLS Educ § 2-d (2014); "Student Data Accessibility, Transparency, and Accountability Act of 2013," 70 Okl. St. § 3-168 (2014); "An act relating to education research centers and the sharing of educational data between state agencies; redesignating certain fees as charges," Tex. Educ. Code § 1.005 (2014).

98. Kansas requires specification of use only when the data is shared. North Carolina and Wyoming law imply a need for specification because they require the data to be destroyed when its specified use is complete; "An act to add Section 49073.6 to the Education Code, relating to pupil records," Cal Ed Code § 49073.6 (2015); "An act to add Section 49073.1 to the Education Code, relating to pupil records," Cal Ed Code § 49073.1 (2015); "Student Online Personal

Information Protection Act," Cal Bus & Prof Code § 22584 (2015); "Student Data Protection, Accessibility, Transparency, and Accountability Act of 2014," C.R.S. 22-2-309 (2014); "Student Data Accessibility, Transparency and Accountability Act of 2014," Idaho Code § 33-133 (2014); "Kansas Student Data Privacy Act," K.S.A. § 72-6214 (2013); "An Act to Ensure the Privacy and Security of Student Educational Records, as Recommended by the Joint Legislative Oversight Committee on Information Technology," N.C. Gen. Stat. § 115C-402.5 (2014), N.C. Gen. Stat. § 115C-402.15 (2014); NY CLS Educ § 2-c (2014), NY CLS Educ § 2-d (2014); Wyo. Stat. § 21-2-202 (2014); "Student Data Accessibility, Transparency, and Accountability Act of 2013," 70 Okl. St. § 3-168 (2014).

99. "An act to add Section 49073.6 to the Education Code, relating to pupil records," Cal Ed Code § 49073.6 (2015); "An act to add Section 49073.1 to the Education Code, relating to pupil records," Cal Ed Code § 49073.1 (2015); "Student Online Personal Information Protection Act," Cal Bus & Prof Code § 22584 (2015); "Student Data Protection, Accessibility, Transparency, and Accountability Act of 2014," C.R.S. 22-2-309 (2014); "Student Data Accessibility, Transparency and Accountability Act of 2014," Idaho Code § 33-133 (2014); "Kansas Student Data Privacy Act," K.S.A. § 72-6214 (2013); "An act to enact R.S. 17:3913 and 3996(B)(34), relative to student information; to limit the type of information to be collected on students; to prohibit the collection of certain information; to prohibit the sharing of student information; to provide exceptions; to provide for access by parents and specified others to certain student information stored in public school computer systems; to provide for student identification numbers; to provide definitions; to provide criminal penalties; and to provide for related matters," La. R.S. § 17:3913 (2015); "An Act to Ensure the Privacy and Security of Student Educational Records, as Recommended by the Joint Legislative Oversight Committee on Information Technology," N.C. Gen. Stat. § 115C-402.5 (2014), N.C. Gen. Stat. § 115C-402.15 (2014); NY CLS Educ § 2-c (2014); NY CLS Educ § 2-d (2014); Wyo. Stat. § 21-2-202 (2014).

100. "An act to add Section 49073.6 to the Education Code, relating to pupil records," Cal Ed Code § 49073.6 (2015); "An act to add Section 49073.1 to the Education Code, relating to pupil records," Cal Ed Code § 49073.1 (2015); "Student Online Personal Information Protection Act," Cal Bus & Prof Code § 22584 (2015); "Student Data Protection, Accessibility, Transparency, and Accountability Act of 2014," C.R.S. 22-2-309 (2014); "Student Data Accessibility, Transparency and Accountability Act of 2014," Idaho Code § 33-133 (2014); "Kansas Student Data Privacy Act," K.S.A. § 72-6214 (2013); "An act to enact R.S. 17:3913 and 3996(B)(34), relative to student information; to limit the type of information to be collected on students; to prohibit the collection of certain information; to prohibit the sharing of student information; to provide excep-

tions; to provide for access by parents and specified others to certain student information stored in public school computer systems; to provide for student identification numbers; to provide definitions; to provide criminal penalties; and to provide for related matters," La. R.S. § 17:3913 (2015); 20-7-104, MCA (2013); "An Act to Ensure the Privacy and Security of Student Educational Records, as Recommended by the Joint Legislative Oversight Committee on Information Technology," NY CLS Educ § 2-c (2014); NY CLS Educ § 2-d (2014); R.I. Gen. Laws § 16-103-3 (2014); R.I. Gen. Laws § 16-103-4 (2014); Wyo. Stat. § 21-2-202 (2014).

101. "Children's Online Privacy Protection Act,"15 U.S. Code Chapter 91. Retrieved January 8, 2015, from http://www.law.cornell.edu/uscode/text/15/chapter-91.

102. Harris, J. L., Heard, A., & Schwartz, M. B. (2014, January). *Older but still vulnerable: All children need protection from unhealthy food marketing.* Rudd Center for Food Policy and Obesity. Retrieved January 28, 2015, from http://www.yaleruddcenter.org/resources/upload/docs/what/reports/Protecting_Older_Children_3.14.pdf.

103. The Secretary of Education designated the Family Policy Compliance Office (FPCO) of U.S. Department of Education to "Investigate, process, and review complaints and violations under [FERPA]"; 34 CFR § 99.60(b)(1). In April 2014, EPIC submitted a Freedom of Information Act request to the U.S. Education Department for documents detailing parent and student complaints about the misuse of educational records. According to EPIC, the documents reveal that the Department failed to investigate many FERPA complaints; Electronic Privacy Information Center (2014, October 15). EPIC Student Privacy Freedom of Information Act Request: Department of Education's FERPA Enforcement. Author. Retrieved February 11, 2015, from https://www.epic.org/foia/ed/ferpa/default.html.

104. Barnes, K. (2014, March 6). Why a 'Student Privacy Bill of Rights' is desperately needed. *Washington Post.* Retrieved January 7, 2014, from http://www.washingtonpost.com/blogs/answer-sheet/wp/2014/03/06/why-a-student-privacy-bill-of-rights-is-desperately-needed/.

105. Privacy Technical Assistance Center (2014, February). *Protecting Student Privacy While Using Online Educational Services: Requirements and Best Practices.* U.S. Department of Education. Retrieved February 16, 2015, from http://tech.ed.gov/wp-content/uploads/2014/09/Student-Privacy-and-Online-Educational-Services-February-2014.pdf.

8

CLOSING THOUGHTS

It's sometimes hard to understand why school districts don't "just say no" to marketing programs in their schools. If you strip away the rosy language of "school-business partnership," "win-win situation," "good corporate citizen," "giving back to the community," and the like, what you see when you look at corporate marketing activities in the schools is example after example of the exploitation of children for financial gain.

Yet school districts often eagerly welcome marketers. There are several possible reasons for this, and in any given instance, it is likely that more than one of them is at play. Perhaps in these corporate-friendly times educators want to be seen to be responsive to the "business community"; or they may hold the naïve belief that allowing marketing to children in schools will provide significant financial benefits; or they may view children as too "savvy" to be taken in by marketing messages; or they may themselves be so thoroughly in tune with the mercantile consumption values of our culture that they are no longer capable of seeing advertising for what it so plainly is—propaganda.

Whatever the reasons that educators sign on to advertising in schools, there is little doubt in our minds that the chronic underfunding of public education over the last thirty-five years has made school districts ever more desperate for money, and thereby ever more susceptible to the lure of corporations that promise, no matter how implausibly, to provide some.[1]

Sadly, as things now stand, such policy as there is tends to either support commercial activities in schools or doesn't address it at all, and children are left to bear the brunt of the marketing assault on schools.

Selling products and services in the moment is important to marketers who take aim at children in school, but even more important is the prize of long-term influence. Over the long run the financial benefit marketing in schools delivers to corporations rests on the ability of advertising to "brand" students and thereby help ensure that they will be customers for life.

More generally, the process of "branding" involves inculcating the value of consumption as the primary mechanism for achieving happiness, demonstrating success, and finding fulfillment. Along the way, "branding" children—just like branding cattle—inflicts pain.

Marketers torment students with images of themselves as inadequate, unpopular, ugly, and undesirable—images that can, marketers imply, be erased when students purchase the advertised deodorant, or jeans, or hair gel. Foods of little or no nutritional value—junk food in everyday language—are heavily promoted by marketers in ads that emphasize that good times, popularity, and junk food go together like sweet cola and salty French fries.

Children of all ages are vulnerable to marketing designed to take advantage of their particular developmental stage. Younger children are vulnerable because they are often unable to distinguish advertising messages from editorial content.[2] In other words, they don't understand when the school curriculum leaves off and an ad begins. Early adolescents and teens are vulnerable because marketing is designed to exploit the particular psychological vulnerabilities associated with their age, such as their reduced ability to control impulsive behaviors and to resist immediate gratification, and their susceptibility to peer influence and image advertising.[3]

All students, regardless of their age, are vulnerable to assuming that their teachers and schools have their best interests at heart, and would allow promotion only of products or ideas they believe in. That is, regardless of whether it claims to endorse particular products or not, the school implicitly endorses any products or points of view marketed in its domain. Even the most savvy, cynical teens are unlikely to expect their caretakers to sell them out for cash.

After studying the nature, scope, and intensity of marketing in schools as it has developed over the past thirty-five years, it is clear to us that marketing to children, particularly in school, poses serious threats to children's physical and psychological well-being and to the integrity of the education they receive.

Unlike an educational program whose focus is on deepening children's understanding, increasing their skills, and encouraging their competence, marketing programs are intended to manipulate children for the particular benefit of a corporation. Toward that end corporations will attach themselves to any desirable values they believe will effectively promote what they have to sell.

Corporations even adopt values that contradict each other to market different product lines. Consider, for example, the Unilever brands Dove and Axe. The Dove brand is currently marketed to girls. The Axe brand focuses on boys. Dove's marketing creates the pretense of teaching girls that beauty is more than skin deep and that they should not be controlled by other people's ideas about beauty. Axe's marketing uses highly sexualized ads to convince boys that a good dose of Axe will make them irresistible to hordes of stereotypically beautiful girls who are uncontrollably attracted to Axe-scented boys.

Digital technologies now make it possible to turn information about students into a marketable commodity that marketers can use to more precisely target students. Parents are right to be concerned that information about their children collected in schools could be shared, sold, and used in a variety of ways about which they are unaware and over which they have no control.

State and federal laws that currently address student privacy rights most often address only students' educational record data and focus in particular on personally identifiable information. However, students' educational record data is only one access point for marketers.

Schools, for example, now routinely require students to use proprietary software programs and Internet applications as part of their required academic work, and these also become sources of information about students that marketers can use to promote products to them.

For the most part, schools appear to have neither an interest in nor the resources required to establish and maintain safeguards that would help ensure that academic assignments are not used as portals to sites that gather information about children, or attempt to sell the children products, or expose children to unwholesome material of a variety of kinds.

Our survey of recent state legislation found evidence of some interest in limiting access to student data and some legislation that explicitly forbids the commercial use of certain types of student data. Overall, however, policy reform has been halting, piecemeal, and inadequate to the threats now posed to student privacy and the use of student data by marketers.

We recognize that not all marketing in schools is equally threatening to children's well-being. The sponsoring entity, the nature of the product, and the advertising itself help determine the magnitude of threats posed by a given ad or advertising program. However, given that all ads in school pose some threat, it is past time for considering whether marketing activities belong in school. In our view, the evidence is clear: schools should be ad-free zones.

NOTES

1. Brent, B. O., & Lunden, S. (2009). Much ado about very little: The benefits and costs of school-based commercial activities. *Leadership and Policy in Schools, 8*(3), 307–36.

2. Wilcox, B., Kunkel, D., Cantor, J., Dowrick, P., Linn, S., & Palmer, E. (2004). Report of the APA task force on advertising and children. Washington, DC: American Psychological Association. Retrieved March 31, 2010, from http://www.chawisconsin.org/Obesity/O2ChildAds.pdf.

3. For simplicity's sake we include "adolescents" in with "children," but adolescents are even more susceptible than younger children to the psychological harms caused by advertising because of the sensitivities associated with their developmental stage. Self-regulation guidelines for advertisers have only very recently begun to recognize adolescents' susceptibility; and up until now adolescents have been grouped with adults. For research on adolescents, see Food Marketing Workgroup (2011, July). Re: Interagency Working Group on Food Marketed to Children: General Comments and Proposed Marketing Definitions: FTC Project No. P094513 (Comment on Marketing Definitions) (pp. 10–13). Retrieved September 9, 2011, from http://www.ftc.gov/os/comments/foodmarketedchildren/07843-80010.pdf/; Montgomery, K. C., & Chester, J. (2009). Interactive food and beverage marketing: Targeting adolescents in the digital age. *Journal of Adolescent Health, 45*, S18–S29; Giedd, J. N. (2008). The teen brain: Insights from neuroimaging. *Journal of Adolescent Health, 42*,

335–43. Retrieved October 15, 2010, from http://download.journals. elsevierhealth.com/pdfs/journals/1054-139X/PIIS1054139X0800075X.pdf? refuid=S1054-139X(09)00149-9&refissn=1054-139X&mis=.pdf/; Pechmann, C., Levine, L., Loughlin S., & Leslie, F. (2005). Impulsive and self-conscious: Adolescents' vulnerability to advertising and promotion. *Journal of Public Policy Marketing, 24*, 202–21; Steinberg, L. (2008). A social neuroscience perspective on adolescent risktaking. *Development Review, 28*, 78–106.

APPENDIX A

Gubbins's Matrix of Thinking Skills[1]

Problem Solving

Identifying general problem

Clarifying problem

Formulating hypothesis

Formulating appropriate questions

Generating related ideas
Formulating alternative solutions

Choosing best solutions

Applying the solution

Monitoring acceptance of the solution

Drawing conclusions

Decision Making

Stating desired goal/condition

Stating obstacles to goal/condition

Identifying alternatives

Examining alternatives

Ranking alternatives

Choosing best alternatives

Evaluating actions

Inferences (Inductive and Deductive)

Inductive

Determining cause and effect

Analyzing open-ended problems

Reasoning by analogy

Making inferences

Determining relevant information

Recognizing relationships
Solving insight problems

Deductive

Using logic

Spotting contradictory statements

Analyzing syllogisms

Solving spatial problems

Divergent Thinking Skills

Listing attributes of object/situation

Generating multiple ideas (fluency)

Generating different ideas (flexibility)

Generating unique ideas (originality)

Generating detailed ideas (elaboration)

Synthesizing information

Evaluative Thinking Skills

Distinguishing between facts and opinions

Judging credibility of a source

Observing and judging observation reports

Identifying central issues and problems

Recognizing underlying assumptions

Detecting bias, stereotypes, clichés

Recognizing loaded language

Evaluating hypotheses

Clarifying data

Predicting consequences

Demonstrating sequential synthesis of information

Planning alternative strategies

Recognizing alternative strategies

Recognizing inconsistencies in information

Identifying stated and unstated reasons

Comparing similarities and differences

Evaluating arguments

Philosophy and Reasoning

Using dialogical/dialectical approaches

NOTE

1. Gubbins, E.J. (1985). *Matrix of thinking skills.* Unpublished document. Hartfort, CT: State Department of Education. Cited in Sternberg, Robert J. (1986). *Critical thinking: Its nature, measurement, and improvement.* ERIC Document Reproduction Service No. 272882. Retrieved March 30, 2011, from http://www.eric.ed.gov/PDFS/ED272882.

APPENDIX B

State Laws and Regulations as of May 2004

State statutory and regulatory provisions relating to commercial activities as of May 2004. Italicized entries reflect policy that addresses product sales.

All information in this table was drawn from the 2004 Government Accountability Office (GAO) analysis of state legislature Web sites. Information from this analysis was reorganized into the categories in this table.[1]

State	Policy Permitting Commercializing Activities in Schools	Policy Restricting Commercializing Activities in Schools	Policy Neither Permitting nor Restricting Commercializing Activities in Schools	Policy Delegating Authority to School Boards or Other Entities, or Requires Process
AL		*Prohibits requiring students participate in school fundraising.*		
AK		Prohibits students from participating in survey or questionnaire		

without parental
consent.

AZ   Permits advertising
        on school buses
        under restrictions.

AR   1. Prohibits vending
                                    machines in
                                    elementary schools;
                                    2. Prohibits
                                    students from
                                    participating in
                                    survey or
                                    questionnaire
                                    without parental
                                    consent.

CA   *1. Restricts individual*   Prohibits schools
                                    food items sold at   from contracting
                                    elementary schools to   for electronic
                                    those complying with   products or
                                    fat, sugar content   services
                                    restrictions;   disseminating
                                    2. Restricts beverages   advertising to
                                    sold at middle, junior   students unless
                                    high schools during   notice
                                    school day to water,   requirements
                                    milk, fruit-based   followed.
                                    drinks, electrolyte
                                    replacement
                                    beverages meeting
                                    restrictions;
                                    3. Restricts beverages
                                    sold at elementary
                                    schools during school
                                    day to water, milk,
                                    100% fruit juice,
                                    unsweetened fruit-
                                    based drinks
                                    containing at least
                                    50% fruit juice;
                                    Restricts school
                                    boards, schools from

contracting for carbonated beverages, non-nutritious foods;
4. Prohibits teachers, dentists, optometrists from soliciting students on school grounds;
5. *Prohibits advertising of tobacco products on any outdoor billboard within 1,000 feet of any public (or private) school;* 6. Prohibits states, local boards from adopting basic instructional materials providing unnecessary exposure to brand names, products or company logos.

CO

1. Prohibits operation of competitive food service beginning half hour before, ending half hour after school breakfast, lunch period;
2. Prohibits student participation in any survey without written parental consent.

Student editors determine advertising content of school-sponsored publications.

CT

Prohibits selling coffee, soft drinks, tea, candy half hour before, during, after lunch or breakfast.

FL	1. Permits school boards to establish fundraising policies; 2. Permits school boards to establish policies regarding advertising.	*Foods of minimal nutritional value can only be sold in secondary schools for 1 hour after lunch.*	
GA		Prohibits selling foods of minimal nutritional value in elementary schools until after lunch, in other schools during mealtime in dining, serving, kitchen areas.	
HI	Permits schools to have vending machines, concessions if operated by blind or individuals with visual handicaps;	*Prohibits selling cigarettes from lunch wagon engaging in any sales activity within 1,000 feet of elementary or secondary school grounds.*	
IL		1. Prohibits disclosure of student's name, address, tel. no., Social Security no., email address, other personal identifying information to business or financial institution issuing credit or debit cards; 2. *Elementary*	1. Prohibits solicitation of students by certain private businesses or vocational schools unless approved by superintendent; 2. Prohibits certain private businesses or vocational schools from advertising for student enrollees

		schools in National School Lunch Program prohibited from selling competitive food during breakfast, lunch periods.	unless approved by superintendent.
KY		*Prohibits selling any food outside National School Breakfast or Lunch program until half hour after lunch period.*	
LA	Permits donor decals on school buses acknowledging donations of cellular telephone service.	*Prohibits sale of competitive foods until last 10 minutes of each lunch & in food service areas.*	
ME	*Permits school districts to fundraise for their benefit.*		
MD	Permits advertising on school bus shelters under restrictions.		
MA		*Prohibits outdoor advertising of cigarettes within 1,000-foot radius of any school.*	Requires school committee establish travel policy addressing expectations for fundraising by students.

MN	1.School board may contract with advertisers or others to sell naming rights, advertising rights to school facilities; 2. Permits advertising on school buses under restrictions.	Prohibits school boards from contracting for computer or related equipment requiring advertising disseminated to students unless parents given opportunity to opt child out of exposure to advertising.	
MS	Permits commercial advertising on protective textbook covers.	Prohibits selling any food item for 1 hour before school meal.	Requires school boards to include disclosure statement advising what portion of proceeds from board-authorized fundraising (eg: school pictures, cap, gown rentals, etc.) for which board receives commission, rebate, or fee, shall be contributed to school activity fund.
NV	Permits advertising on, in school buses.		
NH	Permits advertising on school bus shelters.	Prohibits advertising on school bus exterior except for manufacturer's logo.	

NJ	Permits advertising on school bus stop shelters subject to governmental approval.	*Prohibits selling foods of minimal nutritional value before end of last school lunch period.*
NM	Permits commercial advertising inside, on sides of school buses.	Prohibits sale or use of personally identifiable information for marketing unless parent consents in writing for legitimate educational purposes.
NY		*1. Generally prohibits selling soft drinks, candy during school day until last scheduled meal period.* 2. Generally prohibits commercial promotional activities on school premises except where commercial entity sponsors school activity which does not involve promoting sponsor's product or service.
NC	Permits school boards adopt instructional materials containing commercial advertising so long	1. Prohibits individual ("a la carte") sale of foods of minimum nutritional value, limits sale of

	as materials relate to academic curricula.	individual food items until after established lunch hour has ended; 2. Requires local school boards assure students not regularly required to observe, listen to, read commercial advertising.	
ND			Requires school boards approve fundraising involving students.
RI		Prohibits school officials from soliciting any pupil in any public school, generally prohibits sale of commercial goods or services in schools, requires school committee issue rules related to fundraising activities.	Prohibits distribution to students of commercial materials unless approved by local school committee.
TN	Permits commercial advertising on school buses, in accordance with policy established by local school board.		Requires districts to develop policy setting forth rights of parents, students, guidelines for teachers, principals with respect to administration of surveys, analyses, evaluations of students

TX	1. Permits commercially sponsored high school athletic programs; 2. Permits advertising on exterior of school bus, provided it does not distract from effectiveness of required safety warning equipment.		
VA	Permits school boards to contract for telephone service or credit card that, without endorsement, bears name of school board, provides portion of revenues to public school fund.	*All foods sold in school from 6:00 a.m. until after breakfast period must be of sound nutritional value.*	Requires each school board develop policy on commercial, promotional, corporate partnerships, sponsorships involving public schools.
WV		Prohibits sale of candy, soft drinks, chewing gum, flavored ice bars during school day, except county boards may permit sale of soft drinks in high schools except during breakfast, lunch periods.	
WI	School board may adopt written resolutions governing sale, promotion of		

goods, services on
school district
property, with
restrictions.[2]

NOTES

1. Government Accountability Office (GAO) (2004). *Commercial activities in schools: Use of student data is limited and additional dissemination of guidance could help districts develop policies* (GAO-04-810), pp. 22-31. Retrieved January 14, 2014, from http://www.gao.gov/assets/250/243777.pdf.

2. This legislation was not included in the GAO's compilation of laws governing school commercialism, although it was in place before May 2004. Original text can be found at http://statutes.laws.com/wisconsin/118/118.12.

APPENDIX C

State Bills Addressing School Commercialism Signed into Law, 2011–2014

Category of School Commercialism	Number of Bills Signed into Law	Bill Detail [1]
Appropriation of Space	2	TN HB 2851 (2012): Permits commercialism: removes a limitation on the lettering of advertisements on school buses. NJ A1637 (2011): Permits commercialism; permits advertising on exterior of school buses.
Fundraising	1	CA AB 626 (2013): Adjusts nutrition allowances, primarily making them stricter; makes small changes in the hours drinks not meeting state nutrition requirements may be sold in schools; allows people other than students to sell permitted food products at fundraisers.
Sponsored Educational Materials	1	KS HB 2253 (2013): Restricts commercialism: prohibits entities that provide abortions from providing educational materials to schools.

NOTE

1. Bills were accessed from the OpenStates database (openstates.org).

APPENDIX D

Websites Associated with Relevant Topics

The following websites associated with advertising and marketing, health care and nutrition, government policy, education, and academic research were regularly reviewed for material.

*Subscription required for access online

Source	Website
Advertising Age*	http://www.adage.com
American Advertising Federation	http://www.aaf.org/
American Association of Advertising Agencies	http://www2.aaaa.org/Portal/Pages/default.aspx
American Beverage Association	http://www.ameribev.org/ http://www.ameribev.org/blog/
Association of National Advertisers	http://www.ana.net/
Center for Science in the Public Interest	http://www.cspinet.org/
Consumers International	http://consumersinternational.org/
Food Marketing Workgroup	http://www.foodmarketing.org/
Consortium for Media Literacy	http://www.consortiumformedialiteracy.org

Source	Website
Federal Communications Commission	*http://www.fcc.gov/*
Federal Trade Commission	*http://www.ftc.gov*
Institute of Medicine	*http://www.iom.edu/Reports.aspx*
Interactive Food and Beverage Marketing—Montgomery & Chester	*http://www.digitalads.org/*
Kidscreen	*http://www.kidscreen.com*
British Psychological Society Research Digest Blog	*http://www.bps.org.uk/publications/rd/rd_home.cfm*
Campaign for Commercial Free Childhood	*http://www.commercialfreechildhood.org/*
Canadian Centre for Policy Alternatives	*http://www.policyalternatives.ca/*
Commercial Alert	*http://www.commercialalert.org/*
Empowered by Play	*http://www.empoweredbyplay.org/*
Journal of Consumer Research*	*http://www.press.uchicago.edu/ucp/journals/journal/jcr.html/*
Medpage Today	*http://www.medpagetoday.com*
Product Placement News	*http://productplacement.biz/*
Youth Markets Alert	*http://www.epmcom.com/*

APPENDIX E

State Laws Addressing Student Data Privacy: Synopses of Major Provisions With Significant Gaps in Protection, Exclusions and Omissions Noted (2011-2014)

STATE LAWS ENACTED IN 2011

20-1-213, MCA (2013)
Montana House Bill 208 (2011)

Summary:	Requires that information that a student has dropped out to be sent to the Montana Youth Challenge program (i.e., a narrowly defined bill not intended to establish broad data collection or privacy rights)
Major Provisions:	- Applies to name, address, and dates of attendance only (i.e., information to be transferred to another state agency).
	- Parents can opt out of sharing data with third parties.
	- Implies that LEA would be held accountable for breaches.
Gaps in Protection, Exclusions and Omissions:	- Does not restrict the use of data collection for advertising and marketing purposes, but those are irrelevant in this case.
	- Does not give parents the right to see data collected about their child.

- Does not specifically give parents the right to challenge and correct data.

- Does not specifically require implementation of data security procedures.

- Does not require de-identification of personally identifying information.

- Does not require the data's intended use to be specified in advance.

- Does not require data to be destroyed following intended use.

Ohio Rev. Code Ann. § 149.381 (2014)
Ohio House Bill 153 (2011)

Summary:	As part of the state budget bill, excludes pupil records and FERPA-protected records from review by state historical society.
Major Provisions:	- Applies to educational record data with personally identifying information. - Written parental request is required for data release.
Gaps in Protection, Exclusions and Omissions:	- Does not restrict the use of data collection for advertising and marketing purposes.
	- Does not give parents the right to see data collected about their child.
	- Does not specifically give parents the right to challenge and correct data.
	- Does not specifically require implementation of data security procedures.
	- Does not require de-identification of personally identifying information.
	- Does not require the data's intended use to be specified in advance.
	- Does not require data to be destroyed following intended use.
	- Contains no provision regarding accountability for breaches.

Utah Code Ann. § 53A-13-301 (2014)
Utah House Bill 145 (2011)

Summary:	Applies FERPA to state and provides for rules to protect confidentiality of student information and records.
Major Provisions:	- Applies to educational record data.

Gaps in Protection, Exclusions and Omissions:	- Does not restrict the use of data collection for advertising and marketing purposes.
	- Although it does not explicitly give parents the right to see data, it refers to FERPA, which does.
	- Makes no provision for parents to opt out of data collection, storage, or use.
	- Does not specifically require implementation of data security procedures.
	- Does not require de-identification of personally identifying information
	- Does not require the data's intended use to be specified in advance.
	- Does not require data to be destroyed following intended use.
	- Contains no provision regarding accountability for breaches.

STATE LAWS ENACTED IN 2012

***A.R.S. § 15-241 (2014)
Arizona House Bill 2663 (2012)

Summary:	Relates to underperforming school districts, relates to reclassification of such schools. Establishes criteria for letter grading of schools, requires schools to submit the data and provides for family educational rights and privacy of student records.
Major Provisions:	- Applies to educational record data.
	- Holds LEA accountable for breaches.
Gaps in Protection, Exclusions and Omissions:	- Does not restrict the use of data collection for advertising and marketing purposes
	- Although it does not explicitly give parents the right to see data, it refers to FERPA, which does.
	- With respect to challenging the accuracy of data, refers to FERPA.
	- Makes no provision for parents to opt out of data collection, storage, or use.
	- Does not specifically require implementation of data security procedures.

- Does not require de-identification of personally identifying information.

- Does not require the data's intended use to be specified in advance.

- Does not require data to be destroyed following intended use.

W. Va. Code § 18B-2A-3 (2014)
WV SB 661 (2012)

Summary:	Provides for the collection, synthesis, and dissemination of data from state agencies; relates to communication and cooperation among state education providers; directs institutional boards of governors to cooperate in certain data-related operations; requires reports; provides for privacy protection; authorizes the Commissioner of Workforce West Virginia to share data with certain education providers.
Major Provisions:	- Applies to educational record data.
	- Holds individuals accountable for breaches of the law.
Gaps in Protection, Exclusions and Omissions:	- Does not restrict the use of data collection for advertising and marketing purposes.
	- Does not give parents the right to see data collected about their child.
	- Does not specifically give parents the right to challenge and correct data.
	- Makes no provision for parents to opt out of data collection, storage, or use.
	- Does not specifically require implementation of data security procedures.
	- Does not require de-identification of personally identifying information
	- Does not require the data's intended use to be specified in advance.
	- Does not require data to be destroyed following intended use.

STATE LAWS ENACTED IN 2013

"An act relating to school safety," KRS § 158.448 (2014)
Kentucky House Bill 354 (2013)

Summary:	Among other items related to school safety, requires the Kentucky Department of Education to develop protocols for student records within the student information system that (1) provide notice to schools receiving the records of prior offenses committed by a student transferring to a new school or district and (2) protect the privacy rights of students and parents guaranteed under FERPA; requires school council to review performance data annually.
Major Provisions:	- Applies to educational record data.
Gaps in Protection, Exclusions and Omissions:	- Does not restrict the use of data collection for advertising and marketing purposes.
	- Although it does not explicitly give parents the right to see data, it refers to FERPA, which does.
	- Refers to FERPA regarding parents' right to challenge the accuracy of data.
	- Makes no provision for parents to opt out of data collection, storage, or use.
	- Does not specifically require implementation of data security procedures.
	- Does not require de-identification of personally identifying information
	- Does not require the data's intended use to be specified in advance.
	- Does not require data to be destroyed following intended use.
	- Contains no provision regarding accountability for breaches.

"An act relating to reorganization," KRS § 151B.132 (2014)
Kentucky HB 240/SB 83 (2013)

Summary:	Establishes Office for Education and Workforce Statistics to oversee and maintain Kentucky Longitudinal Data System.
Major Provisions:	- Applies to educational record data.
	- Requires implementation of data security procedures.
	- Requires the de-identification of personally identifying information.

Gaps in Protection, Exclusions and Omissions:	- Does not restrict the use of data collection for advertising and marketing purposes.
	- Although it does not explicitly give parents the right to see data, it refers to FERPA, which does.
	- With respect to challenging the accuracy of data, refers to FERPA.
	- Makes no provision for parents to opt out of data collection, storage, or use.
	- Does not require the data's intended use to be specified in advance.
	- Does not require data to be destroyed following intended use.
	- Contains no provision regarding accountability for breaches of the law.

20-7-104, MCA (2013)
Montana Senate Bill 175 (2013)

Summary:	As part of a larger bill, applies FERPA and strengthens safeguards with respect to personally identifying information; prohibits superintendent from releasing personally identifying information to any entity without parental consent.
Major Provisions:	- Applies to educational record data, especially personally identifying information.
	- Specifically restricts the use of data collection for advertising and marketing purposes.
	- Parental opt-in is required for release of personally identifying information.
	- Implies that the Superintendent of Public Instruction would be held accountable for breaches.
Gaps in Protection, Exclusions and Omissions:	- Although it does not explicitly give parents the right to see data, it refers to FERPA, which does.
	- With respect to challenging the accuracy of data, refers to FERPA.
	- Does not specifically require implementation of data security procedures.
	- Does not require de-identification of personally identifying information.
	- Does not require the data's intended use to be specified in advance.
	- Does not require data to be destroyed following intended use.

"Current Operations and Capital Improvements Appropriations Act of 2013," 2013
N.C. Sess. Laws 360
North Carolina SB 402 (2013)

Summary:	As part of a comprehensive bill, a nonpublic school that gets scholarship grant money must report aggregate scores of students.
Major Provisions:	- Applies to educational record data.
	- Holds the nonpublic school that enrolls scholarship students accountable for breaches.
Gaps in Protection, Exclusions and Omissions:	- Does not restrict the use of data collection for advertising and marketing purposes.
	- Does not give parents the right to see data collected about their child.
	- Does not specifically give parents the right to challenge and correct data.
	- Makes no provision for parents to opt out of data collection, storage, or use.
	- Does not specifically require implementation of data security procedures.
	- Does not require de-identification of personally identifying information.
	- Does not require the data's intended use to be specified in advance.
	- Does not require data to be destroyed following intended use.

ORC Ann. 3301.0714 (2014)
Ohio House Bill 59 (2013)

Summary	As part of a larger bill, requires the assignment of a data verification code to each student; prohibits the state Board of Education and the Education Department from having access to information that would enable any data verification code to be matched to personally identifying student data.
Major Provisions:	- Applies to educational record data.
	- Requires de-identification of personally identifying information.
Gaps in Protection, Exclusions and Omissions:	- Does not restrict the use of data collection for advertising and marketing purposes.
	- Does not give parents the right to see data collected about their child.
	- Does not specifically give parents the right to challenge and correct data.

- Makes no provision for parents to opt out of data collection, storage, or use.

- Does not specifically require implementation of data security procedures.

- Does not require the data's intended use to be specified in advance.

- Does not require data to be destroyed following intended use.

- Contains no provision regarding accountability for breaches.

"Student Data Accessibility, Transparency, and Accountability Act of 2013," 70 Okl. St. § 3-168 (2014)
Oklahoma House Bill 1989 (2013)

Summary:	Requires compliance with FERPA, provides for data inventory, requires a data security plan, requires contracts to include privacy and security provisions.
Major Provisions:	- Applies to educational record data; excludes biometric data from the educational record.
	- Requires implementation of data security procedures.
	- Requires the de-identification of personally identifying information.
	- Requires specification of how collected data will be used.
	- State Board of Education and private vendors, when relevant, would be held accountable for breaches.
Gaps in Protection, Exclusions and Omissions:	- Does not restrict the use of data collection for advertising and marketing purposes.
	- Although it does not explicitly give parents the right to see data, it refers to FERPA, which does.
	- Refers to FERPA regarding challenging the accuracy of data.
	- Makes no provision for parents to opt out of data collection, storage, or use.
	- Does not require data to be destroyed following intended use.

"An act relating to education research centers and the sharing of educational data between state agencies; redesignating certain fees as charges," Tex. Educ. Code § 1.005 (2014)
Texas House Bill 2103 (2013)

Summary:	Establishes rules for sharing of education data with education research centers.

Major Provisions:	- Applies to educational record data.
	- Requires implementation of data security procedures.
	- Implies that the researcher involved would be held accountable for breaches in the law.
Gaps in Protection, Exclusions and Omissions:	- Does not restrict the use of data collection for advertising and marketing purposes.
	- Although it does not explicitly give parents the right to see data, it refers to FERPA, which does.
	- Refers to FERPA regarding challenging the accuracy of data.
	- Makes no provision for parents to opt out of data collection, storage, or use.
	- Does not require de-identification of personally identifying information.
	- Does not require the data's intended use to be specified in advance.
	- Does not require data to be destroyed following intended use.

Utah Code Ann. § 53A-1-413 (2014)
Utah Senate Bill 82 (2013)

Summary:	Creates "Student Achievement Backpack" and requires ability for parents and authorized LEA representatives to access it.
Major Provisions:	- Applies to educational record data.
	- Gives parents the right to see data collected about their child.
	- Requires implementation of data security procedures.
	- Holds State Board of Education accountable for breaches.
Gaps in Protection, Exclusions and Omissions:	- Does not restrict the use of data collection for advertising and marketing purposes.
	- Does not specifically give parents the right to challenge and correct data.
	- Makes no provision for parents to opt out of data collection, storage, or use.
	- Does not require de-identification of personally identifying information.
	- Does not require the data's intended use to be specified in advance.
	- Does not require data to be destroyed following intended use

STATE LAWS ENACTED IN 2014

"An act to add Section 49073.6 to the Education Code, relating to pupil records," Cal Ed Code § 49073.6 (2015):
California Assembly Bill 1442 (2014)

Summary:	Restricts use of information gathered from social media to school/student safety; restricts use of that information and requires it to be destroyed when no longer needed for original use.
Major Provisions:	- Applies to data obtained from social media.
	- Explicitly restricts the use of data collection for advertising and marketing purposes; data can only be used to satisfy terms of contract, and cannot be sold or shared.
	- Gives parents the right to see data collected about their child.
	- Gives parents the right to challenge and correct the data.
	- Requires specification of use before data is collected; data may be used only for school or student safety.
	- Requires destruction of data after its use for its intended purpose is completed.
	- Implies that LEA will be held accountable for breaches.
Gaps in Protection, Exclusions and Omissions:	- Does not give parents the right to opt out of data collection, storage, or use.
	- Does not require implementation of data security procedures.
	- Does not require de-identification of personally identifying information.

"An act to add Section 49073.1 to the Education Code, relating to pupil records," Cal Ed Code § 49073.1 (2015)
California Assembly Bill 1584 (2014)

Summary:	Amends existing law to authorize an LEA to enter into a contract with a third party to provide services for the digital storage, management, and retrieval of pupil records, or to provide digital educational software, or both.
Major Provisions:	- Applies to educational record data.
	- Specifically restricts the use of data collection for advertising and marketing purposes.

- Gives parents the right to see data collected about their child.

- Gives parents the right to challenge and correct data collected about their child.

- Requires implementation of data security procedures.

- Specification of use of the data is implied (by requirement to destroy the data after its intended use is completed).

- Requires destruction of data after its use for its intended purpose is completed.

- Holds both LEA and private company accountable for breaches of the law.

Gaps in Protection, Exclusions and Omissions:

- Does not give parents the right to opt out of data collection, storage, or use.

- Does not require deidentification of personally identifying information.

"Student Online Personal Information Protection Act," Cal Bus & Prof Code § 22584 (2015)
California Senate Bill 1177 (2014)

Summary:

Prohibits an operator or an Internet website, online service, online application, or mobile application from knowingly engaging in targeted advertising to students or their parents or legal guardians, using covered information to amass a profile about a K-12 student, selling a student's information or disclosing covered information. Requires security procedures and practices of covered information, to protect information from unauthorized access, destruction, use, modification, or disclosure.

Major Provisions:

- Applies to Internet sites and applications.

- Specifically restricts the use of data collection for advertising and marketing purposes.

- Requires implementation of data security procedures.

- Requirement to de-identify personally identifying information is implied, but not specifically discussed.

- Specification of use of the data is implied.

- Requires destruction of the data upon completion of intended use.

- Holds LEA accountable for breaches of the law.

Gaps in Protection, Exclusions and Omissions:

- Does not give parents the right to see data collected about their child.

- Does not specifically give parents the right to challenge and correct data.

- Makes no provision for parents to opt out of data collection, storage, or use.

"Student Data Protection, Accessibility, Transparency, and Accountability Act of 2014," C.R.S. 22-2-309 (2014)
Colorado House Bill 1294 (2014)

Summary: Requires the state's Board of Education to maintain and publish an inventory of student-level data currently in the student data system, to develop policies to comply with federal privacy law, to use aggregate data; and to a develop data security template for LEAs. Prohibits the Department of Education from providing individual student data to organizations or agencies outside the state except under specified circumstances.

Major Provisions: - Applies to educational record and to on-line education services, including websites and applications.

- Specifically restricts the use of data collection for advertising and marketing purposes.

- Gives parents the right to see data collected about their child.

- Requires implementation of data security procedures.

- Requires de-identification of personally identifying information.

- Requires specification of how collected data will be used.

- Requires destruction of the data upon completion of intended use.

- Holds state Board of Education, Department of Education, or both accountable for breaches of the law.

Gaps in Protection, Exclusions and Omissions: - Does not specifically give parents the right to challenge and correct data.

- Makes no provision for parents to opt out of data collection, storage, or use.

- Does not specifically give parents the right to challenge and correct data.

Fla. Stat. § 1002.22 (2014); Fla. Stat. § 1002.221 (2014); Fla. Stat. § 1008.386 (2014); Fla. Stat. § 1011.622 (2014)
Florida Senate Bill 188 (2014)

Summary: Requires notification of privacy rights, defines and prohibits collection of biometric information, and provides for student identification numbers other than Social Security number (the original law applies to educational record data; the 2014 amendment specifically addresses biometric data).

Major Provisions:	- Applies to educational record data; specifically references biometric data.
	- Requires the assignment of a code rather than the use of Social Security numbers.
	- Although it does not specify de-identification as the reason for the code assignment, it seems clear that the code provides for de-identification.
	- Holds state agency or LEA accountable for breaches of the law.
Gaps in Protection, Exclusions and Omissions:	- Does not restrict the use of data collection for advertising and marketing purposes.
	- Although it does not explicitly give parents the right to see data, it refers to FERPA, which does.
	- Refers to FERPA regarding challenging the accuracy of data.
	- Makes no provision for parents to opt out of data collection, storage, or use.
	- Does not specifically require implementation of data security procedures.
	- Does not require the data's intended use to be specified in advance.
	- Does not require data to be destroyed following intended use.

"Kansas Student Data Privacy Act," K.S.A. § 72-6214 (2013)
Kansas Senate Bill 367 (2014)

Summary:	Restricts which data contained in a student's educational record can be disclosed and to whom it may be disclosed.
Major Provisions:	- Applies to educational record data and specifically to biometric data.
	- Give parents the right to see data collected about their child.
	- Requires parental "opt-in" for biometric data only; otherwise there are no opt-out provisions
	- Required implementation of security procedures is implied.
	- Requires the de-identification of personally identifying information.
	- Data use must be specified if it is to be shared with another agency; otherwise language is vague.
	- When the data are shared, requires destruction of the data upon completion of their intended use; otherwise language is vague.
	- Holds state agency, employees or agents of the agency, or anyone with data accountable for breaches of the law.

Gaps in Protection, Exclusions and Omissions:
- Does not restrict the use of data collection for advertising and marketing purposes.

- Does not specifically give parents the right to challenge and correct data.

"Student Data Accessibility, Transparency and Accountability Act of 2014," Idaho Code § 33-133 (2014)
Idaho Senate Bill 1372 (2014)

Summary:
Defines and establishes provisions for data collected as part of educational record, for confidential data, for data security

Major Provisions:
- Applies to educational record data.

- Specifically restricts the use of data collection for advertising and marketing purposes.

- Gives parents the right to see data collected about their child.

- Parental "opt-in" is required for secondary uses of the data only.

- Requires implementation of data security procedures.

- Requires the de-identification of personally identifying information.

- Requires specification of how collected data will be used.

- Requires destruction of the data upon completion of intended use.

- Holds State Board of Education accountable for breaches.

Gaps in Protection, Exclusions and Omissions:
- Does not specifically give parents the right to challenge and correct data.

"Personal Online Account Privacy Protection Act," La. R.S. §§ 51:1951-1955 (2014)
Louisiana House Bill 340 (2014)

Summary:
Prohibits employers and educational institutions from requesting or requiring certain individuals to disclose information that allows access to or observation of personal online accounts.

Major Provisions:
- Applies to personal electronic devices or accounts.

- Implies that the educational institution will be held accountable for breaches.

Gaps in Protection, Exclusions and Omissions:
- Does not restrict the use of data collection for advertising and marketing purposes.

- Does not give parents the right to see data collected about their child.

- Does not specifically give parents the right to challenge and correct data.

- Makes no provision for parents to opt out of data collection, storage, or use.

- Does not specifically require implementation of data security procedures.

- Does not require de-identification of personally identifying information.

- Does not require the data's intended use to be specified in advance.

- Does not require data to be destroyed following intended use.

"An act to enact R.S. 17:3913 and 3996(B)(34), relative to student information; to limit the type of information to be collected on students; to prohibit the collection of certain information; to prohibit the sharing of student information; to provide exceptions; to provide for access by parents and specified others to certain student information stored in public school computer systems; to provide for student identification numbers; to provide definitions; to provide criminal penalties; and to provide for related matters," La. R.S. § 17:3913 (2015) and La. R.S. § 3996(B) **Louisiana House Bill 1076 (2014)**

Summary:	Provides for limitations and prohibitions on the collection and sharing of student information and provides penalties for violations.
Major Provisions:	- Applies to educational record data and specifically to personally identifying information.
	- Specifically restricts the use of data collected for advertising and marketing purposes.
	- Gives parents the right to see data collected about their child.
	- Parental "opt-in" is required for release of personally identifying information.
	- Requires implementation of data security procedures.
	- Requires de-identification of personally identifying information; but if LEA contracts with a provider, it can transfer personally identifying information.
	- Requires destruction of the data upon completion of intended use.
	- Any person who violates the law can be held accountable.
Gaps in Protection, Exclusions and Omissions:	- Does not specifically give parents the right to challenge and correct data.
	- Does not require the data's intended use to be specified in advance.

Resolve, Directing a Study of Social Media Privacy in School and in the Workplace,
Maine HP 838 – Legislative Document 1194 - R. 112 (2014)
Maine House Proposal 838 (2014)

Summary:	Directs the Joint Standing Committee on Judiciary to study issues about social media and personal email privacy in school and the workplace.
Major Provisions:	- Applies to personal email and social media accounts; requires study of privacy concerns.

"An act to make appropriations to aid in the support of the public schools, the intermediate school districts, community colleges, and public universities of the state; to make appropriations for certain other purposes relating to education; to provide for the disbursement of the appropriations; to authorize the issuance of certain bonds and provide for the security of those bonds; to prescribe the powers and duties of certain state departments, the state board of education, and certain other boards and officials; to create certain funds and provide for their expenditure; to prescribe penalties; and to repeal acts and parts of acts," MCLS § 388.1694a (2014), MCLS § 388.1817 (2014), MCLS § 388.1704c (2014).
Michigan House Bill 5314 (2014)

Summary:	Education appropriations bill creates Center for Educational Performance and Information to create, maintain, and enhance this state's P-20 longitudinal data system; Requires state and/or LEAs to maintain data privacy and institute procedures to that effect.
Major Provisions:	- Applies to educational record data.
	- Gives parents the right to see data collected about their child.
	- Requires the de-identification of personally identifying information.
Gaps in Protection, Exclusions and Omissions:	- Does not restrict the use of data collection for advertising and marketing purposes.
	- Does not specifically give parents the right to challenge and correct data.
	- Makes no provision for parents to opt out of data collection, storage, or use.
	- Does not specifically require implementation of data security procedures.
	- Does not require the data's intended use to be specified in advance.
	- Does not require data to be destroyed following intended use.
	- Contains no provision regarding accountability for breaches.

"An Act to Ensure the Privacy and Security of Student Educational Records, as Recommended by the Joint Legislative Oversight Committee on Information Technology," N.C. Gen. Stat. § 115C-402.5 (2014) and N.C. Gen. Stat. § 115C-402.15 (2014)

North Carolina Senate Bill 815 (2014)

Summary:	Directs the State Board of Education (State Board) to ensure student data accessibility, transparency, and accountability relating to the student data system. Requires LEAs to notify parents of their rights under state and federal law regarding student records.
Major Provisions:	- Applies to educational record data; addresses biometric data.
	- Gives parents the right to see data collected about their child.
	- Requires implementation of data security procedures.
	- Specification of data use is implied by the requirement to produce an annual report that includes use.
	- Destruction of data after its specified use is implied in the security requirements.
	- Contracts must include penalties for noncompliance with the law, but the law does not specify who is held accountable.
Gaps in Protection, Exclusions and Omissions:	- Does not restrict the use of data collection for advertising and marketing purposes.
	- Does not specifically give parents the right to challenge and correct data.
	- Makes no provision for parents to opt out of data collection, storage, or use.
	- Does not require de-identification of personally identifying information.

"An act relative to the collection and disclosure of student data," N.H. Rev. Stat. Ann. §§ 189:65 - 189: 68 (2014)

New Hampshire House Bill 1587 (2014)

Summary:	Regulates the collection and distribution of student data; limits disclosure of personally relevant information.
Major Provisions:	- Applies to educational record data; also specifically to biometric data, student physical tracking, and surveillance of electronic devices.
	- Gives parents the right to see data collected about their child.
	- Requirement to specify the data's intended use in advance is implied by the requirement to destroy the data upon completion of its intended use.

- Requires destruction of the data upon completion of intended use.

- Implies that the school and/or the state Department of Education would be held accountable for breaches.

Gaps in Protection, Exclusions and Omissions:

- Does not restrict the use of data collection for advertising and marketing purposes.

- Does not specifically give parents the right to challenge and correct data.

- Makes no provision for parents to opt out of data collection, storage, or use.

- Does not specifically require implementation of data security procedures.

- Does not require de-identification of personally identifying information.

NY CLS Educ § 2-c (2014) and NY CLS Educ § 2-d (2014)
New York Senate Bill 6356-D/Assembly Bill 8556-D (2014)

Summary:

A budget bill that among other things, amends the education law in relation to prohibiting the release of student information to certain entities (Subpart K); and in relation to protecting student privacy and ensuring data security (Subpart L)

Major Provisions:

- Applies to educational record data and specifically refers to biometric data.

- Specifically restricts the use of data collection for advertising and marketing purposes.

- Gives parents the right to see data collected about their child.

- Gives parents the right to challenge and correct data, but specifically denies private right of action.

- The law does not specifically give parents the right to opt out of data collection, but it does require parental "opt-in" for a company to further release the child's information.

- Requires implementation of data security procedures.

- Requires specification of how collected data will be used.

- Requires destruction of the data upon completion of intended use.

- Holds private company accountable for breaches of the law.

Gaps in Protection, Exclusions and Omissions:

- Does not require de-identification of personally identifying information.

Ohio Rev. Code Ann. § 3301.0714 (2014)
Ohio House Bill 487

Summary:	Adds language on standards for statewide information management system to protect confidentiality of student data; also adds language barring collection of certain data in the course of school testing.
Major Provisions:	- Applies to educational record data and specifically addresses biometric data.
	- Requires implementation of data security procedures.
	- Requires the de-identification of personally identifying information.
Gaps in Protection, Exclusions and Omissions:	- Does not restrict the use of data collection for advertising and marketing purposes.
	- Does not give parents the right to see data collected about their child.
	- Does not specifically give parents the right to challenge and correct data.
	- Makes no provision for parents to opt out of data collection, storage, or use.
	- Does not require the data's intended use to be specified in advance.
	- Does not require data to be destroyed following intended use.
	- Contains no provision regarding accountability for breaches.

"Parents' Bill of Rights," 25 Okl. St. § 2001 (2014), 25 Okl. St. § 2002 (2014), 25 Okl. St. § 2003 (2014)
Oklahoma House Bill 1384 (2014)

Summary:	Creates parents' bill of rights.
Major Provisions:	- Applies to educational record data and specifically to biometric and other biological records.
	- Gives parents the right to see data collected about their child.
	- Requires parental "opt-in" for biometric or biological data; allows parents to opt out except for "necessary items" of the educational record.
Gaps in Protection, Exclusions and Omissions:	- Does not restrict the use of data collection for advertising and marketing purposes.
	- Does not specifically give parents the right to challenge and correct data.
	- Does not specifically require implementation of data security procedures.

- Does not require de-identification of personally identifying information.

- Does not require the data's intended use to be specified in advance.

- Does not require data to be destroyed following intended use.

- Contains no provision regarding accountability for breaches of the law.

R.I. Gen. Laws § 16-103-3 (2014), R.I. Gen. Laws § 16-103-4 (2014)
Rhode Island House Bill 7124 (2014)

Summary:	Forbids school from demanding private social media account info; cloud providers can't use data for commercial purposes.
Major Provisions:	- Applies to any data created by a student or processed by cloud provider.
	- Specifically restricts the use of data collection for advertising and marketing purposes.
	- Holds educational institution accountable for breaches of the law.
Gaps in Protection, Exclusions and Omissions:	- Does not give parents the right to see data collected about their child.
	- Does not specifically give parents the right to challenge and correct data.
	- Makes no provision for parents to opt out of data collection, storage, or use.
	- Does not specifically require implementation of data security procedures.
	- Does not require de-identification of personally identifying information.
	- Does not require the data's intended use to be specified in advance.
	- Does not require data to be destroyed following intended use.

S.D. Codified Laws § 13-3-51 (2014), S.D. Codified Laws §§ 13-3-51.1 - 13-3-51.6 (2014)
South Dakota Senate Bill 63 (2014)

Summary:	- Provides that the state's existing student record statute does not authorize the collection of information that is not necessary for funding calculations, student academic progress determinations, or reports required by law, prohibits students from being surveyed without consent on personal topics, prohibits the submitting of personally identifying

information to the US Department of Education and requires the Education Department to develop security measures for the data.

Major Provisions:

- Applies to educational record data, especially personally identifying and private information.

- Requires implementation of data security procedures.

- Holds the State Department of Education accountable for breaches.

Gaps in Protection, Exclusions and Omissions:

- Does not restrict the use of data collection for advertising and marketing purposes.

- Does not give parents the right to see data collected about their child.

- Does not specifically give parents the right to challenge and correct data.

- Makes no provision for parents to opt out of data collection, storage, or use.

- Does not require de-identification of personally identifying information.

- Does not require the data's intended use to be specified in advance.

- Does not require data to be destroyed following intended use.

Utah Code Ann. § 63J-1-602.3 (2014), Utah Code Ann. §§ 53A-1b-101 – 53A-1b-111 (2014)
Utah House Bill 96 (2014)

Summary:

Creates the School Readiness Board, which provides grants to certain early childhood education programs, and may enter into certain contracts with private entities (including providers of education tech for school readiness) to provide funding for early childhood education programs for at-risk students.

Major Provisions:

- Applies to educational record data.

- Requires the de-identification of personally identifying information.

- Implies that the School Readiness Board would be held accountable for breaches.

Gaps in Protection, Exclusions and Omissions:

- Does not restrict the use of data collection for advertising and marketing purposes.

- Does not give parents the right to see data collected about their child.

- Does not specifically give parents the right to challenge and correct data.

- Makes no provision for parents to opt out of data collection, storage, or use.

- Does not specifically require implementation of data security procedures.

- Does not require the data's intended use to be specified in advance.

- Does not require data to be destroyed following intended use.

Va. Code Ann. § 22.1-287.01 (2014)
Virginia HB 449 (2014)

Summary: Forbids members/employees of local school boards or the state Department of Education from transmitting a student's "personally identifying information" (as FERPA defines it) to a federal agency or its representative.

Major Provisions: - Applies to educational record data.

Gaps in Protection, Exclusions - Does not restrict the use of data collection for advertising
and Omissions: and marketing purposes.

- Does not give parents the right to see data collected about their child.

- Does not specifically give parents the right to challenge and correct data.

- Makes no provision for parents to opt out of data collection, storage, or use.

- Does not specifically require implementation of data security procedures.

- Does not require de-identification of personally identifying information.

- Does not require the data's intended use to be specified in advance.

- Does not require data to be destroyed following intended use.

- Contains no provision regarding accountability for breaches.

Wyo. Stat. § 21-2-202 (2014)
Wyoming Senate Bill 79 (2014)

Summary: Requires a data security plan for education accountability and assessment data by the Department of Enterprise Technology Services to include privacy and security, breach planning, the prohibition of the sale of student information to private entities or organizations, and the security of all personally identifying information.

Major Provisions:	- Applies to educational record data.
	- Specifically restricts the use of data collection for advertising and marketing purposes.
	- Requires implementation of data security procedures.
	- Specification of data use is implied.
	- Requirement to destroy data after intended use is implied.
Gaps in Protection, Exclusions and Omissions	- Although it does not explicitly give parents the right to see data, it refers to FERPA, which does.
	- With respect to challenging the accuracy of data, refers to FERPA.
	- Makes no provision for parents to opt out of data collection, storage, or use.
	- Does not require de-identification of personally identifying information.
	- Contains no provision regarding accountability for breaches.

INDEX

ABOUT THE AUTHORS

Alex Molnar is research professor at the University of Colorado Boulder, where he serves as publications director of the National Education Policy Center (NEPC) and director of the Commercialism in Education Research Unit (CERU). His work has examined curriculum and instruction topics, market-based education reforms, and policy formation. He directed the Center for Education Research, Analysis, and Innovation (CERAI) at the University of Wisconsin-Milwaukee and for six years (1995–2001) was the principal investigator for the research evaluation of Wisconsin's SAGE class size reduction program. From 2001 to 2011 he directed the Education Policy Studies Research Laboratory (EPSL) at Arizona State University. Molnar is an internationally recognized expert on school commercialism; his annual reports on commercializing trends in schools have become standard reference works for experts in the field. His most recent books are *Commercialism in Education: From Democratic Ideal to Market Commodity* (2005) and *Think Tank Research Quality: Lessons for Policymakers, the Media, and the Public* (with Kevin Welner, Pat Hinchey, and Don Weitzman) (2010). Molnar has a BA in history, political science, and education; master's degrees in history and in social welfare; a specialist's certificate in educational administration; and a PhD in urban education.

Faith Boninger is a research associate at the University of Colorado Boulder, specifically at the university's National Education Policy Center (NEPC) and Commercialism in Education Research Unit (CERU). Since 2007 she has coauthored CERU's *Annual Report on Trends in School-*

house Commercialism. Additional publications include *A National Survey of the Types and Extent of the Marketing of Foods of Minimal Nutritional Value in Schools* (with Alex Molnar, David Garcia, and Bruce Merrill, 2006) and *Policy and Statutory Responses to Advertising and Marketing in Schools* (with Alex Molnar and William S. Koski, 2010). She brings to this work a background in social psychology (PhD, Ohio State University), particularly an interest in persuasion and communication processes.

Made in United States
Orlando, FL
12 January 2022

13368265R10176